Lecture Notes in Computer Science 7525

Commenced Publication in 1973
Founding and Former Series Editors:
Gerhard Goos, Juris Hartmanis, and Jan van Leeuwen

Paul Groth   James Frew (Eds.)

Provenance and Annotation of Data and Processes

4th International Provenance
and Annotation Workshop, IPAW 2012
Santa Barbara, CA, USA, June 19-21, 2012
Revised Selected Papers

 Springer

Volume Editors

Paul Groth
VU University Amsterdam
Department of Computer Science
De Boelelaan 1081a, 1081 HV Amsterdam, The Netherlands
E-mail: p.t.groth@vu.nl

James Frew
University of California
Bren School of Environmental Science and Management
2400 Bren Hall, Santa Barbara, CA 93106-5131, USA
E-mail: frew@bren.ucsb.edu

ISSN 0302-9743   e-ISSN 1611-3349
ISBN 978-3-642-34221-9   e-ISBN 978-3-642-34222-6
DOI 10.1007/978-3-642-34222-6
Springer Heidelberg Dordrecht London New York

Library of Congress Control Number: 2012949280

CR Subject Classification (1998): I.2.4, H.2.4, H.2.8, H.3.3-5, H.4.1, K.6.m, K.4.3

LNCS Sublibrary: SL 3 – Information Systems and Application, incl. Internet/Web
and HCI

Typesetting: Camera-ready by author, data conversion by Scientific Publishing Services, Chennai, India

Printed on acid-free paper

Springer is part of Springer Science+Business Media (www.springer.com)

Preface

"Provenance of a resource is a record that describes entities and processes involved in producing and delivering or otherwise influencing that resource. Provenance provides a critical foundation for assessing authenticity, enabling trust, and allowing reproducibility. Provenance assertions are a form of contextual metadata and can themselves become important records with their own provenance."

This quotation is from the W3C Provenance Incubator Group Final Report (http://www.w3.org/2005/Incubator/prov/XGR-prov-20101214/).

2012 is a watershed year for provenance/annotation research. Under the stewardship of the World Wide Web Consortium, the global community of provenance practitioners is converging on standardized definitions, models, representations, and protocols for provenance. An infrastructure may soon be in place that could potentially support universal access to the provenance of online artifacts. The time is ripe to explore the implications of ubiquitous provenance.

Provenance is understood to be a critical component of information trustworthiness. Provenance is also increasingly understood to be essential to scientific reproducibility – the provenance and annotation of a digital scientific artifact often fulfills the same function that a paper notebook did for earlier laboratory experiments. In many cases provenance offers the only coherent picture of ad-hoc digital workflows. Provenance is also a requirement for long-term preservation of digital information.

The spread of automatic systems for provenance capture and management will allow provenance to be associated with digital artifacts whose complexity (e.g., social networks) or volume (e.g., environmental satellite data) would make manual annotation prohibitive. Furthermore, the availability of large corpora of provenance records is enabling research into automatic exploration of and reasoning about provenance.

The Fourth International Provenance and Annotation Workshop (IPAW 2012) built on the success of previous workshops held in Troy (2010), Salt Lake City (2008), Chicago (2006, 2002), and Edinburgh (2003). IPAW 2012 was held in Santa Barbara, California at the Bren School of Environmental Science and Management at the University of California, Santa Barbara. The 50 attendees represented both academia and industry, and came from the US, the UK, the Netherlands, Brazil, and Germany.

In response to our call for papers, we received 49 full paper, poster, and demo submissions. Full papers received a minimum of 3 reviews and poster and demo papers received at least 2 reviews. After review, 14 full papers, 4 demo papers, and 12 poster papers were accepted. Many papers covered classic themes of the provenance literature including research on provenance for workflow systems, databases, the web, and applications to science. However, new themes emerged including the application of network analysis techniques to provenance, as well as investigating the ability to reconstruct or recreate provenance traces.

In addition to the papers, posters and demos, the workshop had a session providing updates on related provenance events. Philip E. Bourne from the Skaggs School of Pharmacy and Pharmaceutical Sciences at the University of California, San Diego gave an outstanding keynote, The Provenance Divide, on the gap between fundamental provenance research and the demand for provenance in the biomedical and scientific domains. He encouraged the community to close that gap.

As with prior IPAW workshops, there were additional events surrounding the core workshop. A tutorial on the W3C Provenance Working Group's emerging specifications for interchanging was attended by 28 participants. Likewise, the Data Observation Network for Earth (DataONE) organized a meeting on provenance and scientific workflow. Finally, the W3C Provenance Working Group held their third face-to-face meeting after the conclusion of the workshop. IPAW has become a nexus in the community not just for communicating results but also for starting and maintaining collaborations.

IPAW 2012 was a fantastic event driven by an active and engaged community of provenance researchers facilitated by a beautiful and well-organized venue at the Bren School. We thank B.J. Danetra and her staff for their support during the conference, and Kim Fugate for handling conference registration and billing. We also thank the Program Committee for their thoughtful reviews.

July 2012   Paul Groth
                                                            James Frew

Organization

Program Committee

Ilkay Altintas	University of California, San Diego
Eddy Banks	Lawrence Livermore National Laboratory
Bruce Barkstrom	SGA
Khalid Belhajjame	University of Manchester
Shawn Bowers	Gonzaga University
Remco Chang	Tufts University
Adriane Chapman	The MITRE Corporation
Paolo Ciccarese	Harvard Medical School / Massachusetts General Hospital
Oscar Corcho	Universidad Politécnica de Madrid
Helena Deus	Digital Enterprise Research Instutite, NUIG
Kai Eckert	Mannheim University Library
Peter Edwards	University of Aberdeen
Todd Elsethagen	Pacific Northwest National Laboratory
Juliana Freire	Polytechnic Institute of New York University
James Frew	University of California Santa Barbara
Yolanda Gil	Information Sciences Institute, University of Southern California
Jose Manuel Gomez-Perez	Intelligent Software Components (iSOCO) S.A.
Paul Groth	VU University Amsterdam
Olaf Hartig	Humboldt-Universität zu Berlin
Jan Hidders	Delft University of Technology
Jane Hunter	University of Queensland
H.V. Jagadish	University of Michigan
Qing Liu	CSIRO ICT Centre
Shiyong Lu	Wayne State University
Bertram Ludäscher	UC Davis
Marta Mattoso	COPPE – Federal Univ. Rio de Janeiro
Deborah L. McGuinness	Tetherless World Constellation, Rensselaer Polytechnic Institute
Simon Miles	King's College London
Paolo Missier	Newcastle University
James Myers	CCNI/Rensselaer Polytechnic Institute
Edoardo Pignotti	University of Aberdeen
Paulo Pinheiro Da Silva	University of Texas at El Paso
Beth Plale	Indiana University

Satya Sahoo   Case Western Reserve University
Amit Sheth   Kno.e.sis Center, Wright State University
Eric Stephan   Pacific Northwest National Laboratory
Kerry Taylor   CSIRO ICT Centre
Curt Tilmes   NASA GSFC
Jan Van Den Bussche   Hasselt University and Transnational
                               University of Limburg
Jun Zhao   University of Oxford

Additional Reviewers

Chen, Yuhui   Michaelis, James
Dey, Saumen   Nguyen, Vinh
Dias, Jonas   Oliveira, Daniel
Koehler, Sven   Palmer, Doug
Koop, David   Ritze, Dominique
Lebo, Timothy   Sarkar, Anandarup
McCusker, Jim

Table of Contents

Science Applications

Networks

Demonstrations

Posters

SourceTrac: Tracing Data Sources within Spreadsheets

Hazeline U. Asuncion

Computing and Software Systems
University of Washington, Bothell
Bothell, WA USA
hazeline@u.washington.edu

Abstract. Analyzing data from multiple sources is a common task in scientific research. In particular, spreadsheet data is often aggregated from a variety of sources to identify patterns and synthesize reports. Yet, techniques are lacking for automatically capturing the provenance of such data within spreadsheet environments like Excel. We present a novel approach for fine-grained tracing of tabular data that may have been obtained from files, databases, or the Web. Our approach provides relevant provenance information at both the micro-level (per cell) and the macro-level (per sheet). Initial results suggest that our approach is scalable and beneficial to data analysts.

Keywords: data provenance, spreadsheets, multiple sources.

1 Introduction

Aggregating data from multiple sources is a fundamental operation in data-intensive domains, including the natural sciences, social sciences, and business. In the eScience domain, raw scientific data may be stored by different instruments in different file locations or may be obtained from different research organizations. As an example, the Jaffe Atmospheric Research Group at UW Bothell analyzes tabular data from their own field sites as well as published data from the EPA, NOAA, and NASA on a weekly basis to understand global and regional sources of air pollution.

While methods exist for tracking multiple sources of data in the context of scientific workflows, databases, and grid computing [5, 6, 7, 11, 14], provenance techniques are lacking in spreadsheet environments (like Microsoft Excel) which are ubiquitously used by data analysts and researchers. Because spreadsheet environments are highly interactive, multiple data sets are often merged together into one spreadsheet at multiple time points. Thus, without provenance it becomes difficult for researchers to recover the original source(s) of a record. In addition, it is difficult to determine updates to downstream files if a source file has changed or contains an error.

In response to these challenges, we present SourceTrac, a novel approach for tracing multiple sources of data within a spreadsheet. Our approach captures the source as the users are obtaining data (e.g., from the Web), annotates the immediate source of each record at the granularity of individual cells, calculates source ancestors of formulas, and provides mechanisms for connecting a file to parent files as well as

P. Groth and J. Frew (Eds.): IPAW 2012, LNCS 7525, pp. 1–10, 2012.

visualizing this provenance data. In this paper, our approach is tailored towards Microsoft Excel but can be generalized to other environments.

In previous work, we focused on capturing the operations that users perform on a spreadsheet while analyzing data [2]. This paper, meanwhile, is complimentary since the focus is on capturing operations that pertain to fine-grained tracking of data sources.

The rest of the paper is organized as follows. The next section discusses techniques we use to track data sources. Section 3 describes the implementation details of the SourceTrac tool. Section 4 presents use cases, initial user feedback, and scalability measures. Section 5 covers related work. Finally, we conclude with a discussion of future avenues of research.

2   Provenance Technique

In this section, we delve into the core aspects of our provenance technique for tracking sources within spreadsheets.

2.1   Tracking the Source as the User Obtains the Data

To support the tracking of heterogeneous data sources, we capture the data source *in situ,* at the time a user obtains the data. Otherwise, retrospectively determining the source may be difficult, if not impossible. Users also explicitly specify when they wish to track data sources. This avoids the accidental capturing of sources that are unnecessary to researchers. Users may obtain data from the Web, a database, or other tabular files.

There are several ways that sources can be recorded when users obtain data from the internet. Within Excel, SourceTrac can detect data scraped from the web through Excel's "Get External Data From Web" interface. If data is manually copied from a Web page or if a file is downloaded from a web site, it is also possible to determine the source by automatically inspecting the immediate history of the user's web browser (e.g., Firefox) and obtaining the visited URL (using a traceability technique [3]). Once the URL is captured, the cells are annotated with this URL.

Figure 1 shows data scraped using the Excel interface (background) which is then pasted onto a spreadsheet (foreground). After the extracted data has been cleaned up and formatted, we see that each cell is automatically annotated with the source, shown as a small red triangle at the top-right of each cell. In this example, the annotation reveals that the data comes from one source, indicated by "1", followed by the URL of the source. The "100" at the end indicates that the data in the cell is 100% derived from the specified URL.

Another source of data is external files, such as other spreadsheet files or text files. In this case, we can record the name of the file (including the file path) when the user copies the data. When the data is pasted onto the spreadsheet, the cells are then annotated with the file name of the source. In principle, it is also feasible to perform provenance tracking as users query a database, using Excel's facilities. In this case, the

SQL query would be the recorded source. It is worth noting that once a cell is anno-tated with a data source, the annotation will remain with the cell even if the user cop-ies the cell to another sheet.

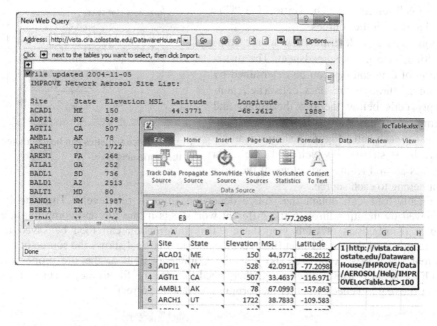

Fig. 1. Data obtained from the Web are annotated with the URL

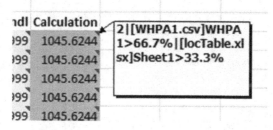

Fig. 2. Data sources are annotated at the cell level

2.2   Querying Data Sources at Multiple Levels of Granularity

Since sources, or provenance metadata, are recorded at the cell level, SourceTrac allows for provenance reporting at multiple levels of granularity: the cell level, the spreadsheet level, and the file level. At the cell level, individual cells are annotated with the source. If the data contained within a cell is a function or a calculated formula, the sources of the dependency cells are indicated. For instance, Figure 2 shows that the calculated cell is derived from two sources (as indicated by the number 2 at the beginning of the annotation): two-thirds of the cells which the calculated cell de-pends on is derived from the file "WHPA1.csv", while one-third comes from worksheet

"Sheet1" of the file "locTable.xlsx". These ratios are based on the number of cell references specific to a source and the total number of cell references. The vertical bar "|" is used to delimit the sources.

One may also determine the source composition for a given spreadsheet. The distribution of data sources can be determined by scanning through the data cells (i.e., non-empty cells below the row headings) and summing up the individual source distributions for each cell. Figure 3 shows example worksheet statistics which list the data sources as well as the percentage of the cells that belong to each source.

Fig. 3. Source statistics can be calculated at the worksheet level

Finally, one can obtain the source dependencies at a file level. This can be achieved by iterating through the different worksheets in the file and compiling the source distributions of each worksheet. This information can then be saved as the metadata of the spreadsheet file. As an example, Figure 4 shows the source of the current file ("WHPA_process.xlsx") in the Comments field of the file properties. Such metadata is useful when researchers need to trace the file to the parent spreadsheet file (e.g., to check whether the formulas used were correct).

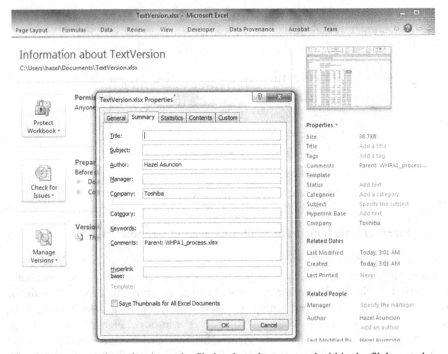

Fig. 4. Data source dependencies at the file level can be annotated within the file's metadata

2.3   Calculating the Ancestors of the Data

While the previous techniques allows for tracking to the immediate source, there are situations where tracking the line of source ancestors (across files) is necessary (e.g., when an error appears in a descendant spreadsheet). There are two possible ways to track the ancestors of data within a cell. The first method is by following the backward links from the cell to the immediate source and on to its source until we arrive at an external root source, which is can be a web URL, a database connection, or another file with no source annotations.

Another method is to build source trees as the user obtains data from the different sources. Root nodes are created each time data is extracted externally. Branches are created each time the extracted data is copied to another file or is inserted via an Excel "lookup" function across files. Branch nodes contain the filename of the descendant spreadsheet, as well as specific location in the spreadsheet where the data has been copied or inserted, such as the worksheet name and the range of cells.

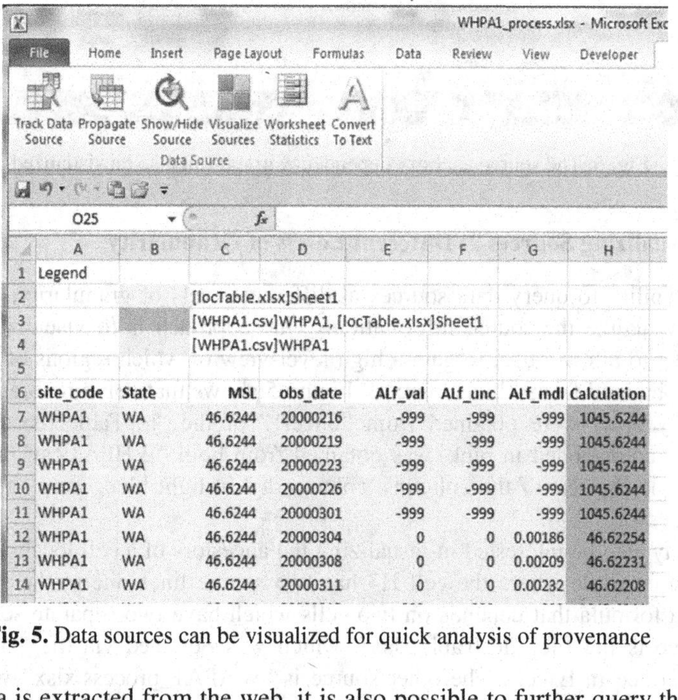

Fig. 5. Data sources can be visualized for quick analysis of provenance

If the data is extracted from the web, it is also possible to further query the source of the published data on the web. This will require the existence of structured metadata or a web service that takes in a URL of a data source and outputs the source(s) of the data. In the event that the data has been obtained from a published source of another research organization, one can envision the output of the web service to be another URL, or perhaps another web service that points to yet another published data source on the web.

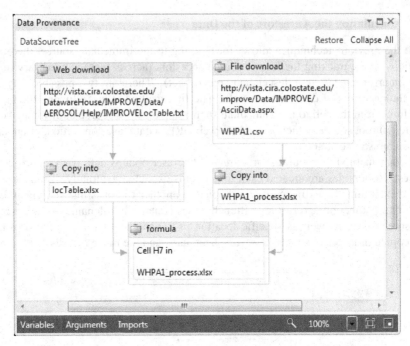

Fig. 6. The source ancestry dependency graph can also be visualized

2.4   Visualizing Sources at Different Levels of Granularity

With the ability to query data sources at different levels of granularity, SourceTrac can also visualize the source information. One approach is to visualize the entire spreadsheet to allow a user to gain a high level-view of which regions of the spreadsheet are obtained from which sources. Figure 5 shows that columns B and C, color-coded in yellow, were obtained from "Sheet1" of the "locTable.xlsx file", while column H, color-coded in pink, was obtained from both "WHPA1.csv" and "locTable.xlsx" and the rest of the columns, color-coded in light blue, were obtained from "WHPA1.csv".

One may also be interested in visualizing the ancestors of a cell location. Figure 6 depicts an example where the cell H7 has two source lines due to the fact that H7 contains a formula that depends on two cells which have two separate sources. The first source is the file, "locTable.xlsx", which was obtained via the "Get External Data" interface in Excel. The other source is "WHPA1_process.xlsx" which originated from a download. Thus, this view allows a user to quickly identify the various sources of a calculated field.

3   SourceTrac Tool Support

The following sections describe the tool's design and implementation as well as use cases of interest to data analysts.

3.1   Tool Design and Implementation

We designed the SourceTrac tool to be easy to use and accessible, requiring minimal setup and configuration. To this end, we provide a user interface within the Excel environment (specifically Excel 2010). The functionalities mentioned in the previous section are accessible via the Excel ribbon (seen in Figure 1). To set up the tool, users would simply run an installation file.

SourceTrac also leverages Excel's interfaces for obtaining data from the Web and from a database. For example, we use Excel's XLQueryType property of the QueryTable object to obtain the URL of the source data. SourceTrac automatically determines which sections of the spreadsheet received the data and annotates the cells with the sources.

We use various means of storing the source annotations. At the cell level, sources are stored as comments to individual cells. At the file level, sources are stored as a file property (within the "Comments" metadata field). Users also have the option of viewing or hiding the cell comment indicator (i.e., the red triangle at the top-right corner).

The current tool implementation includes most of the capabilities mentioned in the previous section. Dependency tracking is only partially implemented. We also plan to integrate the capture of the source URL from the Firefox browser's history into our tool.

3.2   Use Cases

We envision the following use cases for SourceTrac. A researcher obtains data published on the Web through Excel's "Get External Data" interface. The researcher then obtains another data set online by downloading a spreadsheet from a different URL. The researcher proceeds to combine the two data sets by using an Excel "vlookup" function in the downloaded spreadsheet to get the data from the first file. After the data has been combined, the researcher adds formulas to the spreadsheet.

At a later point in time, the researcher discovers that the first data set has been corrected by the publishers of the data. The researcher opens the aggregated file, visualizes the sources, and immediately identifies which regions of the spreadsheet to update using the SourceTrac tool.

When the researcher decides to publish his results, he proceeds to duplicate his spreadsheet by pasting the data values and removing the formulas. Sometime later, he wishes to double-check whether he used the correct statistical formula in his published result. Looking at the "Comment" metadata field in the file properties of the published file, he finds the path to the parent file and verifies that he has indeed used the correct formula.

4   Evaluation

In this section, we discuss the provenance queries that can be answered by the tool as well as initial user feedback and a discussion of the tool's overhead.

4.1   Provenance Queries

The SourceTrac tool can answer the following important provenance queries.

1. Where did the data from this spreadsheet file come from? This query can be answered in multiple ways. One may view the individual annotations at the cell-level (Figure 2), or one may choose to look at the worksheet source distribution statistics (Figure 3). Furthermore, file-level annotation is saved in the "Comment" field in the file properties (Figure 4).

2. How was the data in this cell derived? Again, one may view the cell annotation, which would show the sources from which that cell was derived. This query can also be answered by viewing the ancestor source tree (Figure 6).

3. If a source file changes, which parts of the worksheet need to be updated? This query can be answered by visualizing sources (Figure 5). If the first source file, "locTable.xlsx", has been changed, then one can find (by color) the regions of the spreadsheet to change.

4. Does my final accuracy in cell H18 depend at all on faulty data source X? One can look at the cell annotation or the ancestor tree. Moreover, SourceTrac returns the degree (percentage) to which H18 depends on data source X.

4.2   User Feedback

We have solicited feedback regarding our tool from a senior scientist in the Jaffe Atmospheric Research Group at the University of Washington, Bothell. This scientist analyzes data from multiple sources frequently, at least on a weekly basis. A typical size of his resulting dataset is 30,000 records with 10 to 50 columns. He performs environmental analyses of data from multiple data sources.

His current approach to tracking sources is naming the spreadsheet based on the source and manually entering the data sources in another worksheet within the same file. A drawback to this approach is that there are times where he may forget to document the data source. In addition, since he transforms his spreadsheet data into another spreadsheet by pasting by value, the formulas he used in the original spreadsheet are not readily available. In order to find this information, he needs to search through his file system to find the parent file (or the source file) of the text file.

According to the scientist, the tool will allow him to improve his documentation of the sources. It will also save him a substantial amount of time by avoiding the duplication of his analysis. Without the tool, if he is unsure of the data source or the version of the data source, he would have to re-analyze the source data again to verify his results. He comments that he is looking forward to using the tool in day-to-day analysis operations.

4.3   Scalability of Tool

Since we provide a source annotation for each data cell in the spreadsheet, a potential concern is that the spreadsheet files would become too large in size due to the necessity to store this additional metadata. However, we find that the space overheads are reasonable. For an Excel spreadsheet containing 5,000 cells with formulas and annotations, the file size is only 3.25 times larger than the equivalent spreadsheet without annotations. With 10,000 cells, the file size is only 3.69 times larger. With 100,000 cells, the file size is only 4.63 times larger than the corresponding spreadsheet without annotations. In all these cases, the file size is less than a few megabytes. These numbers suggest that the overhead cost of adding annotations at a cell-level is reasonable.

5   Related Work

Tracking multiples sources of data has been addressed in different contexts: databases, scientific workflows, grid computing, and web pages. In databases, one technique analyzes the database query issued to obtain the source of data [6]. Other techniques include propagating source annotation along with the data [5] or using provenance polynomials [14]. In the context of scientific workflows, one can show the derivation path of information [7] and a dataset derivation graph [15] or one can use the notion of a strong link to connect a workflow instance with the input and derived data [11]. In the context of grid computing, one may track files and processes [12] or use a web crawler [4]. In the context of the web, multiple data sources may be presented in a web page. To determine the data sources, one can extract provenance metadata embedded on the page [1, 8].

Within Excel spreadsheets, tracking and visualizing dependent data sources within a spreadsheet can be performed with Excel's built-in "Trace Precedents" or "Trace Dependents" interface [13]. A more intuitive visualization of data sources within a spreadsheet has also been proposed [9]. Excel also has a built-in mechanism for linking to external data when a formula, chart, pivot table, or object link is created [13]. However, for the usage scenarios of importing data or copying/pasting data into a spreadsheet, tracking sources is not provided. Another technique can trace the relationships between spreadsheets, but only at the file level [10].

6   Conclusion

In this paper, we presented SourceTrac, a provenance technique for spreadsheets that supports capturing data sources in situ, querying data sources at different levels of granularity, calculating ancestors of data, and visualizing source compositions at different levels of granularity. Preliminary results suggest that this tool has minimal overhead and is beneficial to data analysts and researchers. There are many potential directions for future work. An interesting future work is tracking whether the source data has moved or has been modified. Combining source tracking with provenance techniques for analyzing data manipulations is also another promising direction to pursue in the future.

Acknowledgement. The author thanks Alex Dioso for development support and Dan Jaffe for helpful feedback. Research was supported in part by the University of Washington Royalty Research Fund No. A65951 and the UWB Collaborative Undergraduate Research Grant.

References

[1] EXIF, http://www.exif.org/

[2] Asuncion, H.U.: In Situ data provenance capture in spreadsheets. In: Proc. of the 7th International Conference on e-Science (2011)

[3] Asuncion, H.U., Taylor, R.N.: Automated Techniques for Capturing Custom Traceability Links Across Heterogeneous Artifacts. In: Software and Systems Traceability, pp. 129–146. Springer (2012)

[4] Benabdelkader, A., Santcroos, M., Madougou, S., van Kampen, A.H.C., Olabarriaga, S.D.: A provenance approach to trace scientific experiments on a grid infrastructure. In: Proc. of the 7th International Conference on e-Science (2011)

[5] Bhagwat, D., Chiticariu, L., Tan, W.-C., Vijayvargiya, G.: An annotation management system for relational databases. VLDB Journal 14 (2005)

[6] Buneman, P., Khanna, S., Tan, W.-C.: Why and Where: A Characterization of Data Provenance. In: Van den Bussche, J., Vianu, V. (eds.) ICDT 2001. LNCS, vol. 1973, pp. 316–330. Springer, Heidelberg (2000)

[7] Greenwood, M., Goble, C., Stevens, R., Zhao, J., Addis, M., Marvin, D., Moreau, L., Oinn, T.: Provenance of e-science experiments - experience from bioinformatics. In: The UK OST e-Science Second All Hands Meeting (2003)

[8] Groth, P.: ProvenanceJS: Revealing the Provenance of Web Pages. In: McGuinness, D.L., Michaelis, J.R., Moreau, L. (eds.) IPAW 2010. LNCS, vol. 6378, pp. 283–285. Springer, Heidelberg (2010)

[9] Hermans, F., Pinzger, M., van Deursen, A.: Supporting professional spreadsheet users by generating leveled dataflow diagrams. In: Proc. of ICSE (2011)

[10] Jensen, C., Lonsdale, H., Wynn, E., Cao, J., Slater, M., Dietterich, T.G.: The life and times of files and information: A study of desktop provenance. In: Proc. of International Conf. on Human Factors in Computing Systems, pp. 767–776. ACM (2010)

[11] Koop, D., Santos, E., Bauer, B., Troyer, M., Freire, J., Silva, C.T.: Bridging Workflow and Data Provenance Using Strong Links. In: Gertz, M., Ludäscher, B. (eds.) SSDBM 2010. LNCS, vol. 6187, pp. 397–415. Springer, Heidelberg (2010)

[12] Malik, T., Gehani, A., Tariq, D., Zaffar, F.: Sketching Distributed Data Provenance. In: Liu, Q., Bai, Q., Giugni, S., Williamson, D., Taylor, J. (eds.) Data Provenance and Data Management in eScience. SCI, vol. 426, pp. 85–108. Springer, Heidelberg (2013)

[13] Microsoft Corporation. MS Excel, http://office.microsoft.com/en-us/excel/

[14] Olteanu, D., Zavodny, J.: On factorisation of provenance polynomials. In: USENIX Theory and Practice of Provenance (2011)

[15] Osterweil, L.J., Clarke, L.A., Ellison, A.M., Boose, E., Podorozhny, R., Wise, A.: Clear and precise specification of ecological data management processes and dataset provenance. IEEE Trans. on Automation Science & Engr. 7, 189–195 (2010)

Towards Integrating Workflow and Database Provenance

Fernando Chirigati and Juliana Freire

Polytechnic Institute of NYU
Computer Science and Engineering Department
fernando.chirigati@gmail.com, juliana.freire@nyu.edu

Abstract. While there has been substantial work on both database and workflow provenance, the two problems have only been examined in isolation. It is widely accepted that the existing models are incompatible. Database provenance is fine-grained and captures changes to tuples in a database. In contrast, workflow provenance is represented at a coarser level and reflects the functional model of workflow systems, which is stateless—each computational step derives a new artifact. In this paper, we propose a new approach to combine database and workflow provenance. We address the mismatch between the different kinds of provenance by using a temporal model which explicitly represents the database states as updates are applied. We discuss how, under this model, reproducibility is obtained for workflows that manipulate databases, and how different queries that straddle the two provenance traces can be evaluated. We also describe a proof-of-concept implementation that integrates a workflow system and a commercial relational database.

Keywords: Workflow Provenance, Database Provenance, Reproducibility.

1   Introduction

Provenance for digital objects is becoming increasingly important both in industry and science, not only due to regulations such as HIPAA and Sarbanes Oxley, but also due the fact that computational scientific results must be reproducible [6]. The area of provenance management has been very active and there is a rich body of work on different aspects of provenance. Work on *database provenance* has focused on techniques to represent provenance for tuples in a relational database and to propagate provenance through queries [3]. For *scientific workflows*, there have been proposals that address issues such as capture, modeling, storage, and querying for provenance information [4,8].

However, an important problem has received much less attention: how to combine database and workflow provenance. For scientific workflows that interact with data stored in databases, unless there is a model that combines the different kinds of provenance, it is not possible to maintain accurate provenance of the complete process, and consequently, results cannot be reproduced. Consider the

P. Groth and J. Frew (Eds.): IPAW 2012, LNCS 7525, pp. 11–23, 2012.
© Springer-Verlag Berlin Heidelberg 2012

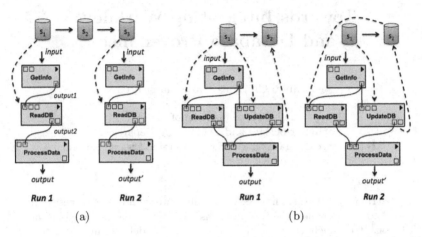

Fig. 1. This figure illustrates challenges in reproducing a workflow run when database access is involved. (a) shows two runs of the same workflow which accesses a database; because the database has changed in between the two runs, even though the workflows have the same structure and input data (i.e., *input*), their results differ—one derives *output* and the other derives *output'*. (b) shows a workflow that, due to its DAG structure, can have two different execution orderings, and depending on the ordering, the outputs may also be different.

example shown in Fig. 1a. The workflow on the left receives as input *input* and outputs *output*. One of its modules, *ReadDB*, consumes data from a database. If this workflow is executed at a later time, even if it uses the same input, there is no guarantee that it will produce the same result. In particular, agents that are external to and not observable by the workflow system may modify the database in between the executions. This happens even in scenarios where database access is always observable by the workflow system. For example, Fig. 1b shows a workflow that both reads from and writes to a database. Note that either *ReadDB* or *UpdateDB* modules can be executed after *GetInfo*. The workflow has two possible execution orderings: if *ReadDB* is executed first (*Run 1*), it will read the initial state s_1 of the database; otherwise, it will read the state that results from the changes applied by *UpdateDB* (*Run 2*). Depending on the execution order, the result produced by the workflow might be different, and without information about how the database changed, the workflow run might not be reproducible.

Combining database and workflow provenance is challenging because of an inherent mismatch in the models used to represent them. Workflows adopt a functional, stateless model where each module is a function that receives some input data and generates a new output: the workflow structure and inputs uniquely identify the outputs [12]. Databases, in contrast, adopt a stateful model: every time a transaction commits, there is a new state that reflects the changes applied in the transaction. Thus, accesses to databases *break* the stateless (and deterministic) scientific workflow model.

In this paper, we propose a new model to integrate database and workflow provenance. To the best of our knowledge, this is the first approach that supports reproducibility of workflows in the presence of database accesses. This model was inspired by the observation that transaction temporal databases provide a suitable abstraction to represent database changes that is compatible to the execution model of scientific workflows. The key intuition here is that, because transaction temporal databases keep track of each state of the database by its transaction time, it is possible to uniquely identify and retrieve each state [9]. Consequently, by recording information about the database states it observes or generates, a workflow system is able to faithfully reproduce workflow executions that involve database access. Because our model relies on a temporal model that is currently supported by commercial relational databases such as Oracle RDBMS [14] and DB2 [5], it is practical and amenable to implementation. In fact, we describe how we have implemented this model in the VisTrails system [7] using the Oracle Total Recall functionality [15].

Besides the ability to accurately reproduce a workflow run, our approach also supports queries that straddle database and workflow provenance. Because the provenance information from the different systems is connected, we have a graph that allows the complete lineage of data artifacts to be computed, e.g., the workflow modules that affected a given database relation, or the relation states that contributed to the derivation of a data product by a workflow. As we discuss in Section 2, it is also possible to obtain the provenance for individual tuples and to answer *how provenance* queries [3].

Related Work. Also with the goal of integrating database and workflow provenance, Acar et al. [1] proposed the use of a *common* provenance model. Their proposal was motivated by the fact that workflow specifications, unlike databases, are seldom accompanied by a formal specification, and this, they argue, makes it difficult to integrate database and workflow provenance. Amsterdamer et al. [2] proposed a framework to integrate the fine-grained database-style provenance with workflows that consist of Pig Latin [13] modules. To capture fine-grained provenance for modules, they translate Pig Latin expressions into nested relational calculus expressions. We attack an orthogonal problem: our goal is to *connect* the two different kinds of provenance so as to support reproducibility. Our approach makes no assumption about the semantics of workflow modules, which can be black boxes, and it also does not prescribe the use of a unified provenance model. Nonetheless, the information captured by our model makes it possible to answer queries that combine database and workflow provenance.

Outline. The remainder of the paper is organized as follows. We present our model that integrates workflow and database provenance in Section 2, where we also discuss how this model supports reproducibility as well as provenance queries. In Section 3, we describe our prototype that combines VisTrails provenance with Oracle Total Recall. We conclude in Section 4 where we outline directions for future work.

2 A Model for Integrating Workflow and Database Provenance

In this section, we begin by introducing some basic concepts about workflows and databases, and then formally define our integrated provenance model.

2.1 Background

Stateless Workflows. We assume a dataflow model for workflows. A workflow is represented as a directed acyclic graph (DAG), where vertices are modules (functions) that perform computations, and data flows through the edges which connect modules.

Definition 1. *A workflow instance W is described by the tuple (M, C), where M is the set of modules and C is the set of connections. Each module $m \in M$ is represented by a function f_m, such that*

$$f_m : D_m^I \to D_m^O \tag{1}$$

where D_m^I is the domain of input values and D_m^O is the domain of output values. Since the definition of f_m is unknown, it is considered a black box[1]. A connection $c \in C$ that connects module m to module n is described as the tuple (m, n, d), where d corresponds to the data product that flows from m to n and that creates the dependency between these modules.

In the remainder of the paper, we represent a module m as $f_m(I_m) = <O_m>$, where I_m represents the input set and O_m is the output set of m. For instance, the workflow presented in the left side of Fig. 1a can be described by the following functions:

$$f_{GetInfo}(input) = <output_1>, f_{ReadDB}(output_1) = <output_2>,$$
$$f_{ProcessData}(output_2) = <output>$$

Stateful Databases. Transaction temporal databases keep track of the different states of a database as tuples are added, deleted or updated. Thus, these databases have all the necessary elements to support fine-grained provenance [9,10] and to achieve reproducibility of results [10].

To model transaction temporal relations, we adapt the backlog scheme proposed by Jensen et al. [11]. A *backlog* is a relation that contains the complete history of changes in another relation. Any tuple affected by an update is added to the append-only backlog, and tuples in the backlog are never updated. Backlogs thus maintain a complete record of modifications in tuples of the database. Each tuple in the backlog can be uniquely identified by its valid and transaction

---

[1] A module is also associated with a set of parameters whose values may also be used by f_m, and thus contribute to the output of the module. To keep the notation simple, we do not explicitly show these parameters and their values.

times. In our model, it is sufficient to consider only transaction time. We also restrict the data manipulation language to the operations *select*, *insert*, *update* and *delete*. While to simplify the presentation, we focus on single-relation queries and transactions; as we discuss below, the model can naturally handle multiple relations. Similarly, while we assume that separate states are maintained for each relation, rather than for the whole database, states covering all relations can also be supported[2]. This scheme is defined below.

Definition 2. *Given a schema* $\Re = (K, A)$ *from a transaction temporal relation* R, *where* K *is the tuple identifier and* A *is the set of attributes for* R, *the schema* $\Re_B$ *of the corresponding backlog relation* R_B *is defined as*

$$\Re_B = (K, A, T, Op, U), \tag{2}$$

where T *is the transaction time when the tuple was included in the backlog, Op is the operation applied to the tuple at time T (I for insertion and D for deletion) and U is the user who managed the operation in the tuple.*

When a set of tuples is first inserted into a relation, they are also inserted into the backlog; the transaction time T when the insertion took place is recorded for each tuple, and Op is set to "I". If a tuple is deleted, this tuple is inserted again in the backlog, but with T set to the transaction time when the deletion was performed, and Op set to "D". An update operation is represented by a deletion followed by an insertion, both with the same transaction time T.

The transaction time corresponds to the timestamp when the transaction was successfully committed. Consequently, all tuples with the same transaction time T were inserted in the backlog by the same transaction, i.e., they belong to the same state of the relation. A state represents a snapshot of a given relation at a certain time point. Since a new state is created for each successful transaction, we can uniquely identify a state by the transaction time. Because backlogs are append-only, they maintain all information needed to reconstruct each database state, and thus, they provide complete provenance for all tuples.

Definition 3. *The tuples in the backlog relation* R_B *represent the sequence of states* $\mathcal{S}(R)$ *for* R:

$$\mathcal{S}(R) = \{(S_1(R), T_1(R)), \ldots, (S_n(R), T_n(R))\}, \tag{3}$$

where $T_i(R)$, *for* $1 \leq i \leq n$, *represent transaction times recorded in* R_B, *and* $S_i(R)$ *corresponds to the state of* R *at time i. A state $S_i(R)$ is defined as*

$$S_i(R) = \{t_j \in R_B \mid time(t_j) \leq T_i(R)\}, \tag{4}$$

where t_j *is a tuple of* R_B *and* $time(t_j)$ *is the transaction time recorded for* t_j.

---

[2] In practice, these choices will be determined by the underlying implementation of the temporal features in the database.

Note that the indices in the states indicate their order in time. Given the states $S_i(R)$ and $S_j(R)$, and $i < j$, then $T_i(R) < T_j(R)$. Using this model, besides being able to identify the states by the transaction times, it is also possible to identify the differences between two states. Below, we use a concrete example to illustrate this.

Definition 4. *The difference (or delta) between two states $S_i(R)$ and $S_j(R)$, where $i < j$, is computed as follows:*

$$\Delta_{j,i}(R) = S_j(R) - S_i(R) \tag{5}$$

Example 1. Consider the following scenario. We have an empty relation *Emp*. A transaction that inserts two tuples in *Emp* is executed and successfully committed at transaction time 10 by user *fchirigati*. Then, at transaction time 15, user *jfreire* commits a transaction that corrects the job information about employee *Robert*. Finally, at transaction time 20, a new tuple is inserted in the relation by user *fchirigati*. The backlog which reflects these operations is shown below.

K	Name	Job	T	Op	U
1	Robert	Researcher	10	I	fchirigati
2	Claire	Assistant Director	10	I	fchirigati
1	Robert	Researcher	15	D	jfreire
1	Robert	Research Assistant	15	I	jfreire
3	Eric	Administrative Director	20	I	fchirigati

The set of states $\mathcal{S}(Emp)$ corresponds to the different timestamps in the backlog:

$$\mathcal{S}(Emp) = \{(S_1(Emp), 10), (S_2(Emp), 15), (S_3(Emp), 20)\}$$

The delta $\Delta_{3,1}(Emp)$ between $S_1(Emp)$ and $S_3(Emp)$ is:

1	Robert	Researcher	15	D	jfreire
1	Robert	Research Assistant	15	I	jfreire
3	Eric	Administrative Director	20	I	fchirigati

2.2   Integrating Workflow and Database Provenance

As discussed in Section 1, a key challenge in integrating database and workflow provenance to support reproducibility stems from the inherent mismatch between the two provenance models. In what follows, we show how this problem can be addressed for databases which adopt a temporal transaction model. In order to connect the workflow provenance to the database provenance, we need to capture information about the database states observed by the workflows. Given a module m in a workflow instance W that either consumes or modifies data in a relation R of a transaction temporal database, for each execution of

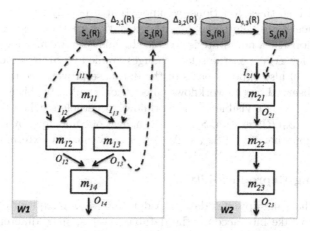

Fig. 2. In the integrated provenance model, database states observed by the workflow are recorded in the provenance (*dashed arrows* represent the database accesses.) Together with the workflow provenance, they not only provide the complete derivation chain for the workflow results, but also enable result reproducibility.

m, we store, in the provenance, information about the states before and after the module execution:

$$f_m(I_m, [R, T_b(R)]) = \; <O_m, [R, T_a(R)] > \qquad (6)$$

where $T_b(R)$ and $T_a(R)$ are the transaction times of the states of relation R before and after the module execution, respectively. Since a transaction time uniquely determines a state, by storing this information, we can retrieve the state.

If $T_a(R)$ and $T_b(R)$ are the same, it means that m did not modify R. Otherwise, if the transaction times are different, a new state was created, and this implies that data was being inserted, updated or deleted from R.

To simplify the presentation, so far we have assumed single-relation queries and transactions. However, it is straightforward to extend the model to work with multiple relations: transaction times must be stored for all relations used in a query. For instance, if a module m retrieves data from relations R_1 and R_2, states of both relations need to be explicit in the model:

$$f_m(I_m, [R_1, T_b(R_1)], [R_2, T_b(R_2)]) = \; <O_m, [R_1, T_a(R_1)], [R_2, T_a(R_2)] > \quad (7)$$

Fig. 2 shows an example of the information captured by our model. Both workflows (W_1 and W_2) have modules that manipulate data in relation R. The sequence of states for R, which is maintained by the database system, is also shown in the figure. For instance, modules m_{12} and m_{13} of W_1 can be represented by functions

$$f_{m_{12}}(I_{12}, [R, T_1(R)]) = \; <O_{12}, [R, T_1(R)] > \qquad (8)$$
$$f_{m_{13}}(I_{13}, [R, T_1(R)]) = \; <O_{13}, [R, T_2(R)] > \qquad (9)$$

respectively. Given these functions, we know that m_{12} only retrieves data from relation R, since states before and after the execution are the same, and that m_{13} modifies relation R—a new state is created. In this case, we also know that m_{13} is responsible for $\Delta_{2,1}$, i.e., the set of changes applied to $S_1(R)$. Note that the integrated model also exposes parts of the database provenance that, although not directly observed by the workflows, affect their results. In this example, only the changes in $\Delta_{2,1}$ are visible to the workflow. Nonetheless, when W_2 executes, m_{21} reads state $S_4(R)$; as state $S_2(R)$ was the last one managed by the workflow system, we know that $\Delta_{4,2}$ ($\Delta_{4,3} + \Delta_{3,2}$) was performed by external agents.

2.3   Enabling Reproducibility

When a workflow manipulates data in a database, to ensure reproducibility, it is necessary to take into account the database states, since different database states might lead to different results (see Fig. 1a). In our model, database states are uniquely identified and made explicit in the provenance as input and output for the workflow. Because states before the execution of a module are captured in the provenance, by re-enacting the workflow instance using the stored state, it is possible to reproduce its results. Consider, for example, workflow W_2 of Fig. 2. Reproducing this workflow instance is possible because we have recorded the following information:

$$f_{m_{21}}(I_{21}, [R, T_4(R)]) = \; < O_{21}, [R, T_4(R)] >$$

In this case, if the current state of relation R is not $S_4(R)$, module m_{21} needs to retrieve data from R as if R were in this state. Because we know that the transaction time for the original execution was $T_4(R)$, we can retrieve the corresponding state $S_4(R)$. Then, m_{21} can use this state in its execution, and the results can be correctly reproduced.

2.4   Querying Provenance

With workflow and database provenance integrated, it is possible to perform queries that straddle the workflow and database systems. Below, we use examples to illustrate different queries that are supported by the integrated model.

Lineage of an output. Consider Fig. 2. Using our model, through the set of workflow connections and links to the database states, we can trace the complete provenance of output O_{14}, which includes information about both input data I_{11} and database state $S_1(R)$, which is used to produce outputs that are fed into m_{14}.

$$lineage(O_{14}) = \{W_1, I_{11}, [R, T_1(R)]\}$$

Another important benefit of our model is that the combined provenance includes information about changes to the database which may affect the results of the workflow, even though they may not be directly observed by the workflow system.

Consider for example a query to find the lineage of output O_{23}. Even though the changes in $\Delta_{3,2}(R)$ were performed by agents external to the workflow system, the set of operations are present in the backlog and can thus be retrieved from the database. In addition, by following the provenance links, we can also infer that states $S_1(R)$ and $S_2(R)$, as well as workflow W_1 with input I_{11}, have contributed to O_{23}.

Lineage of a database state. Consider module m_{13} in Fig. 2. The function corresponding to this module that is stored as provenance is shown in Equation 9. From this function, we can infer that the output of m_{13} (O_{13}) depends on its input (I_{13}) as well as on state $S_1(R)$ ($T_1(R)$). Besides, we can also infer that state $S_2(R)$ is derived by this module using input I_{13} and state $S_1(R)$. In this case, we have the following:

$$lineage(S_2(R)) = \{W_1, f_{m_{13}}, I_{13}, [R, T_1(R)]\}$$

Note that, as we have both $T_1(R)$ and $T_2(R)$, we can not only retrieve $S_1(R)$ and $S_2(R)$ from $\mathcal{S}(R)$, but also $\Delta_{2,1}(R)$. Consequently, it is also possible to construct answers that include fine-grained information about the effect of m_{13} on relation R. In other words, we know exactly which tuples were inserted, updated or deleted by m_{13}.

Lineage of a tuple. Using our model, it is also possible to retrieve the lineage of individual tuples. Given a tuple s inserted in the database by a workflow, we compute its lineage as follows. First, we search the backlog relation for s. By using its unique identifier K (Definition 2), a *select* operation can be performed in the backlog relation to get the set of transaction times T associated with s. Then, we search for each transaction time in $T_i \in T$ in the set M of the modules in workflow instance W. If T_i is an output, and not an input, of function f_m, it means that f_m created the state identified by T_i, i.e., f_m modified s. In this case, W and f_m are included in the lineage of s. We can also retrieve Op from the backlog relation to know exactly what was the modification that f_m performed in s.

How-provenance. If a workflow module modifies a relation R, using our model, it is possible to identify exactly which modifications were performed. As we can retrieve the set $\Delta_{j,i}(R)$ of modifications from the backlog, we know exactly *how* a module modified the relation from $S_i(R)$ to $S_j(R)$.

3 Implementation

As a proof-of-concept for our model, we have implemented it using the VisTrails system [7,16] and the Oracle RDBMS [14]. VisTrails is workflow-based data exploration system that provides support for provenance. Oracle is a leader in the relational database market and in their released system, they support temporal database features. Notably, the Total Recall [15] sub-system makes it possible to automatically track every change to the database as well as to query the historical information. Once the Total Recall option is enabled for a relation in the database, an append-only *history table* is created, which keeps track of the tuple-level changes applied to the relation. Like in the backlog scheme [11], each change to the relation recorded in the history table is identified by the transaction time of the modification.

An interesting aspect of Oracle Total Recall is the ability to query in a relation as of a time in the past. Given an identifier to a time in the past, Total Recall recovers the state associated with this time so queries can be performed. The identifier can be either a timestamp or a system change number (SCN), which is an integer that uniquely maps to a timestamp. Total Recall also allows the user to query versions of the relation within a time range, which includes all the modifications that occurred within that range. The syntax of these queries in SQL is as follows:

```
SELECT "column_name" FROM "table_name"
     AS OF "time"
```

```
SELECT "column_name" FROM "table_name"
     VERSIONS BETWEEN "time_1" AND "time_2"
```

Note that querying as of a time in the past is similar to retrieving a state from $S(R)$ given its corresponding transaction time. Consequently, this syntax can be used to reproduce previous results. Also, querying between ranges of time is similar to retrieving the difference between states, i.e., the delta (Δ).

The VisTrails Total Recall Package. To support the integration between VisTrails and Oracle Total Recall provenance, we have created a *Total Recall* package for VisTrails[3]. This package consists of three modules: *DBConnection*, *CloseDBConnection* and *OracleSQLSource*. The first two modules are used to open and close a connection with an Oracle database, respectively. The third one is the module used to execute commands in the database. We assume that this module corresponds to the execution of a single transacation.[4] When *OracleSQL-Source* is executed, it automatically retrieves from the database provenance the transaction times, represented as SCN, associated with states before and after its execution ($T_b(R)$ and $T_a(R)$). This information is then recorded in the workflow provenance.

So that users can reproduce prior workflow executions, we have extended the VisTrails provenance exploration interface: a user can select a particular execution and request it to be reproduced by clicking on the *reproduce* button (see Fig. 3). When users request to reproduce a workflow execution, the package checks the transaction times for the modules in the workflow that access

---

[3] For more information about package creation in VisTrails, we refer the reader to the VisTrails' Users Guide [17].

[4] Note that if multiple transactions are required, they can be modeled using multiple modules.

Fig. 3. Users may request workflows to be reproduced through the VisTrails provenance exploration interface

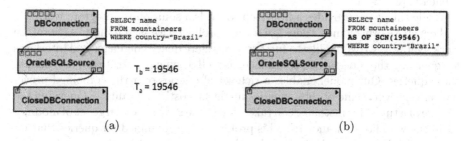

(a)   (b)

Fig. 4. When the workflow is executed (a), transaction times before and after the execution are retrieved. If this workflow instance is to be reproduced (b), the transaction times are detected to be the same, and then, the query is modified so the correct state can be used.

the database. To simplify the discussion, let us assume there is only one such module. If $T_b = T_a$, it means that the transaction only retrieves data from the relation. For this case, the original query is automatically rewritten: the "AS OF" construct is used to ensure that the query will be run over the database state associated with T_b. It is important to note that the query rewrite is transparent to the user. Fig. 4 illustrates this process. The module *OracleSQLSource* performs a *select* operation over the relation *mountaineers*. When the workflow is executed (Fig. 4a), transaction times before and after the module execution are retrieved from the database provenance ($T_b = T_a = 19546$). When the workflow instance of Fig. 4a is reproduced (Fig. 4b), the system first detects that both T_b and T_a are the same; then, the module automatically modifies the query to retrieve the state associated with SCN = 19546.

If $T_b < T_a$, it means that the workflow module modified the relation. In theory, an approach similar to the read-only queries could be used. However, in practice, this operation is more complicated and its performance depends on the implementation of the underlying database system. The reason for this is the fact that, for the update to be re-applied, the original state must be reconstructed and materialized: all transactions that committed between T_a and T_b must be rolled back. If there are many such transactions, this operation can be time consuming.

4 Conclusion and Future Work

In this paper, we present a model that integrates database and workflow provenance. Inspired by work on transactional temporal databases, to bridge the gap between the stateless model of scientific workflow systems and stateful databases, our model explicitly captures and stores information about the database states observed by workflows. With this additional information, it is possible not only to reproduce workflow executions, but also to support lineage queries that go across provenance information in a database and workflow system. We have also described a prototype implementation of our model using the VisTrails system and the Oracle RDBMS. This implementation provides evidence that our approach is practical.

While this work provides a first step towards a solution to integrate workflow and database provenance, there are several problems we plan to address in future work. Notably, we would like to further investigate query languages and interfaces for querying the integrated provenance, as well as efficient strategies to evaluate these queries. Our model enables a rich set of queries over the combined provenance. However, some of these queries might be costly to evaluate. Querying the lineage of a tuple, for instance, can take a long time if we have a large set of modules M in the workflow instance W. This problem is compounded for queries that involve multiple workflow instances. Another potentially interesting aspect to consider are changes to the structure of relations, i.e., the data definition language (DDL) operations, which are not captured in the backlog scheme.

Acknowledgments. We thank Dieter Gawlick and Venkatesh Radhakrishnan for insightful discussions on the Oracle Total Recall option and for their guidance in the implementation of our prototype. We also thank Jan Van den Bussche for his feedback on our initial ideas for the integrated model.

References

1. Acar, U., Cheney, J., Bussche, J.V.D., Vansummeren, S., Buneman, P., Kwasnikowska, N.: A graph model of data and workflow provenance. In: Proceedings of the USENIX Workshop on the Theory and Practice of Provenance (TaPP), p. 11 (2010)

2. Amsterdamer, Y., Davidson, S.B., Deutch, D., Milo, T., Stoyanovich, J., Tannen, V.: Putting lipstick on pig: enabling database-style workflow provenance. Proceedings of VLDB Endowment 5(4), 346–357 (2011)
3. Cheney, J., Chiticariu, L., Tan, W.C.: Provenance in databases: Why, how, and where. Foundations and Trends in Databases 1(4), 379–474 (2009)
4. Davidson, S.B., Freire, J.: Provenance and scientific workflows: challenges and opportunities. In: Proceedings of the ACM SIGMOD, pp. 1345–1350 (2008)
5. A matter of time: Temporal data management in DB2 for z/OS (2010)
6. Fomel, S., Claerbout, J.: Guest editors' introduction: Reproducible research. Computing in Science & Engineering 11(1), 5–7 (2009)
7. Freire, J., Koop, D., Santos, E., Scheidegger, C., Silva, C.T., Vo, H.T.: VisTrails. In: The Architecture of Open Source Applications. Lulu.com (2011)
8. Freire, J., Koop, D., Santos, E., Silva, C.T.: Provenance for computational tasks: A survey. Computing in Science and Engineering 10(3), 11–21 (2008)
9. Gawlick, D., Radhakrishnan, V.: Fine grain provenance using temporal databases. In: Proceedings of the USENIX Workshop on the Theory and Practice of Provenance (TaPP) (2011)
10. Huq, M.R., Wombacher, A., Apers, P.M.G.: Facilitating fine grained data provenance using temporal data model. In: Proceedings of the International Workshop on Data Management for Sensor Networks (DMSN). ACM (2010)
11. Jensen, C.S., Soo, M.D., Snodgrass, R.T.: Unifying temporal data models via a conceptual model. Information Systems 19, 513–547 (1993)
12. Koop, D., Santos, E., Bauer, B., Troyer, M., Freire, J., Silva, C.T.: Bridging Workflow and Data Provenance Using Strong Links. In: Gertz, M., Ludäscher, B. (eds.) SSDBM 2010. LNCS, vol. 6187, pp. 397–415. Springer, Heidelberg (2010)
13. Olston, C., Reed, B., Srivastava, U., Kumar, R., Tomkins, A.: Pig latin: a not-so-foreign language for data processing. In: Proceedings of the ACM SIGMOD, pp. 1099–1110 (2008)
14. Oracle database, http://www.oracle.com/technetwork/database/enterprise-edition/overview
15. Oracle total recall with oracle database 11g release 2 (2009)
16. The VisTrails Project, http://www.vistrails.org
17. The VisTrails Users' Guide, http://www.vistrails.org/usersguide

DEEP: A Provenance-Aware Executable Document System

Huanjia Yang[1], Danius T. Michaelides[1], Chris Charlton[2], William J. Browne[3], and Luc Moreau[1]

[1] Electronics and Computer Science, University of Southampton, UK
{hy2,dtm,L.Moreau}@ecs.soton.ac.uk
[2] Graduate School of Education, University of Bristol, UK
c.charlton@bristol.ac.uk
[3] School of Veterinary Science, University of Bristol, UK
william.browne@bristol.ac.uk

Abstract. The concept of executable documents is attracting growing interest from both academics and publishers since it is a promising technology for the the dissemination of scientific results. Provenance is a kind of metadata that provides a rich description of the derivation history of data products starting from their original sources. It has been used in many different e-Science domains and has shown great potential in enabling reproducibility of scientific results. However, while both executable documents and provenance are aimed at enhancing the dissemination of scientific results, little has been done to explore the integration of both techniques. In this paper, we introduce the design and development of DEEP, an executable document environment that generates scientific results dynamically and interactively, and also records the provenance for these results in the document. In this system, provenance is exposed to users via an interface that provides them with an alternative way of navigating the executable document. In addition, we make use of the provenance to offer a document rollback facility to users and help to manage the system's dynamic resources.

1 Introduction

e-Science aims to make available complex computation and analysis to users via tools that are easy to use and understand. In the context of quantitative social science, we observe that cutting edge methodological developments are beyond the reach of some social scientists that might benefit from new and complex analysis tools. The e-Stat project brings together statisticians, social and computer scientists in a collaboration funded by the UK's Economic and Social Research Council to build an environment for social scientists that provides learning pathways to bring these cutting edge developments into their working practices.

We also observe that traditional paper-based documents come short of meeting the goals of disseminating complex scientific research and that executable

P. Groth and J. Frew (Eds.): IPAW 2012, LNCS 7525, pp. 24–38, 2012.

documents may provide a possible solution. In the e-Stat project, we have developed DEEP(Documents with Embedded Execution and Provenance), a system that combines document presentation with a computational back-end, thereby combining the narrative and expository advantages of conventional documents with the interactive and experimental advantages of computational methods, allowing researchers to share research findings and techniques and also document their research process. Our document reading interface allows users to explore beyond the document content and examine the dynamically generated content in detail. This facility allows readers to get a deep understanding of the computation that a DEEP document encapsulates, providing a valuable learning pathway. DEEP is part of the statistical modelling package called Stat-JR[1] developed during the course of the e-Stat project.

It is vital for DEEP to keep track of the computational processes that occur and the dynamic content that they generate. This information is essential to understand artifacts created in context and is required in order that results can be validated, reproduced and reused. This matches the principle of data provenance models, which represent the information that can help determine the nature and derivation history of a data product[2]. In DEEP, we integrate provenance generation based on a specialization of the PROV Data Model (PROV-DM)[3]. The contributions of this work are threefold: firstly, we have designed a *provenance data model* to describe the internal behaviour and the resource organization of our executable document system; secondly, the information expressed according to this data model is used to provide users with novel resource and document *navigation experience*; thirdly, provenance information is also used to drive certain system functions, such as performing *execution status checking* and *document rollback*.

The remainder of this paper is organized as follows: we survey some related work in Section 2 before extracting the requirements and presenting some basic system design principles for the e-Stat executable document system in Section 3. We discuss our integration of provenance in the internal data model of DEEP in Section 4. In Section 5, we introduce the system functions that allow rendering and navigation of provenance information. The provenance-driven system functions are presented in Section 6. Finally we conclude our work in Section 7 before discussing our future work.

2   Related Work

Academic papers have always been the primary approach by which research results are disseminated within the science community. Their shortcomings, however, are also well recognized as not being able to provide sufficient support for verification, reproducibility and reuse of the research results that they describe. With the rapid developments of e-Science, the possibility of making interactive digital publications with more comprehensive information embedded within them has attracted interest from both academics and science publishers [4]. Bechhofer et al. [5] proposed the notion of Research Object (RO), which is defined as an aggregation of essential resources and information relating to experiments and investigations that helps other people to reproduce and reuse research results. One of the key motivations of such RO notion is its potential in supporting "rich publication". Researchers and publishers who are interested in such notion gathered together in the Beyond the PDF [6] workshop, in which a variety of models, publishing tools, and impact metrics were introduced. However, most of them focus on the annotation, linked data and bundling models for static resources, with no concrete design or development for executable document. In their work on verifiable computational scientific research, Gavish and Donoho[7] introduce the notion of identifying computational results via a URL and also establishing public repository services to archive all published results. The authors argue that proper usage of this notion and service structure will simplify the practice of reproducible research and executable papers, but no solution is explicitly given to develop this claim further. The Author-Review-Execute Environment[8] has a similar notion of linked results, but it locates the results archive on authors' own machines. This requires that each author maintains a server and installs the service to expose the data and the execution resources, which raises issues of security and adoption. The SHARE environment[9] shows more progress by providing the execution services directly on its server. However, it still has not achieved an integrated interface for both the paper reading and the executions. Instead, for accessing the original data and executions, users have to use a separate view that just leads to a remote virtual machine with the required execution environment. The Collage system[10] joins the static content in the documents with interactive/dynamic components that enable the readers and reviewers to access original data contained within to validate the results by re-executing the software that generated them, and to get the document dynamically updated with the latest results. Compared to other existing systems, Collage provides a unified, dynamic and interactive document reading interface for an improved reading experience. However, it lacks the flexibility of supporting multiple executions in one document and the ability of navigating the resource structure.

Provenance is well understood in the context of art or digital libraries, where it refers to the documented history of an art work or a digital object respectively[11]. Provenance has also shown great potential in the e-Science domain, as it provides a data product's derivation history, which is crucial information for validating and reproducing the results[2]. It allows users to understand, verify and even reuse the data, and thus helps achieve a better level of research reproducibility. For the past decade, much work has been done to advocate provenance in workflow applications in various scientific domains[12], where provenance has shown some of its promising features in leveraging effective dissemination of research results. However, little has been done to integrate provenance into the field of executable documents. The authors in [13] propose a provenance based infrastructure to support the executable document's life cycle, while in [14] the authors attempt to create paper publications with provenance embedded in them to describe appropriate data and results. However, in both these papers, the proposed designs depend strongly on a specific workflow system for executions and content reading.

Some systems hide the complexities of running workflows from the user by providing easy to use front-ends configured for the the application in mind. VisMashup [15] allows the creation of custom visualization applications using VisTrails as the underlying dataflow system. Web applications are a popular delivery platform such as in the Digital Synthesis Framework[16].

3   DEEP Requirements and Design

The requirements for DEEP documents and the DEEP system, based on the project scenarios are as follows:

Interactive: DEEP documents should provide a compelling, interactive and immersive environment. They should be reactive to user input and authors must be able to write content that can be tailored to the reader's inputs.

Interface with Significant Computation: DEEP should integrate with execution back-ends to perform non-trivial computation. Such integration should be seamless and maintain the document metaphor.

Exploratory: DEEP and documents written for the system should allow the reader to explore the material assembled within the document and should support them in understanding the relationships between elements of the document.

Complete Access: the user should be able to view all static and dynamic resources used and generated the DEEP document and not just those those the author chose to show in the main body of the document. Such material would help improve the user's understanding, and provide a valuable resource as their capability improves.

Dynamic to Static: DEEP documents have a variety of uses and we identify a spectrum of content from dynamic to static. A fully dynamic document would consist of only dynamic or computational resources - such as an electronic notebook. A static document, on the other hand, requires no computational backend as all possible dynamic resources would be contained in the DEEP document. An academic paper would be an example of such a static document. Provenance included in the document describes the relationships between any contained dynamic resources and the author would decide what dynamic resources are included.

3.1   DEEP System Design and Overview

The major components of DEEP are shown in Figure 1. A Web Browser(1) acts as the front-end providing a familiar interface to users with a strong linking and navigation metaphor. HTML is the chosen format for the visual content in DEEP, since we did not want to have to invent a new document and rendering language. In addition, by using a widely known and used format, authors should find it easier to write content (because there is a wealth of material available about writing HTML and they can use a wide range of HTML editing tools).

A significant design decision in the system is the relationship between the visual content and the execution environment. We consider a DEEP document to consist of a collection of resources of different types and uses (for example static HTML content, a dataset to be used in some computation, a graph that was created by an execution). This resource-centric approach informs the design of the interface between DEEP and the execution engine. The action of the user reading a DEEP document establishes relevant resources which are made available to the execution engine, which, in turn, may create new resources. An "execution environment" provides the container to which resources are made available in the system. Resources have their own unique identifiers but are also "bound" into the environment with simple names ("binding names"). The unique identifiers are used by the system whereas binding names are used by the authors to anchor dynamic resources into their document as the resources become available.

The DEEP Server component (4 in Figure 1) maintains the execution environments and generates notifications when resources are created, removed or bound into the execution environments. These notifications trigger activities in the browser front-end for rendering and user interaction, and in the execution engines(9) via the engine API(3) . The DEEP Server uses the Resource Management component(5) for storage of DEEP document files(8), provenance generation(6) and an RDF store(7) for metadata storage and querying. An HTTP server(2) exposes the DEEP Server to the Web Browser and the front-end written in HTML and Javascript.

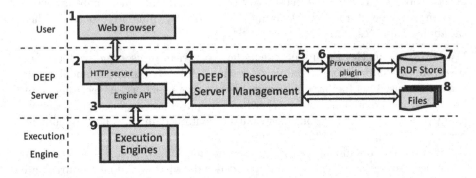

Fig. 1. DEEP system structure

Figure 2 shows the browser based reading interface showing an example DEEP document from the e-Stat project. The interface consists of navigational elements: the menubar at the top, the page number lists top and bottom and the contents list top to the left. The main body of the document shows a number of paragraphs of static content with dynamic content (in boxes with curved corners) placed at certain points between them. The first piece of dynamic content consists of an input widget in which the user can select the explanatory variables for the statistical model. The remaining items of dynamic content (some

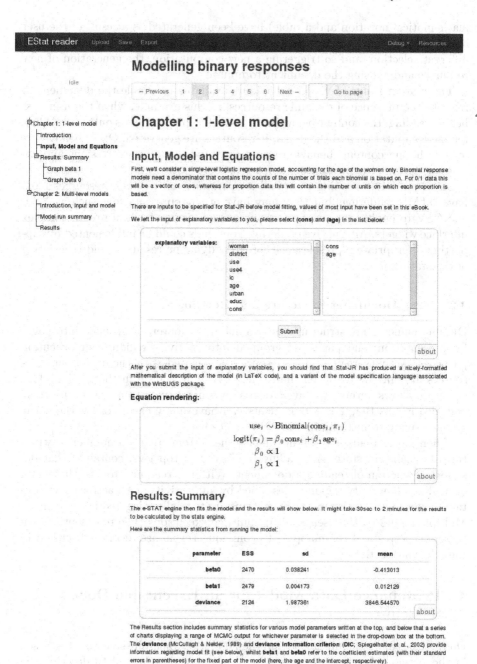

Fig. 2. Screenshot of the reader interface displaying a DEEP document

mathematical notation and a table) have been generated as a result of the user input. At any time, the user is free to return to the input widget and make a different selection, and so triggering a new computation, the generation of new resources and causing the document to update.

There are a range of visual behaviours available to enable the document to react to the presence of dynamic resources. In this example, when the user first begins reading, the content below the input box is hidden and is only revealed after the computation and the dynamic resources are generated. Other behaviours include hiding content, behaviours that are conditional on expressions and extracting specific fragments from resources.

Since the DEEP reading front-end is a browser, all dynamic resources must have HTML renderings but they may have other representations such as XML and CSV to enable exporting of resources and also to facilitate more complex interface widgets. Alternative rendering front-ends could be implemented by supporting appropriate representations of these dynamic resources and translating of the static content.

3.2   DEEP Document Structure and Reading

DEEP documents are structured in two manners: content is grouped into pages for presentation; and pages are grouped into "activity regions" for execution purposes. Activity regions have resources associated with them and these resources are only active when the reader is reading a page in that region. This structure allows authors to have a degree of control over when execution occurs and also means that DEEP documents can have many executions without the system having to instantiate all resources at once.

When a user reads a DEEP document, the system creates a number of structures to maintain state. A "reading process" is a top level container that describes the action of reading a document. Within a reading process, the action of reading an activity region is described by an "activity". An activity can contain one or more "executions". Executions are typically triggered by user input. Multiple inputs by the user result in multiple executions. The representation of these structures and the mapping to common provenance terms is discussed in the following section.

4   Provenance Data Model for an Executable Document System

On the basis of the requirements and the DEEP document file structure discussed in the previous section, we present a provenance data model to describe the system's behaviour and resource organization.

Our model is based on PROV [3], a standardization of a number of provenance vocabularies[17]. As shown in Figure 3, the internal provenance data model consists of two components: the definition component and the runtime component. The definition component consists of information defined by the author in the

DEEP document file, which is loaded and stored in DEEP's RDF store when the file is imported. The information is the DEEP document's descriptive metadata, which provides the basic information for the document as well as the organization structure of the static content and resources contained within it. More specifically, it describes the activity regions contained in the document and the resources associated with each of them. All the resource files contained in the DEEP document, as well as the file itself and the activity regions contained, are considered as PROV entities, and are represented as ellipses in Figure 3. One thing to note is that an activity region is linked to each of its resources via a resource binding, which is a ternary relation that also specifies a "binding name". This allows an actual resource to be bound with multiple activity regions, but with different names in each of them to avoid confusion. It also provides a simple way for DEEP document authors to notate the resources and to place the dynamic content in the document's HTML content.

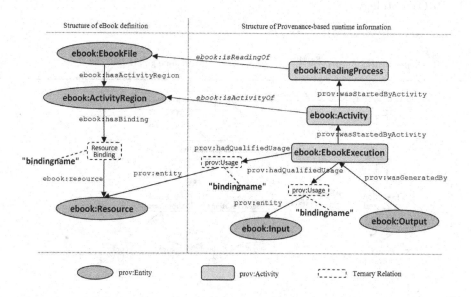

Fig. 3. Structure of data defined in DEEP document files and provenance recorded during reading

The runtime component contains the provenance information recorded automatically during DEEP document reading. For this information, three activity types are defined in an **ebook** namespace: **ReadingProcess**, **Activity** and **EbookExecution**. They are subtypes of **prov:Activity** and represent the reading of an DEEP document, the notion of being in an activity region and a specific execution respectively. The relations **isReadingOf** and **isActivityOf** associate them with appropriate static structures. The PROV **wasStartedByActivity** relation expresses that the **ReadingProcess** initiates an **Activity** when the reader enters an activity region and also that an `Activity` initiates an `EbookExecution` as a result of the execution engine having appropriate resources. All types of resource consumed by the `EbookExecution` processes are subtype of `prov:Entity`, including `ebook:Resource`, which is the resource file already defined in the definition component, and `ebook:Input`, which is the collection of parameters given by the user during reading. They are all linked to the corresponding `EbookExecution` processes with the PROV `Usage` relation. The ternary relation is used so that the "binding name" that the resource used in the execution can be specified. The results generated by `EbookExecution` are of type `ebook:Output`, a subtype of `prov:Entity`, and are linked to the corresponding `EbookExecution` processes with the PROV relation `wasGeneratedBy`.

Using this model, the system can construct a provenance graph for each reading process created by the user. It is a directed graph that grows as the user's reading activity proceeds. As we use a semantic web backend with an RDF store to persist and query data, such provenance graph is recorded with terms from the PROV ontology [18].

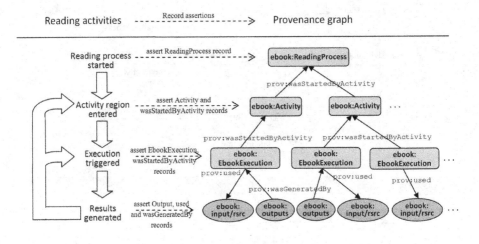

Fig. 4. DEEP document reading activities and the construction of provenance graph

The construction of the provenance graph with respect to the general system activities involved in reading a DEEP document is shown in Figure 4. The assertions of the provenance record are caused by a few key events during reading. Those events include starting a new reading process, entering an activity region, triggering an execution and the generation of an execution result. The first three events are user-triggered events, which cause assertion of `prov:Activity` records with corresponding subtypes and `prov:wasStartedByActivity` records where appropriate. In the case of triggering an execution, the `EbookExecution` instances are also linked to each static resource it consumed with a `used` relation.

The last event, however, is triggered internally when a result is obtained from the execution engine. The system creates an `ebook:Output` instance for the result with a corresponding subtype depending on its nature. For example, an execution may consume statistical template, dataset and input files to generate results in the form of figures, tables, code and LaTeX based equations etc. They are represented in the provenance graph with a URI and an attribute that points to their file location. Moreover, they are directly connected to the instance of the `ebook:EbookExecution` process that generated them by the relation `prov:wasGeneratedBy`.

With the provenance data model and its implementation, the system is able to perform automated recording of the provenance graph that describes the complete system activity and dynamic resource organization within an DEEP document. In the following two sections, we show that by properly presenting or extracting the required information from the provenance recorded, the system can enable additional functionality and provide the users with a better reading experience.

5   Presenting and Navigating Provenance Information - Exposing Provenance to Support Users

Provenance information recorded in existing provenance-aware systems is usually linked to the corresponding resource, so that it can be used by itself or other applications. Whilst this information is traditionally consumed by machines, we also consider it useful in certain circumstances to expose the provenance to human users.

In DEEP, dynamic resources are generated at many stages in the user's reading process. Although an author may write about these dynamic resources in the body of an document, the user may still need additional information regarding these resources and the executions that generated them for the following reasons:

- A reader may want to see an overview of the dynamic resources and the resources used to generate them, either because the document does not go into enough detail or because a clearer view will help in understanding the relationships between the various resources;
- The DEEP document allows the reader to try out different inputs for the same execution. As they do so, corresponding dynamic resources embedded in the DEEP document content are updated with the new results. However, the reader may want to access old results in order to make comparisons;
- Executions triggered by the reading process may generate more outputs than those that the DEEP document author has chosen to show directly in the document. The reader might be interested in these additional resources.

In order to expose this additional information, we have introduced the "resource view" into the reading interface. It is accessible from the menu bar at the top of the reading interface or by clicking on the "About" link next to each dynamic resource embedded in the document content. The resource view, shown in Figure 5, consists of a resource tree view and an information panel, which contains four tabs displaying the content, information, provenance and export links of a selected resource.

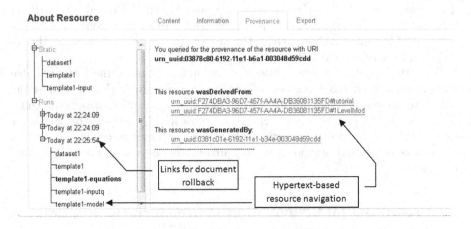

Fig. 5. The resource tree (left) and the provenance tab (right)

The resource tree shows the resources used in the current reading process in two categories: 'Static' and 'Runs'. The 'static' resources are included in the DEEP document to support the executions. In the context of the statistical application these may include statistical model templates (which construct statistical models), datasets and pre-defined input sets. The 'Runs' category lists executions that have been carried out in the current activity region of the document. Each of the executions can be further extended to show a sub-tree of all the resources used and generated allowing the user to gain a deeper understanding of the dynamic nature of the document. These executions could be those triggered by the author and subsequently included in the DEEP document or they could be executions instigated by the reader. The distinction between the two is not clear in the resource tree interface (except via the time labels) and needs improving.

In the information panel, the *Content* tab displays the actual content of the resource, whilst the *Information* tab shows additional metadata associated with it. The *Provenance* tab shows the provenance of a resource including its relationship with the reading process, executions and other resources. The *Export* tab allows the user to extract resources from the DEEP document in appropriate formats. The resource view is designed to let the user navigate around the resources in the usual hypertext manner by clicking on links in both the resource tree and the information and provenance tabs.

The resource view is fully driven by the provenance graph of the current reading process. This graph is obtained from a provenance service in the backend server by making an HTTP GET request on the provenance URL of a reading process. When a provenance request is received, the provenance service traverses the named-graph for the reading process, and builds the provenance graph using Provpy, a Python-based binding for PROV-DM [3] that we have developed. The library serializes the provenance graph into PROV-JSON[19]. On the client side, we have developed a simple JavaScript library "provjs" to parse and query PROV-JSON graphs and the web application uses it to build the resource tree and the information and provenance tabs.

6   Provenance-Aware Interactive Reading - Using Provenance to Drive System Functionality

Many existing provenance-aware systems focus on the ability of automatically recording and sharing of provenance information (provenance is often just recorded, and made available as raw data). In DEEP, we take this a step further by not only exposing provenance information, but also by using it to drive some system functionality: the DEEP document execution status checking and document rollback.

6.1   DEEP Document Execution Status Checking

The document execution status checking is used by DEEP to determine whether a specific computation needs to be performed. By avoiding unnecessary computation, and instead drawing on previously calculated results, DEEP is more responsive to user interaction. The presence of these reusable results arises from two situations. Firstly, they may be stored in the DEEP document file because the author determined that they were important (for example in a static document where all the possible dynamic resources have be pre-calculated). Secondly, as a user reads and interacts with a DEEP document dynamic resources are created. If the user returns to a configuration of inputs that has been explored before, the dynamic resources generated previously can be reused.

Given the resource-centric design of DEEP and execution environment, the query to determine whether a previous execution can be reused is simply stated as: given the current set of inputs, is there an existing execution that has exactly the same set of inputs with exactly the same mapping to bound names. Figure 6 shows the SPARQL query that we generate to determine suitable executions where we have an `prov:Used` for each input and the variables `cur_act_region` and `input1` to `inputN` are passed in as parameters to the query. This query is executed on the named-graph for the current reading process and if there is a matching execution, the system finds all the outputs for that execution and reinstates those resources. Essentially, the combination of resource storage and our provenance information allow us to perform a form of memorization where the focus is on the needs of the document and is agnostic to the execution engine. This caching, however, is similar to caching that occurs in some workflow systems such as the VisTrails Cache Manager[20] in the VisTrails system. Execution status checking is not a frequently triggered activity, so, although performance of the SPARQL queries has not been observed to be critical, the technique of finding existing executions by querying using a signature of inputs could be applied here should the provenance graphs become large (i.e. large numbers of executions or executions with large numbers of inputs).

```
SELECT ?exec WHERE { ?exec rdf:type ebook:EbookExecution.
       ?exec prov:wasStartedByActivity ?activity.
       ?activity ebook:isActivityOf ?cur_act_region.
       ?exec prov:used ?input1.
       ?exec prov:used ?input2.
       ...
       ?exec prov:used ?inputN. }
```

Fig. 6. The SPARQL query used to check for an existing execution

6.2   DEEP Document Rollback

The other system function driven by provenance is document rollback. During the reading of a DEEP document, the user can return to parameter input areas in the document and give different responses. This will trigger new executions and cause the document content to update with different results. Although the resource view allows the inspection of individual results from any execution, the user may prefer to see them in the context of the DEEP document content and therefore wish to revisit a previous execution by returning the state of the document to that point in time. This is performed purely from the point of view of the document and document reading infrastructure and is not reliant on support from the execution engine.

We expose this document rollback facility by allowing the user to click on executions in the resource tree shown in Figure 5. In response, DEEP must reinstate all resources that were generated by the relevant execution. These resources are found by querying the provenance record with a SPARQL query and rebinding them into the execution environment.

These two facilities of DEEP rely on the recording of provenance and the use of RDF and SPARQL to represent and query it.

7   Conclusion and Future Work

Executable documents have become a promising e-Science technology that aims to increase comprehension and reproducibility in the dissemination of scientific results. Data provenance has also shown its potential to enable reproducibility of research results by providing a uniform description of their derivation history. In an attempt to bring together these two technologies, DEEP integrates provenance in an executable document system. This paper reported three main contributions in terms of provenance study. Firstly, we have integrated provenance with the system's internal data structure by using a specialization of the PROV data model to describe the behaviour and resource organization of the system. By recording this provenance for all the dynamic results generated during reading, DEEP is able to provide their full derivation history. Secondly, in terms of the usage of provenance, we have shown that, in our interface, provenance can be exposed to and navigated by DEEP users. This provides the users with a different level of understanding of the resource structure, as well as new ways to navigate the document. Thirdly, we have designed two of DEEP's features, the execution status checking and the document rollback, to be based fully on provenance. This demonstrates that data provenance is not just information to be shown to the reader, but can also be used to drive the system functionality.

DEEP provides a framework that could be applicable to a broad range of scientific domains. With the integration of provenance in our DEEP documents, we can tackle issues of verification and reproducibility and our future work will aim to improve DEEP's infrastructure and functionality to support this. Such work could be twofold: firstly, we aim to make provenance exportable and transferable within the DEEP document files. This means that a user could generate their results in the form of an document and disseminate it to other readers. The provenance carried with the document will help the reader to understand, examine and even reproduce results for the purposes of validating or reusing them. Secondly, our use of a unified representation of provenance, means that we could integrate with other provenance-aware software and provide the user with more detailed provenance, allowing reproducibility and validation at various levels. In terms of modelling and implementation, both of those two points may lead to the notion of provenance accounts being introduced into our system. This would allow us to bundle provenance generated by different users so that DEEP documents can be distributed multiple times to support collaborative work, and, to bundle provenance from different components, including third party software, for better information granularity.

Acknowledgments. This researched was conducted as part of the E-Stat project, funded by the ESRC (RES-149-25-1084) under the Digital Social Research programme. We wish to thank Richard Parker and our other colleagues at the Centre for Multilevel Modelling for their input into the design of our system.

References

1. The eStat Project: Stat-JR, http://www.bristol.ac.uk/cmm/research/estat/
2. Simmhan, Y.L., Plale, B., Gannon, D.: A survey of data provenance in e-science. SIGMOD Rec. 34(3), 31–36 (2005)
3. Moreau, L., Missier, P.: The PROV Data Model and Abstract Syntax Notation, http://www.w3.org/TR/prov-dm/ (retrieved March 28, 2012)
4. de Waard, A.: The Future of the Journal? Integrating research data with scientific discourse. Nature Precedings (713)

5. Bechhofer, S., Buchan, I., Roure, D.D., Missier, P., Ainsworth, J., Bhagat, J., Couch, P., Cruickshank, D., Delderfield, M., Dunlop, I., Gamble, M., Michaelides, D., Owen, S., Newman, D., Sufi, S., Goble, C.: Why linked data is not enough for scientists. Future Generation Computer Systems (2011)
6. Bourne, P., de Waard, A.: Beyond the PDF Workshop (2011),
   `http://sites.google.com/site/beyondthepdf`
7. Gavish, M., Donoho, D.: A Universal Identifier for Computational Results. Procedia Computer Science 4, 637–647 (2011)
8. Müller, W., Rojas, I., Eberhart, A., Haase, P., Schmidt, M.: A-R-E: The Author-Review-Execute Environment. Procedia Computer Science 4, 627–636 (2011)
9. Gorp, P.V., Mazanek, S.: SHARE: a web portal for creating and sharing executable research papers. Procedia Computer Science 4, 589–597 (2011)
10. Nowakowski, P., Ciepiela, E., Hareżlak, D., Kocot, J., Kasztelnik, M., Bartyński, T., Meizner, J., Dyk, G., Malawski, M.: The Collage Authoring Environment. Procedia Computer Science 4, 608–617 (2011)
11. PREMIS Working Group: Data dictionary for preservation metadata. Technical report (2005)
12. Moreau, L.: The Foundations for Provenance on the Web. Found. Trends Web Sci. 2(2-3), 99–241 (2010)
13. Koop, D., Santos, E., Mates, P., Vo, H.T., Bonnet, P., Bauer, B., Surer, B., Troyer, M., Williams, D.N., Tohline, J.E., Freire, J., Silva, C.T.: A Provenance-Based Infrastructure to Support the Life Cycle of Executable Papers. Procedia Computer Science 4, 648–657 (2011)
14. Bauer, B., Gukelberger, J., Surer, B., Troyer, M.: Publishing provenance-rich scientific papers. In: Procs. TAPP 2011 Theory and Practice of Provenance (2011)
15. Santos, E., Lins, L.D., Ahrens, J.P., Freire, J., Silva, C.T.: VisMashup: Streamlining the Creation of Custom Visualization Applications. IEEE Trans. Vis. Comput. Graph. 15(6), 1539–1546 (2009)
16. Myers, J., Marini, L., Kooper, R., McLaren, T., McGrath, R.E., Futrelle, J., Bajcsy, P., Collier, A., Liu, Y., Hampton, S.: A Digital Synthesis Framework for Virtual Observatories, Edinburgh, UK (2008)
17. Sahoo, S., Groth, P., Hartig, O., Miles, S., Coppens, S., Myers, J., Gil, Y., Moreau, L., Zhao, J., Panzer, M., Garijo, D.: Provenance Vocabulary Mappings. Technical report, W3C Provenance Incubator Group (August 2010)
18. Sahoo, S., McGuinness, D.: The PROV Ontology: Model and Formal Semantics, `http://www.w3.org/TR/prov-o/`
19. Huynh, T., Jewell, M., Keshavarz, A., Michaelides, D., Moreau, L., Yang, H.: The PROV-JSON Serialization, `http://users.ecs.soton.ac.uk/tdh/json/`
20. Bavoil, L., Callahan, S., Crossno, P., Freire, J., Scheidegger, C., Silva, C.T., Vo, H.: Vistrails: enabling interactive multiple-view visualizations. In: IEEE Visualization, VIS 2005, pp. 135–142 (October 2005)

Towards Unified Provenance Granularities

Timothy Lebo, Ping Wang, Alvaro Graves, and Deborah L. McGuinness

Tetherless World Constellation
Rensselaer Polytechnic Institute
Troy, NY, USA
{lebot,gravea3}@rpi.edu, {wangp5,dlm}@cs.rpi.edu
http://tw.rpi.edu

Abstract. As Open Data becomes commonplace, methods are needed to integrate disparate data from a variety of sources. Although Linked Data design has promise for integrating world wide data, integrators often struggle to provide appropriate transparency for their sources and transformations. Without this transparency, cautious consumers are unlikely to find enough information to allow them to trust third party content. While capturing provenance in RPI's Linking Open Government Data project, we were faced with the common problem that only a portion of provenance that is *captured* is effectively *used*. Using our water quality portal's use case as an example, we argue that one key to enabling provenance use is a better treatment of provenance granularity. To address this challenge, we have designed an approach that supports deriving abstracted provenance from granular provenance in an open environment. We describe the approach, show how it addresses the naturally occurring unmet provenance needs in a family of applications, and describe how the approach addresses similar problems in open provenance and open data environments.

Keywords: Data Integration, Transparency, Provenance Granularity, Derived Abstractions, Provenance of Provenance, Linked Data.

1   Introduction

Open Data is growing in popularity and is freely available for anyone to use and republish as they wish, with few or no restrictions from copyright, patents or other mechanisms of control. Open Government Data (OGD) is one rapidly growing portion of Open Data. Catalyzed in 2009 by the United States and the United Kingdom, governments from local to national levels are publishing their data for public use [14,5]. These data are available for personal or commercial use and offer the potential to increase government transparency and accountability and create many opportunities for businesses and communities. These data have the potential to help citizens understand important topics such as pollutants near their home [18], crimes in their neighborhood [8], public works[1], the economy [3], natural disasters[2] [9], and political activities [14].

---

[1] https://recollect.net

[2] http://purl.org/twc/lebo/ipaw/2012/od-natural-disasters

P. Groth and J. Frew (Eds.): IPAW 2012, LNCS 7525, pp. 39–51, 2012.

Although individual datasets may be interesting on their own, there is a hope and expectation that combining disparate datasets will lead to even more insight and value – the whole should be greater than the sum of its parts. Linked Open Data is becoming a popular method to connect and publish data on the web [10]. One highly cited view[3] has grown from twelve to 295 datasets between 2007 and 2011. Each of those 295 datasets ranges in size and comprises many more subsets of data. For example, the TWC-LOGD dataset[4] that our group publishes contains almost 10 billion RDF triples created from thousands of datasets. In addition, we have cataloged[5] more than 710,000 other datasets that can be added. The Linked Open Data cloud is continuing to grow and already provides information about a range of topics including Life Sciences, Government, Scholarly Publications, Social Media, and E-Commerce.

Unfortunately, current approaches for creating Linked Data present both implicit and explicit challenges around trust of the Linked Data itself. Because many primary data sources do not publish their material as Linked Data, third parties are left to independently transform and republish it. As illustrated in Figure 1, this forces application developers to choose between two sources of the same content. Although the first option is provided by an authoritative and recognizable source (usually with deep domain knowledge), this data is often not uniformly accessible and not linked to other data. Meanwhile, the second option is uniformly accessible and linked to other datasets, but is not provided by an authoritative source. These third party sources are often experts in technology, but not the particular subject matter. When consumers require more than a vague citation for a transformed dataset, the benefits of Linked Data cannot outweigh the potential risks introduced by a non-authoritative and non-transparent third party.

One obvious approach that third party aggregators can take is to provide transparency for the transformations that they perform as well as the sources used. Application developers would then be able to choose Linked Data instead of the primary source because its lineage is available for inspection. To demonstrate this kind of transparency, RPI's Linking Open Government Data project used the csv2rdf4lod conversion toolset [17] to capture provenance at each stage of Linked Data production. But after 18 months of capture, only a fraction of it has been used in applications.

The pitfall of capturing more provenance than is used is not new. As Chapman warns, *Don't just maintain provenance, maintain good provenance* [2]. But as closed provenance systems become open, homogeneous systems become heterogeneous, and local coordinations become distributed, how does one know what good provenance is *a priori*? Similarly, are there different notions of good provenance in different contexts? With these opening trends, less control of overall systems, and less knowledge of expected usage contexts, the problem of defining and maintaining good provenance becomes more challenging. Indeed, Linked

---

[3] http://richard.cyganiak.de/2007/10/lod/

[4] http://logd.tw.rpi.edu/twc-logd

[5] http://purl.org/twc/links/iogds

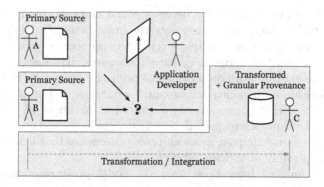

Fig. 1. Linked Data is often produced by third parties that transform data from various sources, which introduces a tradeoff between authoritative content and easier to use linked data. Although provenance enables transparency, excessive granularity may inhibit its use.

Open Data is an open system not only in the Open Data sense, but also in the sense of Moreau's [13] Open Provenance Vision. In the general conversion scenario that we describe above, *many* publishers offer primary data, *many* aggregators convert primary data to Linked Data, *many* developers choose among the data for their applications, and *many* audiences use them. All of these activities are performed across the world with loose, if any, coordination.

As systems become more open and information flows across multiple systems, we need reliable strategies for handling the disparity between what application developers need and what they get. We believe that framing these strategies around provenance granularity promises to address these growing challenges. In this paper, we describe a method to resolve *incongruent provenance granularities* using an open system design.

2 Related Work

Granularity is a widely studied problem in provenance. Gibson et al. [7] point out that the clutter of provenance capture obfuscates the conceptual view of processes. This observation parallels the **provenance granularity disparity** that our approach offers to address: too many details when fewer statements would adequately answer the question at hand. Gibson et al. show how user-defined views along with a high level summary of execution history can improve user understanding of provenance. ZOOM [1] focuses on user needs by offering provenance of customized granularity to achieve benefits like abstraction, privacy, and reuse between workflows. We expand on these ideas by showing how summarizations can be derived by third party consumers in an open environment.

Chapman and Jagadish [2] point out that provenance support needs more than a simple capture-store approach, which is a challenge we address. They also note that a choice in granularity is required and distinguish between a coarse-grained file level and a fine grain attribute level. However, the situation we present here motivates a distinction between coarse and fine granularities about the file level itself. Finally, while they note the importance of enabling *users* to actively view provenance at multiple levels, the approach we present resolves incongruent granularities between *systems* themselves. Ikeda and Widom [11] state that while existing work on provenance primarily focuses on modeling and capturing, there has been inadequate support for querying and using provenance. They also propose that provenance be captured at a variety of granularities. Alternatively, the approach we present here facilitates query and use by providing a mechanism to derive simpler, more abstract provenance that is more suitable for particular, possibly unanticipated uses.

Different techniques have been used to model provenance granularities. Stephan et al. [16] presents a multi-tier provenance model in which each tier has a unique purpose, different characteristics, and distinct levels of granularity. They use the Open Provenance Model (OPM) to encode their provenance and disseminate higher level provenance that are abstracted from provenance captured in different tiers, e.g. instruments used, parameters used, and quality/confidence level, to produce Value Added Products (VAPs). Ding et al.[4] propose *RDF molecules* as a way to handle granularities between a single triple and an entire graph. RDF molecules are generated by decomposing a graph into separate sub-graphs. Although this technique can be used to track the movement of RDF subgraphs across systems, it fails to apply when the graph is abstracted to new forms.

Other granularity techniques are oriented towards the end user or domain expert. WDo [15] is a framework for provenance granularity where domain experts use a graphical interface to specify process composition. Methods are treated as black boxes at one general level and further described at more specific levels in terms of how they transform information types. The results are described using an OWL ontology that extends the Proof Markup Language (PML) ontology [12]. While this approach is helpful to elicit appropriate abstractions from experts, its information types do not allow one to specify the detailed structures that are required for application consumption. Garijo [6] does something similar, but has the same publisher bias for abstraction instead of enabling third parties to derive their own abstractions for their own purposes.

3   csv2rdf4lod's Assertions of Granular Provenance

RPI's Linking Open Government Data (LOGD) project began collecting provenance on June 25th, 2010 using a strategy to encode provenance that might be useful to our anticipated applications. One persisting purpose is to enable transparency for third party transformations when creating well structured and highly connected Linked Data from various disparate sources. To date, the conversion automation has recorded more than a half million instances of the major PML classes (Information, SourceUsage, NodeSet, and InferenceStep) and used more than 200 InferenceEngines. We continue to reflect on what is there, how we are using it, and how we can get more value from it. This section provides an overview of the kinds of provenance captured and highlights some patterns that have worked well throughout the project's development. The granular, context-free provenance that we describe here will contrast with the abstract, user-driven provenance that we describe in the following section.

The Linked Data creation process has four principal stages: retrieval, preparation, conversion, and publishing.[6] While below we list the types of provenance captured in each, different themes emerge between stages. In the **retrieval** stage, it is paramount to distinguish between the materials obtained from the *source* and those that the third party integrator has *derived* from them. In the **preparation** stage, it is important to maintain a distinction between results produced automatically and results produced manually. Finally, in the **conversion** and **publication** stages, it is useful to maintain a distinction between data results and their provenance, which may change even when the results are identical.

During retrieval, data files are obtained from their primary source. A script that retrieves a given URL also records the person and user account initiating retrieval, the URL requested, time requested, HTTP interactions, and the checksum of the file received. This is perhaps the most critical capture because it maintains the connection between the local file on disk and the original URL.

During preparation, manually modifying files retrieved from authoritative sources is avoided because it is error prone and cannot be reliably repeated. Custom software and manual adjustments are minimized by specifying declarative conversion parameters to a common converter. However, human intervention may be necessary in some situations. Transparency of any necessary manual activity is maintained by storing results separately from their originals, associating the adjusted files to their predecessors, indicating the type of process applied, and citing the person and user account reporting the modifications.

Conversion and publishing are automated and is started by software and human agents. Each activity's inputs, parameters, and outputs are published at URLs and are commonly referenced by each actor's provenance assertions. Tabular data files are converted to RDF by csv2rdf4lod, which records its invocation time, version and hash, input file, transformation parameters, the person and user account invoking the conversion, and the generated dump files. Because metadata typically mentions time, it changes more regularly than the generated data and is thus stored in separate files. This way, hashes of unchanging data files can persist through reconversions. Finally, when RDF URLs are loaded into a triple store's named graph, provenance of the activity is stored in the same.

4   SemantAqua's Need for Abstracted Provenance

SemantAqua is one application that uses the provenance captured by csv2rdf4lod during the stages of Linked Data integration. SemantAqua is a water quality web portal[7] that demonstrates a semantic approach to environmental monitoring

---

[6] http://purl.org/twc/links/ipaw/2012/conversion-stages highlights the principal provenance captured for an example dataset.

[7] http://tw.rpi.edu/web/project/SemantAQUA

[18]. It integrates water test results from different government sources and allows users to explore results on a map, see their severity, and hypothetically apply different regulations from different political jurisdictions. One could, for example, classify water tests taken in a particular state against local state regulations, federal regulations, or regulations in states that are known to have stricter rules. SemantAqua introduces a provenance-based search facet that allows the user to select the data organizations he/she trusts, so that the portal will use only data from the selected organizations. This is done by restricting queries to only named graphs that are known to come from the selected organizations.

To achieve this functionality, SemantAqua needs to know the organizations that are attributed to each named graph. The project considered three different strategies to address this need. First, SemantAqua could depend on the attribution made by the data integrator, which is done automatically by csv2rdf4lod using the `source` identifier chosen by the curator. This assertion, however, may not be completely accurate and more cautious consumers may demand more detailed justification. For example, data-gov is commonly cited as a source, when the data is actually provided by specific agencies such as epa-gov or usgs-gov. Second, the application developer could manually maintain the list of attributions. This approach is undesirable because it requires additional effort and cannot be reapplied in other applications. The third approach is to use an automated abstraction of the granular provenance captured at each stage of the data integration process. Although this offers the most accuracy and justification for the attributions, it is not straightforward from the application's perspective to determine the connection from the named graph to the organization. Further, adequate support for this third option was not available prior to this work. To determine the attribution, software would trace the provenance of the named graph load, the conversion invocation, any and all preparations performed, and the retrieval of the original data files provided by the primary source.

Because the first option did not meet application requirements and the third option was not supported at the time, SemantAqua's initial prototype constructed and maintained a separate graph to provide the abstract provenance required to support the data source search facet. This custom work took developer resources away from other portal features and the intermediate solution is difficult to reuse. A more desirable solution is to build on a reusable framework that supports abstracted provenance, which we describe next.

5   Deriving Abstractive Provenance

The prior sections describe two example systems that participate in an Open Provenance Environment. The disparity between application needs and linked data aggregator services provides one example of incongruent granularity issues that we anticipate to grow as more systems realize the Open Provenance Vision.

Our strategy is to resolve incongruent provenance granularities that occur between two systems in an open environment by adding a third, independent component into the same environment. Figure 2 depicts an independent party

D creating a service that abstracts the original provenance in a way that the application can use with relative ease. The service is available for invocation by any system and can be called dynamically or accumulated for local use. We adopt the SADI Semantic Web Services Framework [19] for the design of the services and apply the DataFAQs linked data evaluation framework[8] to accumulate results for specific portions of provenance while capturing the provenance of accumulation. This approach can be applied to resolve incongruences between any systems that expose their provenance in any RDF vocabulary, including the PROV-O vocabulary in development by the W3C Provenance Working Group. The steps to our approach are as follows.

1. Define the type of entity whose provenance is required by the consumer
2. Define the type of provenance required by the consumer
3. Implement and deploy the independent service
4. Optionally find the service based on Steps 1 and 2
5. Accumulate results for the entities of interest, capturing provenance

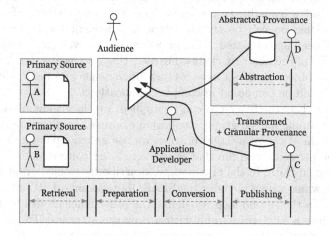

Fig. 2. In addition to Figure 1's situation, party D derives abstracted provenance from party C, which the application developer uses to determine which data to use from C

The first step is to define the type of entity whose provenance is required by the consumer. In our example from the previous sections, the entity type is a named graph in a particular SPARQL endpoint. The type of entity whose provenance is needed will be the topic of a consuming application; whatever an application or system "discusses" is a potential type of entity about which we may want provenance. The second step is to define the type of provenance required by the consumer. In our example, the type of provenance we need for the named graph is the source organization(s) that should be attributed for providing its contents. The third step is to implement and deploy the independent service. Because the

---

[8] http://purl.org/twc/id/software/datafaqs

entity type from Step 1 and the provenance type of Step 2 can be described in RDF using any vocabulary, we use the SADI framework to implement the service. SADI services accept HTTP POSTs of RDF descriptions and return additional RDF descriptions of the same instances. In our example, the service `named-graph-derivation` accepts RDF descriptions of sd:NamedGraph[9] and returns additional descriptions using the prov:wasAttributedTo relation. The fourth step to find the service based on Steps 1 and 2 is necessary in cases where the consumer is not aware of the service. Use of the SADI framework facilitates this search because SADI services use the myGrid vocabulary to specify their input and outputs as OWL classes. The final step is to accumulate results for the entities of interest, capturing provenance of the accumulation. In our example, we create RDF descriptions of sd:NamedGraphs, HTTP POST them to the service `named-graph-derivation`, and store their results in a triple store for query by applications. Although this accumulation can be performed in a variety of ways, we use the DataFAQs linked data evaluation framework because it records the provenance of each service invocation and automatically publishes results.

Applying the five steps above creates an independent collection of abstracted provenance that is available to the application and other systems. Further, the provenance collection can be traced to the independent service regardless of where it has been accumulated. This provenance of provenance enables justifications for any of the abstract claims. Further, this also means that provenance is a first class object that can have its own provenance and has no limitations on the way it can be composed in complex applications.

To illustrate how the five steps can be applied, we show some materials used to solve our running named graph attribution example. To illustrate the longest derivation chain of the conversion process, we use an example dataset that begins as a compressed Excel file that is extracted and converted to CSV before becoming Linked Data. In the first step, we describe the named graph whose attribution we want, which includes the SPARQL endpoint's URL and the name of the graph. In the second step, we define the provenance needed by the application, which is a sd:NamedGraph with a prov:wasAttributedTo relation. The results of these two steps are shown in the RDF fragments below. The third step is to implement `named-graph-derivation`, a SADI service that accepts the description from Step 1 and returns the description in Step 2. The service answers the question, "For a given graph name in a specific SPARQL endpoint, what agent is responsible for the data it contains?" Figure 3 illustrates the output of `named-graph-derivation`. From this graph, one can directly find the attribution by following the prov:wasAttributedTo relations from the #named-graph node. It also includes the named graph in question, and a derivation chain that leads from the named graph to the original download URL. The result is an abstraction of the granular provenance captured throughout all four stages of conversion. The domain name of the original download is used to name the agent responsible for the file. Although this usually represents an organization, it could also represent a person or a specific software agent.

---

[9] See http://prefix.cc/sd http://prefix.cc/prov and http://prefix.cc/moby.

```
# Step 1: Describing the named graph for which we want attribution.
:service a sd:Service;
 sd:endpoint <http://logd.tw.rpi.edu/sparql>;
 sd:availableGraphs [
    a sd:GraphCollection, dcat:Dataset;
    sd:namedGraph :named-graph;
 ] .
:named-graph a sd:NamedGraph;
 sd:name <http://logd.tw.rpi.edu/source/lebot/dataset/golfers> .

# Step 2: Describing the provenance needed.
:named-graph a sd:NamedGraph;
 prov:wasAttributedTo <http://graves.cl>;
  sd:name <http://logd.tw.rpi.edu/source/lebot/dataset/golfers> .
<http://graves.cl> a prov:Agent .
```

6   Discussion

Despite the tendency to focus on modeling and collecting provenance, there are perhaps greater challenges to process and effectively use what has been collected. The approach we present encourages a separation of interests that permits systems to continue to collect with the level of granularity that they deem fit, while contextual applications of the granular provenance may be developed independently to provide direct, easily accessible abstractions derived from the original provenance. A further advantage of deriving abstract provenance from granular is that the provenance of provenance can be used to provide justifications for any high level claims, which can increase their trustworthiness. In contrast, directly asserted abstract records cannot be further justified.

It is important to note that while csv2rdf4lod uses the Proof Markup Language (PML) to record its provenance, the named-graph-derivation service provides its abstraction using W3C's PROV-O vocabulary. We are thus demonstrating interoperability at a fairly granular level between one relatively long lived provenance interlingua and the emerging W3C vocabulary. More importantly, we show how our approach can interoperate between two different provenance vocabularies as was envisioned by the W3C provenance incubator group.[10] This approach also helps advance the W3C Provenance Working Group's objective to enable provenance interchange.

The approach we present also highlights and motivates an outstanding need that, if addressed, would provide significant value in an Open Provenance Environment. In our example, the Linked Data aggregator C would benefit greatly if it were informed of any subsequent processing of its data or granular provenance (i.e., what the abstractor D and application developer did). This way, subsequent visitors to C could be led to derivations that may better suit their

---

[10] http://www.w3.org/2005/Incubator/prov/wiki/
Provenance_Vocabulary_Mappings

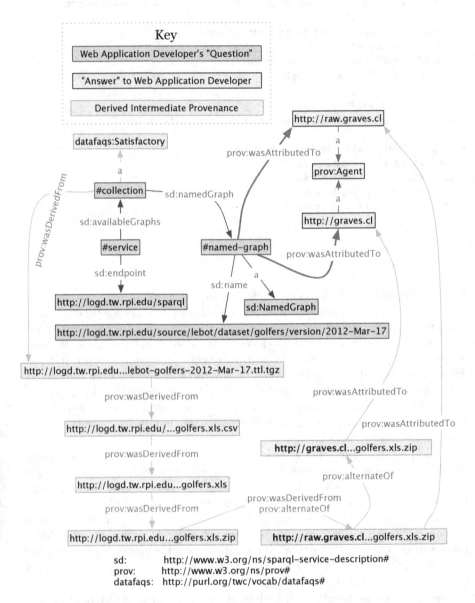

Fig. 3. PROV-O description returned by SADI service `named-graph-derivation` when given an RDF description of the named graph (blue) for which SemantAqua needed provenance (green). The service also returns an intermediate level of abstraction (gray) that can be used to justify the higher level of abstraction. Both the high and intermediate abstractions are derived from the detailed PML provenance about the named graph, which was provided by the data aggregator C.

needs. Similarly, the primary sources would also benefit by being informed about subsequent uses of their publications (i.e., what aggregator C, abstractor D, *and* the application developer did). Consumers should be able to trace provenance in both directions, not just backward. This kind of information can also be essential for evaluating each party's contribution and return on investment. These and other benefits are lost unless the community establishes so-called "ping-back" capabilities in standards such as the W3C PROV recommendation.

Future work could lead in several directions. The framework presented could be used to quantify the interoperability among provenance systems, by building abstraction services to reflect the representation of one system using alternative ontological representations. We currently handle PML and PROV-O, but more could be added. Since PROV-O is an emerging standard, we also expect authors of many other provenance vocabularies to map to it, thus furthering the goal of interoperability. Those authors may use the approach we present to achieve this mapping without interfering with their existing systems. Another direction could use reasoning to chain SADI services based on their OWL inputs and outputs that could lead to some powerful and automated provenance derivations. This would be particularly useful within the Open Provenance Vision, where developers will not know all systems available, may require provenance available in a variety of original representations, but can gather appropriate service descriptions and determine a solution automatically. It would also be interesting to apply the approach we present to the variety of existing abstraction algorithms, including those intended for end users. One advantage is that the summary results would remain as alternative provenance accounts that could be queried, consolidated, and reused by other systems for other purposes at later times. This contrasts with the traditional approach where the abstraction remains in the system and is lost after use.

7   Conclusion

As Open Data grows in popularity, so will the need for and use of Linked Data principles to integrate disparate sources. However, current integration methods provide limited support for transparency, thereby minimizing trust of their results. This causes a tradeoff between authoritativeness and ease of use that needs to be reconciled before Linked Data can be widely adopted. Linked Open Data is one environment that requires – and can realize – the Open Provenance Vision. Using an example from our SemantAqua water quality portal, we show how incongruent provenance granularities can inhibit the use of provenance between systems, and argue that this challenge will grow as more systems participate. We presented an approach and supporting technologies to resolve incongruent provenance granularities between two systems by adding a third independent component that derives abstract provenance from granular provenance sources. We showed how applying this approach fulfilled a real use case that attributes the source organization for the content in a SPARQL endpoint's named graph, which was determined by tracing granular provenance. This same approach can be applied to resolve other incongruent provenance granularities that we anticipate as more systems realize the Open Provenance Vision.

References

1. Biton, O., Cohen-Boulakia, S., Davidson, S.B., Hara, C.S.: Querying and managing provenance through user views in scientific workflows. In: Proceedings of the 2008 IEEE 24th International Conference on Data Engineering, ICDE 2008, pp. 1072–1081. IEEE Computer Society, Washington, DC (2008)
2. Chapman, A., Jagadish, H.V.: Issues in building practical provenance systems. IEEE Data Eng. Bull. 30(4), 38–43 (2007)
3. Craglia, M., Almirall, P.G., Bergadà, M.M., Queraltó Ros, P.: The socio-economic impact of the spatial data infrastructure of catalonia. Institute for Environment and Sustainability, Joint Research Centre, European Commission (2008)
4. Ding, L., Peng, Y., Pinheiro da Silva, P., McGuinness, D.L.: Tracking RDF Graph Provenance using RDF Molecules. Technical report, UMBC (April 2005)
5. Erickson, J.S., Rozell, E., Shi, Y., Zheng, J., Ding, L., Hendler, J.A.: Twc international open government dataset catalog. In: Proceedings of the 7th International Conference on Semantic Systems, pp. 227–229. ACM (2011)
6. Garijo, D., Gil, Y.: A new approach for publishing workflows: abstractions, standards, and linked data. In: Proceedings of the 6th Workshop on Workflows in Support of Large-Scale Science, pp. 47–56. ACM (2011)
7. Gibson, T., Schuchardt, K., Stephan, E.: Application of named graphs towards custom provenance views. In: First Workshop on Theory and Practice of Provenance, TAPP 2009, pp. 5:1–5:5. USENIX Association, Berkeley (2009)
8. Graves, A.: A case study for integrating public safety data using semantic technologies. Information Polity 16(3), 261–275 (2011)
9. Hartung, C., Anokwa, Y., Brunette, W., Lerer, A., Tseng, C., Borriello, G.: Open data kit: Tools to build information services for developing regions. In: Proceedings of the International Conference on Information and Communication Technologies and Development, pp. 1–11 (2010)
10. Heath, T., Bizer, C.: Linked data: Evolving the web into a global data space. Synthesis Lectures on the Semantic Web: Theory and Technology 1(1), 1–136 (2011)
11. Ikeda, R., Widom, J.: Panda: A system for provenance and data. IEEE Data Eng. Bull. 33(3), 42–49 (2010)
12. McGuinness, D., Ding, L., Pinheiro Da Silva, P., Chang, C.: PML 2: A Modular Explanation Interlingua. In: Proceedings of the AAAI 2007 Workshop on Explanation Aware Computing, vol. 7, pp. 49–55. Knowledge Systems Laboratory, Stanford University (2007)
13. Moreau, L.: The Foundations for Provenance on the Web. Foundations and Trends in Web Science 2(2-3), 99–241 (2010)
14. Robinson, D., Yu, H., Zeller, W., Felten, E.: Government data and the invisible hand. Yale Journal of Law & Technology 11, 160 (2009)
15. Salayandia, L., Pinheiro, P., Gates, A.Q.: A framework to create ontologies for scientific data management. Technical Report UTEP-CS-12-03, University of Texas at El Paso, El Paso, TX (2012)

16. Stephan, E.G., Halter, T.D., Ermold, B.D.: Leveraging the Open Provenance Model as a Multi-tier Model for Global Climate Research. In: McGuinness, D.L., Michaelis, J.R., Moreau, L. (eds.) IPAW 2010. LNCS, vol. 6378, pp. 34–41. Springer, Heidelberg (2010)
17. Lebo, T., Erickson, J.S., Ding, L., Graves, A., Williams, G.T., DiFranzo, D., Li, X., Michaelis, J., Zheng, J.G., Flores, J., Shangguan, Z., McGuinness, D.L., Hendler, J.: Producing and Using Linked Open Government Data in the TWC LOGD Portal. In: Wood, D. (ed.) Linking Government Data. Springer (2011)
18. Wang, P., Zheng, J.G., Fu, L., Patton, E.W., Lebo, T., Ding, L., Liu, Q., Luciano, J.S., McGuinness, D.L.: A Semantic Portal for Next Generation Monitoring Systems. In: Aroyo, L., Welty, C., Alani, H., Taylor, J., Bernstein, A., Kagal, L., Noy, N., Blomqvist, E. (eds.) ISWC 2011, Part II. LNCS, vol. 7032, pp. 253–268. Springer, Heidelberg (2011)
19. Wilkinson, M.D., Vandervalk, B., McCarthy, L.: The Semantic Automated Discovery and Integration (SADI) Web service Design-Pattern, API and Reference Implementation. Journal of Biomedical Semantics 2(1), 8 (2011)

Functional Requirements for Information Resource Provenance on the Web

Jamie P. McCusker, Timothy Lebo, Alvaro Graves, Dominic Difranzo,
Paulo Pinheiro, and Deborah L. McGuinness

Tetherless World Constellation
Department of Computer Science
Rensselaer Polytechnic Institute
110 8th Street Troy, NY 12180, USA
http://tw.rpi.edu
Pacific Northwest National Labs
Richland, WA, USA
{mccusj,lebot,gravesa3,difrad}@rpi.edu, paulo.pinheirodasilva@pnnl.gov,
dlm@cs.rpi.edu
http://www.pnnl.gov

Abstract. HTTP transactions have semantics that can be interpreted
in many ways. At a low level, a physical stream of bits is transmitted
from server to client. Higher up, those bits resolve into a message with
a specific bit pattern. More abstractly, information, regardless of the
physical representation, has been transferred. While the mechanisms associated with these abstractions, such as content negotiation, are well
established, the semantics behind these abstractions are not. We extend
the library science resource model Functional Requirements for Bibliographic Resources (FRBR) with cryptographic message and content
digests to create a Functional Requirements for Information Resources
(FRIR) ontology that is integrated with the W3C Provenance Ontology
(PROV-O) to model HTTP transactions in a way that clarifies the many
relationships between a given URL and all representations received from
its request. Use of this model provides fine-grained provenance explanations that are complementary to existing explanations of web resources.
Furthermore, we provide a formal explanation of the relationship between
HTTP URLs and their representations that conforms with the existing
World Wide Web architecture. This establishes the semiotic relationships
between different information abstractions, their symbols, and the things
they represent.

Keywords: World Wide Web, Information Resources, Data Management, multi-level granularity provenance.

P. Groth and J. Frew (Eds.): IPAW 2012, LNCS 7525, pp. 52–66, 2012.

1   Introduction

The architecture of the World Wide Web [1] defines the relations between URLs, Resources, and Representations, which is illustrated in Figure 1[1]. However, these relationships are incomplete, since the content of representations can change over time and content negotiation can result in different data being transferred. For example, the temperature reading in a weather report will change regularly, while different requests for the same weather report can return a variety of formats such as HTML, XML, RDF, and JSON. The ability to explain what an HTTP client sees as a result of a transaction and how, exactly, it relates to the URL that it requested is critical to the understanding of both how information resources[2] work on the web and how the provenance of web information resource access should be represented. We look to library science and provenance models to help provide these explanations, along with some help from the field of semiotics.

There are many reasons to clarify these semantics. For instance, the content of an image is more important than its format. Validating that a pathologist reviewed a particular image relies on the fact that the pathologist saw a particular image, not what file format it was saved in. In fact, transcoding of that image from a database to the client may happen as part of a web application. If it were possible to identify content regardless of format, our doctor would be able to make verifiable claims that she not just read data from a particular file, but that she saw a particular image. Similarly, web site mirroring mechanisms allow the same content to be available from multiple locations. Content-based identity of information would allow users to discover alternative locations for data, and validate that the information is actually the same regardless of source or format.

1.1   A Weather Example

To illustrate some of the issues regarding the relationship between a URL and the variety of representations that its request may return, we use a weather report provided by the National Oceanic and Atmospheric Administration's (NOAA) National Weather Service. Current weather conditions are provided for locations across the United States and include fundamental measures such as time, temperature, wind direction, and visibility distance. The latest hourly reports for Boston are provided in both RSS[3] and XML[4] formats. Although the service reports that it updates every hour on the hour, updates occur at unpredictable intervals. In this particular example, the service updated at 3:00 and 4:00, handled RSS requests at 3:05 and 4:05, and handled XML requests at 3:10 and 4:10.

---

[1] Copyright ©2004 World Wide Web Consortium, (Massachusetts Institute of Technology, European Research Consortium for Informatics and Mathematics, Keio University). All Rights Reserved.
http://www.w3.org/Consortium/Legal/2002/copyright-documents-20021231
[2] Because we consider URLs returning status codes other than 200 to be non-information resources, they are out of scope in this paper.
[3] http://www.weather.gov/xml/current_obs/KBOS.rss
[4] http://www.weather.gov/xml/current_obs/KBOS.xml

Given the current Web Architecture, what can we say about these two URLs and the four representations retrieved by their request? According to the AWWW, [1] the two RSS files *represent* the referent *identified* by the URL, while, because the URL is different, the XML files represent another referent. That these are alternative representations for the same referent means that we need a more sophisticated understanding of how the four files relate to one another and whether each relates to its URL *differently*. How can this be accomplished? We could compare files, but different formats would make it impractical to see their similarities. We could look to the files' creation date to learn when each file was received, but we cannot

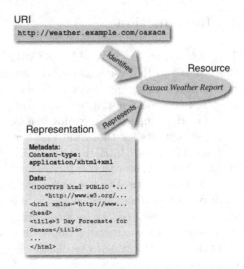

Fig. 1. The relationships between identifier, resource, and representation from Architecture of the World Wide Web

know how content has changed over time or if two transactions returned the same content in different representations. If different clients received the different representations, how can they begin to rationally discuss, compare, and share their individual representations?

2   Background: Existing W3C Recommendations

This leads us to wonder if there are any other existing semantics defined in W3C recommendations relating to how URIs, XML entities and RDF resources are related. This may appear to be a surprising question after years of success of W3C recommendations. However, the latest recommendations for XML [2] and RDF/XML [3] do not illuminate the issue. The XML recommendation [2] comes no closer to the issue than to state the following:

> "Attempts to retrieve the resource identified by a URI may be redirected at the parser level (for example, in an entity resolver) or below (at the protocol level, for example, via an HTTP Location: header). In the absence of additional information outside the scope of this specification within the resource, the base URI of a resource is always the URI of the actual resource returned. In other words, it is the URI of the resource retrieved after all redirection has occurred."

From this definition, one can infer that more than one resource may be returned for a URL and that the exact nature of this resource can be unpredictable. This is because an HTTP-based entity resolver implies the ability to return multiple representations of the same content. Similarly, the RDF/XML recommendation [3] states that:

"nodes are RDF URI references, RDF literals or are blank nodes. Blank nodes may be given a document-local, non-RDF URI references identifier called a blank node identifier. Predicates are RDF URI references and can be interpreted as either a relationship between the two nodes or as defining an attribute value (object node) for some subject node."

but goes no further. An "RDF URI reference" is syntactically described, and the recommendation further discloses that "RDF URI references are compatible with the anyURI datatype as defined by XML schema datatypes [4], constrained to be an absolute rather than a relative URI reference." Again, this leaves the recommendation reader without an explanation of what is the meaning of a URI in an RDF graph.

3 The Semiotics of HTTP URLs

The dereferencing of a URL can be mapped to a semiotic interpretation. For example, it is possible to use Ogden and Richards' Semiotic Triangle [5], a model of how real world objects are related to symbols and how people think about those objects from a linguistic perspective. In order to consider HTTP operations in these terms, it is important to remember that a URL is not only a symbol but also an address for information about that symbol. For example, http://www.weather.gov/xml/current_obs/KBOS.xml indicates that a web page can be accessed using the HTTP protocol against the server denoted by the name www.weather.gov and requesting the document '/xml/current_obs/KBOS.xml'. The document obtained is a representation (an XML document) of the thing

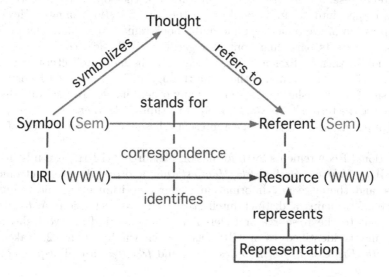

Fig. 2. AWWW's URL and Resource correspond to the semiotic triangle's Symbol and Referent, respectively. A representation is itself another referent that is not identified here, but will be elaborated on in Section 4.

identified by this URL. Figure 2 illustrates the partial correspondence between the semiotic triangle and the web architecture.

While a URL is a Symbol that stands for and identifies a Referent Resource, the correspondence to thoughts (from the Semiotic Triangle) or representations (from the AWWW) isn't immediately clear. The major issue is that the document retrieved cannot be defined only as a representation of a resource: The document can be described in terms of either its content or the set of bytes used to represent it – or both. So, the document needs to be described further. A potential solution is to refine the representation into its constituent identities that are based on different levels of abstraction. In the next section we will introduce a model that, when paired with a provenance model, can provide the necessary distinctions to fully satisfy both the semiotic relationships inherent within HTTP and the means to provide provenance traces for HTTP transactions at the levels of abstraction that are inherent within the protocol.

4   FRBR and FRIR

Functional Requirements for Bibliographic Resources (FRBR) [6] is a mature model from the library science community that distinguishes four aspects of an author's literary work, ranging from purely concrete to completely abstract. For instance, FRBR can describe how different copies of the same book, or different editions of the book, relate to each other. The most concrete aspect is the Item – the physical book that exists in the world. Items are singular entities; making a copy of an Item results in a new Item. Items are exemplars of Manifestations, which represent similar physical structure. For instance, an exact copy of an Item preserves the original Manifestation. If the copy is inexact, or if the book is turned into an audio book, then the Manifestation changes. However, the Expression of the paperback and audio book remains the same, because the Expression reflects particular content regardless of physical configuration. An Expression in turn realizes a Work, which is "a distinct intellectual or artistic creation." [7] A Work remains the same through different realized Expressions that result from translation, revision, or any other change. To facilitate discussion, we use the term *FRBR stack* to refer to a tuple (*frbr:Work*, *frbr:Expression*, *frbr:Manifestation*, *frbr:Item*) that represents these four distinct aspects of a resource.

Functional Requirements for Information Resources[5] (FRIR) extends the use of *frbr:Work*, *frbr:Expression*, *frbr:Manifestation*, and *frbr:Item* to electronic resources, and therefore any information resource. Within electronic resources, a *frbr:Work* remains a distinct intellectual or artistic creation. A *frbr:Work* corresponds to the Resource or Referent in the semiotic framework discussed above, and is identified by a URL, as was shown in Figure 2. Taken together, *frbr:Expression*, *frbr:Manifestation*, and *frbr:Item* are all aspects of the

---

[5] http://purl.org/twc/pub/mccusker2012parallel

Representation, and are each Referents in their own rights. Inasmuch as they can be identified or symbolized, they have symbols that identify them. *frbr:Expression* corresponds to a specific set of content regardless of its serialization. For instance, two files would have the same *frbr:Expression* if they are the same picture stored in two different formats (e.g., JPG and PNG). Similarly, a spreadsheet stored in both CSV and Excel would still have the same *frbr:Expression*. *frbr:Manifestation*s correspond to a specific bit pattern. If a file is an exact copy of another file, they have the same *frbr:Manifestation*. An *frbr:Item* is a specific copy of information stored somewhere or transmitted through a communication link. If a copy of the *frbr:Item* is made, it results in a new *frbr:Item*.

FRIR also integrates FRBR with the W3C Provenance Ontology (PROV-O) by declaring *frbr:Endeavour* to be a subclass of *prov:Entity* and mapping 14 of 18 *frbr:relatedEndeavour* subproperties as subproperties of one or more of *prov:wasDerivedFrom*, *prov:alternateOf*, and *prov:specializationOf*, as shown in Figure 3.

As part of FRIR we have identified two levels of cryptographically computable identity: content and message. Conventional message digests such as MD5 or SHA-1 produce identifiers where the probability of creating the same identifier using different data is vanishingly small. This corresponds very closely to our definition of *frbr:Manifestation* for electronic resources, so we make it possible to identify *frbr:Manifestation*s using message digests. Similarly, a number of *content digests* have been developed for RDF graphs, spreadsheets, images, and XML documents that provide the same digest hash regardless of any particular serialization. We use this to computationally identify *frbr:Expressions*. Further work on creating content digests will allow us to incrementally improve the ability to identify common *frbr:Expressions*. These identifiers fill out the means by which to identify the representation referents, as shown in Figure 4.

5   Explaining HTTP with FRBR, FRIR, and PROV-O

When explaining what is retrieved from a URL, the URL denotes a single *frbr:Work*. We implement these explanations in RDF, which follows the non-unique naming assumption. That is, unless otherwise specified, two identifiers can potentially denote the same thing. URLs are perfect examples of this. If a web site is mirrored, a page on the mirror corresponds to a page on the original. Those two pages can be thought of as the same *frbr:Work* within the FRBR/FRIR perspective. Content retrieved from URLs can change over time, but are expected to have a similar sort of coherence as defined by *frbr:Work* as "a distinct intellectual or artistic creation." [7]

HTTP 1.1 [8] introduced content negotiation, which makes it possible to abstract a URL away from any one particular file format. When a client asks an HTTP server for a mime type at a URL, the server can respond with many different possible files depending on how the content is negotiated. If the client asks for plain text, the server will try to find the best way of representing the

Subclass	Superclass
frbr:Event	prov:Activity
frbr:ResponsibleEntity	prov:Agent
frbr:Endeavour	prov:Entity
nie:DataObject	prov:Entity

(a)

Subproperty	wasDerivedFrom	alternateOf	specializationOf
frbr:adaptionOf	X		
frbr:imitationOf	X		
frbr:reconfigurationOf	X		
frbr:transformationOf	X		
frbr:abridgementOf	X	X	
frbr:arrangementOf	X	X	
frbr:reproductionOf	X	X	
frbr:summarizationOf	X	X	
frbr:translationOf	X	X	
frbr:alternateOf		X	
frbr:revisionOf		X	
frir:redirectsToTransitive		X	
frbr:embodimentOf			X
frbr:exemplarOf			X
frbr:realizationOf			X

(b)

Prefix	URI
frbr:	http://purl.org/vocab/frbr/core#
frir:	http://purl.org/twc/ontology/frir.owl#
prov:	http://www.w3.org/ns/prov#
nie:	http://www.semanticdesktop.org/ontologies/2007/01/19/nie#

(c)

Fig. 3. (a) Class mappings between FRBR and PROV-O. (b) Property mappings between FRBR, FRIR, and PROV. PROV super properties are columns and FRBR and FRIR subproperties are rows. (c) Prefix mappings for (a) and (b).

content of the URL in plain text. This idea of "same content regardless of format" is built into *frbr:Expression*. As previously discussed, the bit sequence of a file aligns very closely with *frbr:Manifestation*, so we use message digests to express this. *frbr:Items* can be files on disk, but they can also be data as streamed over a network connection. We uniquely identify the data streamed over a particular HTTP transaction using the combined message digest of the HTTP header and content. Since the header includes the exact time that the transaction occurred, the likelihood of a *frbr:Item* collision is very low. This enables provenance trace assertions to be applied to individual HTTP transactions without having to store the entire transaction.

An HTTP GET can be a very simple transaction. A client makes a request to a server for a particular URL, the server looks up which file corresponds to that

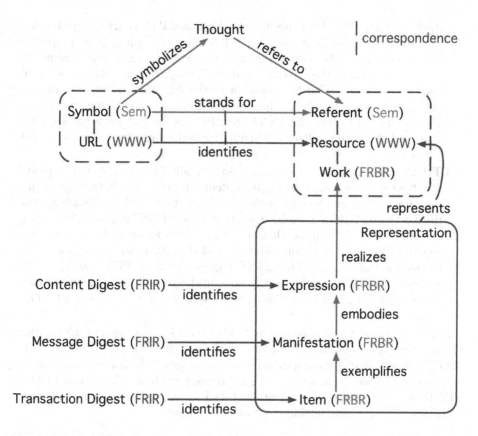

Fig. 4. Relating URIs, Resources, and Representations using FRIR, FRBR, and the semiotic triangle. URLs are symbols that identify resources, which in semiotics are referents and considered *frbr:Works* in FRBR. The representation of that resource is the content that comes from dereferencing the URL, and is composed of an *frbr:Expression*, *frbr:Manifestation*, and *frbr:Item*. The proposed content identities create implicit symbols (URIs) for each level of representation. Users can then use the level of abstraction that suits their task.

URL, and copies it to the network channel in response. The client then copies the data it sees from the network channel and either saves it to disk or displays it on screen. Things can become much more complicated on both ends, but these complications can be explained using current provenance representations, including the emerging W3C Prov standard [9]. This simple case, however, belies the subtleties that we discuss above. The following is a formalization of an HTTP GET request and response composed of common provenance constructs (events, generated by, used, etc.) that are under development in W3C's Prov standard:

HTTP GET: The server and client both share an event, the HTTP connection, which is composed of a request and response. The request is generated by the client and transmitted to the server. It is itself an Item with a singular FRBR stack. The request is for a specific *frbr:Work*, and if there are Accept headers sent, then the request is for a *frbr:Manifestation* with specific properties (the file format). The server then uses the request to generate a response, which is an Item of the URL's *frbr:Work*. This *frbr:Item* only exists on the network channel, and if the client saves the *frbr:Manifestation* to disk, it produces another *frbr:Item*. The response Item is derived from the server's file *frbr:Item*, and the client's file *frbr:Item* is derived from the response Item. All three items share the same Manifestation, Expression and Work (the URL).

HTTP POST: A similar explanation can be made for HTTP POST requests, which send a document as input content. In this case, both request and response content can be represented as FRBR stacks with no explicitly identified *frbr:Work*. Because web servers that handle POST requests derive their responses from the request, their handling can be formalized as a derivation edge in a provenance graph using the POST URL as an agent controlling the transaction process. Two HTTP request methods, PUT and DELETE, are used specifically to change the value of the *frbr:Work* by creating a new *frbr:Expression* (PUT) or invalidating existing *frbr:Expressions* (DELETE).

HTTP also provides other request methods to ask for services and information about a particular resource. These metadata request methods, HEAD and OP-TIONS, do not provide information resources as discussed, and so are not in the scope of the paper. Similarly, the HTTP request methods TRACE and CON-NECT are more functional in nature and deal more with the actual server than its content and are also outside the scope of this paper.

6   Implementation

We provide an implementation of curl called pcurl.py[6] that will record the provenance of an HTTP GET transaction using FRBR[7], FRIR[8], Nepomuk File Ontology (NFO)[9], PROV-O[10], and HTTP-in-RDF[11]. We show a retrieval of the HTTP-in-RDF core classes as an example in Figure 5. We use message and content hashes to generate URIs for *frbr:Expressions*, *frbr:Manifestations*, and *frbr:Items* to allow for automatic aggregation of endeavors that share the same hash. Future use of OWL keys and multiple digest algorithms is enabled through creation of *frir:ContentDigest* and *nfo:FileHash* instances. In Figures 6 and 7 we also show how transcoding and mirroring are represented in the FRIR model.

---

[6] http://purl.org/twc/software/pcurl.py

[7] http://purl.org/vocab/frbr/core

[8] http://purl.org/twc/ontology/frir.owl

[9] http://www.semanticdesktop.org/ontologies/2007/03/22/nfo

[10] http://purl.org/twc/page/prov-o

[11] http://www.w3.org/TR/HTTP-in-RDF/

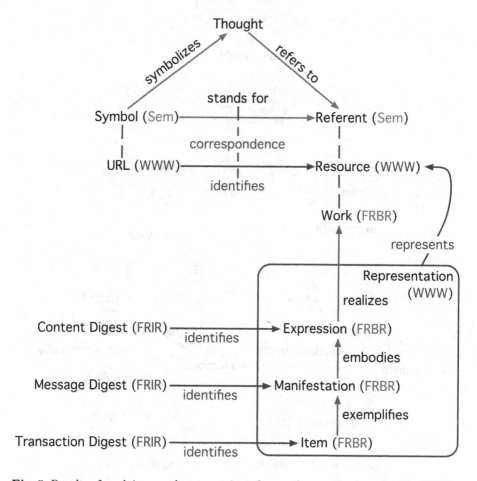

Fig. 5. Results of applying pcurl.py to retrieve the weather result example. The HTTP-in-RDF, FBIR, FRIR, PROV-O, and NFO vocabularies are used to create RDF descriptions of the representation received when the URL is requested. Entities are named using message and content digests, the HTTP transaction Item is associated to the file Item, which in turn has a FRBR stack representing all four aspects from the concrete file to the abstract URL/Referent/Work.

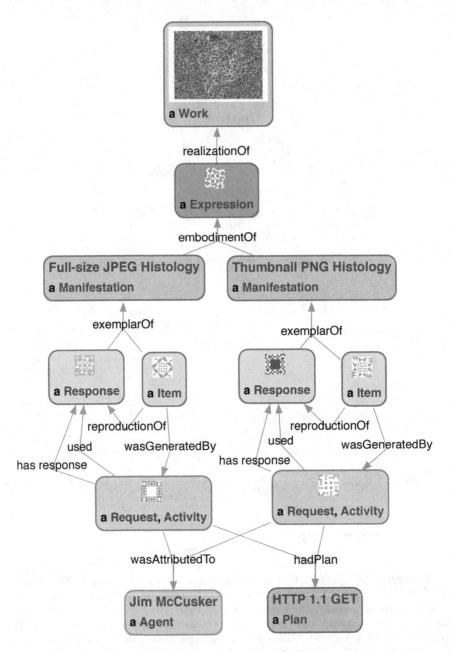

Fig. 6. An example of transcoding a histogram image from a large JPEG to a small thumbnail PNG. The *frbr:Expression* and *frbr:Work* are the same across the transcoding, but the *frbr:Manifestations* and *frbr:Items* are all distinct. This allows, for instance, a patient to verify that the low resolution image shown to them is the same content as the higher resolution image used to actually perform the analysis, even though the format and sizes are different. This graph was produced using pcurl.py.

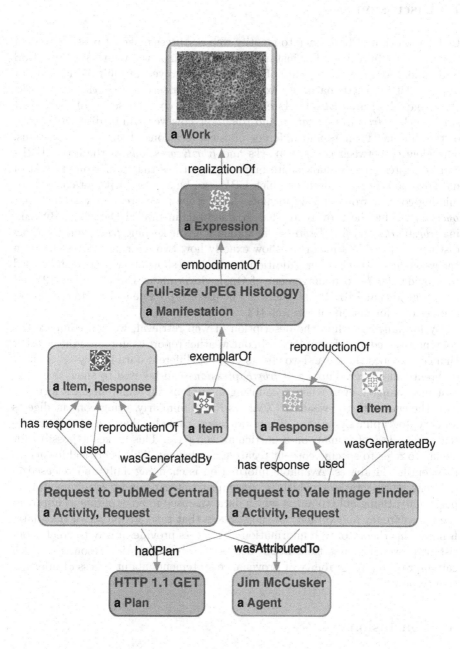

Fig. 7. An example of mirroring content between web sites. Here the Yale Image Finder [10] provides a mirror of an image published at PubMed Central. Since the file is an exact copy, the *frbr:Work*, *frbr:Expression* and *frbr:Manifestation* align, while the individual copies are different. This graph was produced using pcurl.py.

7 Discussion

Using a four-part FRIR stack to identify web resources makes it possible to do a number of useful things. For instance, in cases such as the weather report, RSS feeds and XML files, the same information is conveyed in multiple formats at different URLs. FRIR naturally expresses this by asserting that the *frbr:Work*s (the page URL) are *owl:sameAs* each other. More concrete levels of the FRBR stack, such as *frbr:Manifestation* and *frbr:Item*, however, will be distinct because of the differing formats and different physical locations of the representations. The identity between the *frbr:Work*s and *frbr:Expression*s of these two URLs can be expressed in semantic site maps so that tools that prefer one format of data over another can discover which URLs can be accessed without concern for missing content from varying formats. In fact, we have previously argued that *owl:sameAs* has been overextended to assertions in Linked Data [11]. By linking *frbr:Work*s and *frbr:Expression*s manually while keeping *frbr:Manifestation*s distinct we provide a means to show exactly how two information resources on the web relate to each other. Additionally, we have shown how FRIR can be used to provide clarity to management of Open Government Data (OGD) [12] and have argued that FRBR constructs can be used to provide a clear description of sources of information on the web [13].

By formally modeling the description of web retrieval, we can compare the content received at different levels. In our weather report example, as the weather changes, so does the data. Two clients may see different data if they access it at different times. *frbr:Work*s and *frbr:Expression*s can be used to show that content has changed, even when accounting for potentially different data formats, as is the case with the weather (XML vs RSS). Similarly, using content digests and cryptographic signatures, clients can assert that they have seen specific content, regardless of format, on a particular web page. This makes it possible for clients to refer to specific content regardless of format. This is critical for access to scientific databases. Available information is changing daily and released in different representations, which is convenient but can hinder experimental repeatability. Being able to assert which data was used in an experiment improves the transparency and veracity of the sciences that take advantage of that data. Finally, this theory of web information and access provides a way to create consistent provenance assertions about access of web information resources, which can improve interoperability of provenance statements about access of information resources.

8 Conclusion

We have shown how the use of FRBR and FRIR can help to describe the relation between a URL and the representation obtained using HTTP. We have also shown how this new representation describes a richer set of entities that can be identified by different elements from FRIR. Thus it is possible to use Content, Message and Transaction digests to identify the Expression, Manifestation and Item aspects of the representation. This can lead to a semantically richer description of an HTTP GET operation that includes provenance about the information published and transmitted on the web at each level of abstraction.

As future work, there are several paths we may take: In this paper, our focus has been on URLs that identify information resources. There is also the question of what (and how) non-information resources can be described in terms of FRBR and FRIR. This is particularly interesting when considering the relationships between URL *frbr:Works* that are associated by HTTP 303 redirections. Additionally, the solutions we present here are in principle compatible with the proposed changes to what has been called the HttpRange-14 issue.[12] Applying FRBR and FRIR to address the relationships between a resource, its representations, and its identifiers in a clear manner can serve as a standard pattern for the provenance of web resource access, comparison, and integration.

Acknowledgments. The Tetherless World Constellation is partially funded by grants and/or gifts from DARPA, IARPA, U.S. Department of Energy, Fujitsu, LGS, Lockheed Martin, Microsoft Research, NASA, the National Science Foundation, and Qualcomm. This research was partially funded by the National Science Foundation under CREST Grant No. HRD-0734825.

References

1. Jacobs, I., Walsh, N.: Architecture of the World Wide Web, Volume One (December 2011), http://www.w3.org/TR/2004/REC-webarch-20041215/
2. Bray, T., Paoli, J., Sperberg-McQueen, C.M., Maler, E., Yergeau, F.: Extensible Markup Language (XML) 1.0, 5th edn. (November 2008), http://www.w3.org/TR/2008/REC-xml-20081126/
3. Klyne, G., Carroll, J.J., McBride, B.: Resource Description Framework (RDF): Concepts and Abstract Syntax (February 2004), http://www.w3.org/TR/2004/REC-rdf-concepts-20040210/#section-Graph-URIref
4. Biron, P.V., Malhotra, A.: XML schema part 2: Datatypes (May 2001), http://www.w3.org/TR/2001/REC-xmlschema-2-20010502/
5. Ogden, C.K., Richards, I.: The meaning of meaning. Trubner & Co., London (1923)
6. Madison, O., John Byrum, J., Jouguelet, S., McGarry, D., Williamson, N., Witt, M.: Functional requirements for bibliographic records final report. Technical report, International Federation of Library Associations and Institutions (February 2009), http://www.ifla.org/VII/s13/frbr/
7. Madison, O., John Byrum, J., Jouguelet, S., McGarry, D., Williamson, N., Witt, M.: Functional Requirements for Bibliographic Records (February 2009), http://www.ifla.org/en/publications/functional-requirements-for-bibliographic-records
8. Fielding, R., Gettys, J., Mogul, J., Frystyk, H., Masinter, L., Leach, P., Berners-Lee, T.: Hypertext transfer protocol–HTTP/1.1. Technical report, RFC 2616 (June 1999)

---

[12] http://lists.w3.org/Archives/Public/public-lod/2012Mar/0115.html

9. Lebo, T., Sahoo, S., McGuinness, D.L., Mike Lang, J., Belhajjame, K., Cheney, J., Garijo, D., Soiland-Reyes, S., Zednik, S.: The PROV Ontology: Model and Formal Semantics (December 2011), http://www.w3.org/TR/prov-o

10. Xu, S., McCusker, J.P., Krauthammer, M.: Yale Image Finder (YIF): a new search engine for retrieving biomedical images. Bioinformatics 24(17), 1968–1970 (2008)

11. McCusker, J.P., McGuinness, D.L.: Towards identity in linked data. Proceedings of OWL: Experience and Directions, San Francisco, USA, June 21-22 (2010), http://www.webont.org/owled/2010/papers/owled2010_submission_12.pdf

12. McCusker, J.P., Lebo, T., Chang, C., Pinheiro da Silva, P., McGuinness, D.: Parallel Identities for Managing Open Government Data. IEEE Intelligent Systems Open Government Data Special Issue (2012)

13. McCusker, J.P., Lebo, T., Ding, L., Chang, C., Pinheiro da Silva, P., McGuinness, D.: Where did you hear that? Information and the Sources They Come From. In: Proceedings of Linked Science 2011 (2011)

A PROV Encoding for Provenance Analysis Using Deductive Rules

Paolo Missier[1] and Khalid Belhajjame[2]

[1] Newcastle University,
Newcastle upon Tyne, UK
Paolo.Missier@ncl.ac.uk
[2] University of Manchester
Oxford Road, Manchester, UK
Khalid.Belhajjame@cs.man.ac.uk

Abstract. PROV is a specification, promoted by the World Wide Web consortium, for recording the provenance of web resources. It includes a schema, consistency constraints and inference rules on the schema, and a language for recording provenance facts. In this paper we describe a implementation of PROV that is based on the DLV Datalog engine. We argue that the deductive databases paradigm, which underpins the Datalog model, is a natural choice for expressing at the same time (i) the intensional features of the provenance model, namely its consistency constraints and inference rules, (ii) its extensional features, i.e., sets of provenance facts (called a provenance graph), and (iii) declarative recursive queries on the graph. The deductive and constraint solving capability of DLV can be used to validate a graph against the constraints, and to derive new provenance facts. We provide an encoding of the PROV rules as Datalog rules and constraints, and illustrate the use of deductive capabilities both for queries and for constraint validation, namely to detect inconsistencies in the graphs. The DLV code along with a parser to map the PROV assertion language to Datalog syntax, are publicly available.

1 Introduction

Work towards standardization of a model for expressing the provenance of Web resources has been in progress at the W3C since 2011. The outcome of this community effort comprises (i) a conceptual data model (PROV-DM) [Mor12a], (ii) a set of consistency constraints on the model (PROV-C) [Mor12b], (iii) a formal notation (PROV-N) [Mor12c], and, in the near future, a set-theoretical semantics[1]. Consequently, implementations of the PROV specification should include a parser for the language, a constraint analyzer, and a query model (language and processor) to match the data model. In this paper we propose Datalog as a natural choice of programming model for a PROV implementation that fits these requirements. Rooted in first-order logic, Datalog has been popular amongst the

---

[1] All of these components of the specification are still in progress at the time of writing.

P. Groth and J. Frew (Eds.): IPAW 2012, LNCS 7525, pp. 67–81, 2012.

data management community for a very long time, well past its heyday as a foundation of deductive database theory [CGT90], mostly due to its expressiveness in capturing formal properties of queries and query rewriting methods [Hal01]. Datalog implementations are becoming popular again, thanks in part to the current momentum around Answer Set Programming [BET11], a model for declarative problem solving that is closely related to the Datalog model. Indeed, our prototype implementation is based on DLV[2], a deductive database system based on disjunctive Datalog [EGM97] with additional constraint-solving capabilities.

1.1 Contributions and Approach

Our contribution is threefold. Firstly, we provide a (nearly) complete mapping of PROV constraints to Datalog rules[3], and elaborate on the cases where such mapping is not appropriate. Secondly, we illustrate the expressive power of declarative rules in expressing significant examples of provenance graph queries, highlighting the natural fit of recursive rules to graph traversal. Finally, we apply DLV constraint checking to the problem of validating provenance graphs, for instance to determine temporal consistency.

Our approach involves (i) translating provenance expressed in the native PROV notation into a Datalog database, (ii) encoding PROV constraints as Datalog rules and constraints, and (iii) extending the core set of rules to express specific query patterns on provenance graphs. The resulting prototype implementation is available online[4].

1.2 Related Work

Datalog has a long history as a theoretical tool in data management. Specifically, in data integration, Datalog has been commonly used as a notation to analyze and compare existing query rewriting algorithms [Hal01], where recursive Datalog rewritings are essential. Shen *et al.* [SDNR07] used Datalog rules as a means of developing information extraction programs. Compared with similar techniques that use low-level programming languages such as Perl, C++ or Java, Datalog offers a declarative style along with a powerful mechanism for composing modules, which can be written by multiple users, into larger programs. Datalog has also been used in data exchange to specify schema mappings between heterogeneous schemas [ABR10], and in model translation to transform schemas from one model to another, for example from Relational to XML [ACG07].

Datalog has also been used in workflow provenance literature by a handful of researchers, typically as an illustration of queries at a conceptual level [ABC+10]. For example, Cohen *et al.* [CBD06] chose Datalog as a notation for formally

---

[2] http://www.dlvsystem.com/

[3] This mapping reflects the state of the PROV constraints as of June, 2012. Up-to-date versions of the implementation are maintained online, as indicated here below.

[4] at gitHub: http://bit.ly/HOY15T (code and examples), http://bit.ly/HOYJA8 (PROV-N to Datalog parser), see credits at the end of the paper.

defining provenance views that take into account the chained and nested structure of scientific workflows. We note, however, that the role of Datalog in such proposal is confined to a notation to illustrate provenance queries, as opposed to an actual query language. In this respect, the proposal by Dey *et al.* [DZL11] is closer to our work, in the sense that they use Datalog rules at the core of their *ProPub* system for policy-driven selection of public provenance fragments. This is similar in spirit to our approach, which however is focused on the comprehensive encoding of a set of rules and constraints that are prescribed by a standard specification. Additionally, we highlight the potential of the constraint-solving capabilities of the DLV implementation of disjunctive Datalog, which we argue, will play an important role in provenance analysis and validation.

2 PROV Provenance Graphs as Deductive Databases

We begin by providing an overview of the PROV provenance model by means of an example, and show how it can be encoded as extensional Datalog programs in a natural way.

2.1 Example: Collaborative Document Editing

The example presents an account of how a document was collaboratively edited and published by a group of co-authors, led by Alice and including Bob and Charlie[5]. Bob has produced the initial draft-v1, which includes references to two papers, paper1 and paper2. Alice then left some comments in document draft-comments, including the recommendation to also consider paper3 in the next revision. Bob then used the comments to produce draft-v2. At this point Charlie, who like Bob works for Alice, published the document as Working Draft WD1, using the publication guidelines pub-guide-v1 issued by the W3C. He, however, ignored version pub-guide-v2 of those guidelines, which the W3C had issued as update before the publication process was completed.

A graph depiction of this account of events is shown in Fig. 1, using a non-prescriptive graphical notation. Three types of nodes appear in the graph, namely *entities*, *activities*, and *agents*, and arcs represent directed associations amongst these elements. Node types and their associations are all part of the PROV specification. Notable relations used in the example include the usage (used) of an entity by an activity, the generation (wasGeneratedBy) of a new entity by an activity, the derivation of an entity from another (wasDerivedFrom), the responsibility of an agent for an activity (wasAssociatedWith), and a "chain of responsibility" relation, actedOnBehalfOf. Note also that the publication activity pub involves the additional *plan* pub-guide-v1.

The graph also illustrates a more subtle point, namely that Bob was aware of paper3, although the paper itself was not "consumed" as part of the editing activity. This is achieved by introducing two entities, Bob-1 and Bob-2, both

---

[5] This example is modified version of one that appeared in early versions of the PROV specification draft, and is used with permission from the editors.

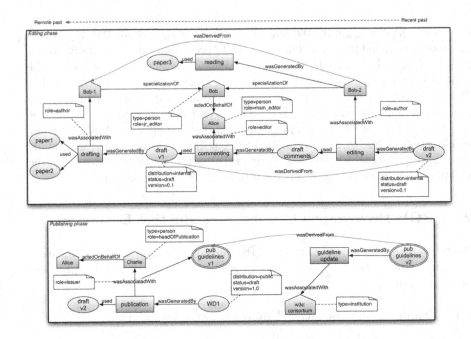

Fig. 1. PROV provenance graph for collaborative document editing

of which *specialize* the more generic Bob. The reading activity used `paper3` and thus accounts for `Bob-2` being "derived from" `Bob-1`. Thus, `Bob-1` and `Bob-2` describe two states of the same person, Bob.

The general idea behind PROV is that the graph of relations embodies the provenance of its entities, for example the genesis of `WD1` is obtained by traversing the graph in the direction of the associations (from the "recent past" back to the "remote past"), or by querying the graph, for example "who was responsible for the comments"? Examples of traversal and queries on provenance graphs are presented throughout the rest of the paper.

2.2 Background: Datalog Basics

In order to make the paper as self-contained as possible, we now briefly recall the basics of the Datalog model. A complete account of Datalog can be found in the classic paper, [CGT89]. A Datalog program consists of a set of rules, which are expressions of the form

$$L_0 : -L_1, \ldots, L_n \tag{1}$$

where the L_i are literals, i.e., either positive or negated *atoms*, of the form $p(t_1, \ldots, t_k)$ where p is a predicate symbol and the *terms* t_i are either constants or variables. L_0 is the *head* of the rule, the remaining L_i form the *body* of the rule. A ground literal is one that contains only constants. Rules with a ground literal in the head and empty body are *ground facts*. The set of ground facts is referred to as the Extensional Database (EDB), in contrast to the Intensional Database (IDB) consisting of rules with non-empty body.

The purpose of rules is to derive new facts from existing ones. For example, the rule:

```
entity(X, Attrs)  :- agent(X, Attrs).
```

(by convention, terms in upper case denote variables) allows for a new fact `entity(x,attrs)` to be derived, where x and attrs are constants, provided there is a substitution of variables $\Theta = \{X/\text{x}, Attrs/\text{attrs}\}$ such that $\Theta(\text{agent}(X, Attrs))$ is a ground fact (either in the EDB or itself derived). In our example, the result includes all the agents, i.e. { `entity(alice,alice_attrs)`, `entity(bob, bob_attrs)`, ... }. In a sense, this rule simply defines "specialization" and has the effect of adding all agents to the EDB as new entities.

In general, a substitution Θ satisfies the body of a rule (1) if the database contains *all* of the ground literals $\Theta(L_i)$. If Θ satisfies the body, the new ground literal $\Theta(L_0)$ is added to the database. Note that Θ must substitute for all variables in the head. This is guaranteed by requiring that the rule be *safe*, i.e., that all variables that appear in the head also appear in the body of the rule[6].

2.3 Datalog Encoding of PROV Graphs

The PROV specification includes a formal notation, called PROV-N, for expressing PROV graphs. Its syntax is so close to that of Datalog ground facts, that we can safely present fragments of the example above using the latter, with nearly no loss of information, with a few exceptions as noted below. For example, the following PROV-N fragment states the existence of entity **draftV1**, activity **drafting** with a start and end time, and the generation of **draftV1** by the **drafting** activity.

```
entity(draftV1, ["distribution"="internal",
                 "status"="draft", "version"="0.1"])
entity(draftComments)
activity(commenting, comment_start, comment_end)
used(u1, commenting, draftV1, -, comm_d1_use).
wasGeneratedBy(g1, draftComments, commenting, -, comm_dc_gen)
```

The first entity is qualified with an optional set of attributes. Start and end events can optionally be specified, e.g. for activity, usage (`comm_d1_use` denotes the time **draftV1** *begins* to be used), and generation (i.e., `comm_dc_gen` the time at which **draftComments** is *complete*). In PROV-N, the '-' symbol indicates a null, or unavailable value. **u1** and **g1** are identifiers for the use and generation relations, respectively, and can be referenced from other relations.

---

[6] The safety property includes the additional condition that each variable in the body appears in at least one positive literal.

Below is the set of Datalog ground facts for the same fragment:

```
entity(draftV1 , draftV1Attrs).
attrList(wd1_attrs , "distribution", "public").
attrList(wd1_attrs , "status", "draft").
attrList(wd1_attrs , "release", "1.0").
entity(draftComments , nil).
activity(commenting, comment_start , comment_end , nil).
used(commenting, draftV1 , nil , comm_d1_use).
wasGeneratedBy(draftComments , commenting , nil , comm_dc_gen).
```

In the mapping from PROV to Datalog, the relation names become predicate names and the relation arguments simply become terms[7]. However, there are a few differences. Firstly, lists of attributes are mapped to a separate predicate symbol **attrList** and linked to their parent element by means of a new identifier, i.e., **draftV1Attrs**. This makes it easy to write queries that involve attributes. A Datalog query, or *goal*, is specified as a conjunction of literals followed by a question mark[8], for example:

```
entity(draftV1s, Attrs), attrList(Attrs ,Name, Value) ?
```

The result of the query includes all ground facts in the EDB that match all the literals in the goal, for some substitution of the variables in the goals' literals. Our example query returns:

```
draftV1_attrs , "distribution", "internal"
draftV1_attrs , "status", "draft"
```

The second difference is that, while in PROV events can be expressed using timestamps, these cannot be used for temporal reasoning, because there is no assumption that they will have been generated by the same clock. Rather, what matters for provenance consistency is only the partial order amongst events. This justifies choosing purely symbolic terms in these examples.

Finally, in this "baseline" mapping we choose not to create new identifiers (which could be done by means of Skolem functions). As a consequence, each new relation created by means of a rule cannot be given an identifier, for example, the following rule generatea a new **used** relation from the presence of others in the EDB:

```
used(A,E1, nil ,Attrs)   :- wasDerivedFrom(E2, E1,_, Attrs),
                              wasGeneratedBy( E2, A, Attrs , _).
```

Since relation identifiers are optional in PROV, in our implementation we choose not to use them.

For reference, additional excerpts of the Datalog EDB for our running example can be found in Appendix A.

3   PROV Constraints as Datalog Rules

In this section we present a selected set of rules that encode PROV constraints, and show them at work on example queries that are relevant for provenance graph analysis.

---

[7] The null symbol "-" is not legal in Datalog, and is replaced by "nil".

[8] The question mark at the end is DLV-specific syntax.

3.1 Mapping PROV Rules to Datalog Rules and Queries

For the most part, PROV rules are of the form if $r_1,\dots,r_n$ then r, where the
antecedents r_i are relations in the provenance graph, and the consequent r is
a new relation. For example: "If wasDerivedFrom(e2,e1,a,g2,u1) holds, for some
a, g2, u1, then tracedTo(e2,e1) also holds."[9] (in some cases, the rule specifies
both sufficient *and* necessary conditions for r). In general, there is a natural
mapping of these rules to Datalog, which involves creating a deductive rule with
head r and body $r_1\dots r_n$ with suitable variables. For example, the entire set of
traceability constraints is encoded in Datalog as follows [10]:

```
tracedTo(E2, E1) :- wasDerivedFrom(E2,E1,_,_).
tracedTo(E2, Ag) :- wasGeneratedBy( E2,A,_,_),
wasAssociatedWith(A,Ag,_,_).
tracedTo(Ag2, Ag1) :- wasGeneratedBy( E2,A,_,_), wasAssociatedWith(A,Ag1,_,_),
                      actedOnBehalfOf(Ag2,Ag1,A,_).
tracedTo(E2, E1) :- wasStartedBy(A,E1,_), wasGeneratedBy( E2,A,_,_).
tracedTo(E3, E1) :- tracedTo(E3, E2), tracedTo(E2,E1).
```

The first rule states that if entity E2 was derived from E1, then it is also true
that E2 can be traced to E1. Rule (2) states that entity E2 can be traced to agent
Ag if E2 was generated by an activity A, and Ag was associated with (i.e., was
responsible for) A. The last rule states transitivity.

In relational database terms, rules define views over the EDB, which can be
used to derive a new set of database facts, in this case of the form tracedTo(e1,
e2). Given the rules, the simple query computes the "traceability" grap *induced*
by the EDB given the rules:

```
tracedTo(E2, E1) ?
```

The set of substitutions for E2, E1 returned by DLV in response to the query are
shown in Table 1, along with an explanation for their derivation (note that one
can ask more specific queries where some of the terms are ground, for example
tracedTo(draftV2,E)? for "what is draftV2 traced to?").

3.2 Limitations of Mapping and Rules as DLV Constraints

We have seen that rules are used to deduce new ground literals from existing
ones. These literals, however, can only contain terms that appear in the body
of the rule. We do not map rules that require the introduction of new constants *that represent new nodes in the provenance graph* (this is also consistent
with our earlier decision not to mint new identifiers)[11]. For example, the rule:
wasRevisionOf(new,old,ag) $\Rightarrow \exists e \mid$ specializationOf(new,e)
is not mapped, as it entails introducing a new entity e into the provenance graph.

---

[9] Quoting [Mor12a], "A traceability relation between two entities e2 and e1 is a generic
dependency of e2 on e1 that indicates either that e1 may have been necessary for e2
to be created, or that e1 bears some responsibility for e2's existence.".

[10] Consistent with our earlier choice for mapping PROV relations, we ignore the relation
identifiers g2 and u1.

[11] Note however, that some of the rules introduce default values for some of the terms,
typically for attribute-value pairs.

Table 1. Substitutions leading to the "traceability" graph induced by the provenance graph on the running example

substitution	rules	facts involved
E2/draftV1, E1/bob_1	(2)	wasGeneratedBy(draftV1, drafting, nil, nil), wasAssociatedWith(drafting, bob_1, nil, waw1_attrs).
E2/draftComments, E1/alice	(2)	wasGeneratedBy(draftComments, commenting, nil, comm_dc_gen). wasAssociatedWith(commenting, alice, nil, waw2_attrs).)
E2/draftV2, E1/draftV1	(1)	wasDerivedFrom(draftV2, draftV1, nil, nil)
E2/draftV2, E1/bob_2	(2)	wasGeneratedBy(draftV2, editing, nil, edit_d2_gen). wasAssociatedWith(editing, bob_2, nil, waw3_attrs).
E2/draftV2, E1/bob_1	(1), (2), (5)	wasGeneratedBy(draftV2, editing, nil, edit_d2_gen). wasAssociatedWith(editing, bob_2, nil, waw3_attrs). wasDerivedFrom(bob_2, bob_1, nil, nil).
E2/pubGuidelinesV2, E1/pubGuidelinesV1	(1)	wasDerivedFrom(pubGuidelinesV2, pubGuidelinesV1, nil, nil).
E2/wd1, E1/charlie	(2)	wasGeneratedBy(wd1, publication, nil, pub_wd1_gen). wasAssociatedWith(publication, charlie, pubGuidelinesV1, nil).
E2/bob_2, E1/bob_1	(1)	wasDerivedFrom(bob_2, bob_1, nil, nil).

Also, a few PROV rules either cannot be captured as Datalog rules, or otherwise lead to unsafety. The following PROV rule, for example, states that the `alternateOf` relation is anti-symmetric, in terms of an inference that leads to a new equality amongst entities being introduced in the model:

$$\texttt{specializationOf(E2,E1)} \wedge \texttt{specializationOf(E1,E2)} \Rightarrow \texttt{E1 == E2.} \quad (2)$$

The new equality in the consequent is problematic, as it cannot be expressed simply by using the built-in equality predicate '=', but instead would require a new predicate, say `equal/2`, as in:

```
equal(E1,E2) :- specializationOf(E1, E2), specializationOf(E2, E1).
```

However, one cannot define the semantics of `equal` in terms of built-in equality, because a rule of the form

```
equal(X,Y) :- X = Y
```

is not safe. As a consequence, such custom equality cannot be used in conjunction with built-in equality when computing a model, and thus rule (2) above escapes our mapping model.

Such rule, however, can be expressed as a *constraint*. Syntactically, DLV constraints are headless rules of the form

$$:-L_1,\ldots,L_n. \quad (3)$$

The models of a program P with such a rule added to it are the models of P that do not satisfy $L_1,\ldots,L_n$. In other words, no model results from a program where the body of the constraint is satisfied. This can be used to express the anti-symmetry property above as a constraint, stating that there cannot be two distinct entities which are each the specialization of the other:

```
:- specializationOf(E3,E2), specializationOf(E2,E3), E2 != E3.
```

DLV enforces constraints and will signal that no model can be found for a given EDB. While this programming approach does not lead to the introduction of new nodes in provenance graphs, it provides a mechanism for checking the consistency of existing graphs with very limited programming effort. Examples of constraints in action are presented in Sec. 4. In the rest of the section we instead present examples of successful rule mappings along with associated provenance queries. A summary of all the rule mappings, including the constraints, indexed by the names given to the rules in [Mor12b], appears in Table B in the Appendix.

3.3   Examples Rules and Queries

Inferring communication amongst activities. The following example illustrates how Datalog rules can be used to match patterns in the graph, and to find paths in the graph which connect instances of those patterns. *Communication* amongst activities is defined in [Mor12a] as "the exchange of an entity by two activities, one activity using the entity generated by the other.". The `wasInformedBy(informed, informant, attrs)` relation is used to represent communication, where `informant` is the activity that provides an input entity to the `informed` activity. [Mor12b] states that a2 was informed by a1, if there is an entity e that has been generated by a1 and used by a2. Furthermore, [Mor12b] also states that if e2 was derived from e1, and e2 was generated by activity a, then one can conclude that a used e1. These two rules are captured as follows:

```
wasInformedBy(A2, A1,nil) :- wasGeneratedBy( E, A1, _, _),
       used( A2, E, _, _).% (1)
used(A,E1,   nil  ,Attrs) :- wasDerivedFrom(E2, E1,_, Attrs),
       wasGeneratedBy( E2, A, Attrs , _).% (2)
```

Each of these two rules capture a pattern in the provenance graph. As an example, `used(editing,draftV1,nil)`, a relation that is not in the graph, is derived from (2), and from this, `wasInformedBy(editing, drafting)` also follows. From these, one can build upon these patterns by introducing further rules such as the following, which states that two agents are related through a path of length n, when they are associated to two activities, one of which is informed by the other. This provides an informal measure of "distance" amongst agents. The rule is recursive:

```
relatedAgents0(Ag2, Ag1) :- wasInformedBy(A2, A1,_),
    wasAssociatedWith(A2,Ag2,_,_),
    wasAssociatedWith(A1,Ag1,_,_).
relatedAgents(Ag2, Ag1, 1)  :- relatedAgents0(Ag2, Ag1).
relatedAgents(Ag3, Ag1, N) :- relatedAgents0(Ag3, Ag2),
    relatedAgents(Ag2, Ag1, M),   #succ(M,N).
```

The built-in predicate #succ(M,N) is true iff N == M+1. The query:

```
relatedAgents(Ag2, Ag1, N) ?
```

returns, amongst others, the triple (`charlie`, `bob_2`, 1), which requires (1) and
(2) for its derivation, and (`charlie`, `bob_1`, 3), which indicates that charlie
and Bob are related by means of the entire chain of activities, from drafting to
publication.

Agents' chains of responsibility. The next rule provides further illustration of
the use of recursion, this time to state that an agent is *ultimate responsibility*
for an activity, if either she is directly responsible or if another agent has acted
on her behalf in the context of that activity[12].:

```
responsible(Ag, Act) :- wasAssociatedWith(Act,Ag,_,_).    %(1)
responsible(Ag, Act) :- specializationOf(Ag1, Ag),
    responsible(Ag1, Act).%(2)
responsible(Ag1, Act) :- actedOnBehalfOf(Ag,Ag1,_,_),
    responsible(Ag, Act). %(3)
```

This reveals for example that `alice` is ultimately responsible for drafting, com-
menting, editing, and publishing. Finally, the following rule uses aggregation, a
feature of DLV with an intuitive syntax, rather than recursion to determine
that `alice` is at the head of a chain of responsibility (and so is, trivially,
`w3c_consortium`):

```
headOfChain(Ag) :- wasAssociatedWith(A,Ag,_,_),
    #count{ Ag2:  actedOnBehalfOf(Ag,Ag2,A,_)} = 0.
```

Entities with limited provenance. A final example of simple and potentially useful
pattern query involves finding entities that have been used, but whose generation
is unknown, making for "incomplete" provenance. The next rules makes use of
aggregation for the purpose[13]:

```
ungenerated(E) :- used(_, E, _, _),
    #count{ A:  wasGeneratedBy(E, A, _,_)} = 0.
```

4   Provenance Validation by Constraint Checking

As anticipated in Sec. 3.2, constraints can be used in DLV as a way to map some
of the PROV rules. Here we show constraints at work in two scenarios, both
involving cycles in the graph. The first concerns temporal events, which are
optionally associated with activities and most relations (Sec.2). PROV defines
temporal consistency by means of a number of *event ordering rules*, from the
simplest: "the start of an activity precedes its end", to more involved ones:

---

[12] The additional literal `specializationOf(Ag1, Ag)` in (2) is needed to associate
responsibility to an agent in its abstract form.

[13] Note that using negation-as-failure, a potentially more natural formulation, would
result in an unsafe rule, i.e., `ungenerated1(E,T,Attrs) :- used(_, E, _, _), not
wasGeneratedBy(E, A, T,Attrs)`.

"if entity e is generated by a, then its generation time follows the start time of a". A provenance graph is temporally consistent if there exists a partial order amongst events, which satisfies all the temporal rules. Our encoding of these rules can be found in Appendix B and is based on the temporal precedence predicate precedes(T1,T2). Precedence is anti-symmetric and transitive:

```
:- precedes(T1,T2), precedes(T2,T1),    T1 != T2.  % anti-symmetry
% transitivity
precedes(T1,T3)   :- precedes(T1,T2),       precedes(T2,T3), T1 != T3.
```

Query precedes(T1,T2)? returns all partial order relations in the graph. In particular, temporal inconsistencies in the EDB are detected when no stable model is found. Fig. 2 shows an example of cyclic graph. Cycles in PROV graphs are in some cases acceptable, as shown in the temporal logic for the Open Provenance Model [KMV10]. Indeed in this example, the query returns a valid partial order (depicted in the bottom part of the figure). However, the program has no model when the precedence relation: precedes(t_u ,a1Start) is explicitly added to the graph (not shown).

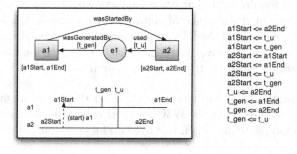

Fig. 2. Example of legal cycle in a PROV graph

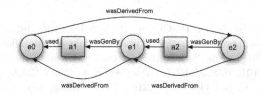

Fig. 3. Example of illegal cycle in a PROV graph

In contrast, some cycles in the provenance graph lead to inconsistencies, as in the example of Fig. 3. Here the cycle consisting of derivation relations is invalid, as derivation implies a time ordering amongst implicit use and generation events that accounts for it. Unless we accept to collapse all such events into one [KMV10], no order is possible.

The following rules are designed to detect these cycles:

```
derivable(E2, E1) :- wasDerivedFrom(E2, E1,_,_) , E1 != E2. % base case
derivable(E2, E1) :-  derivable(E2, E0),  derivable(E0, E1). % induction
:- derivable(E2, E1), derivable(E1, E2). % cycle constraint
```

5   Conclusions

PROV is the emerging W3C recommendation for a provenance data model and language. We have presented an encoding of PROV provenance graphs and inference rules and constraints as Datalog EDB and IDB, and we have shown how such encoding leads to intuitive, declarative-style queries on the graphs. Furthermore, we have used the constraint-solving capabilities of the DLV Datalog engine, which is freely available for non-commercial use, to show automated validation of PROV constraints, i.e., to detect temporal inconsistencies and illegal cycles in the provenance graph. An implementation of PROV-to-Datalog mapper is available online[14], along with the complete set of Datalog rules and the examples used in the paper[15].

In this work we have not addressed issues of efficient execution of queries on large graphs, a requirement that often conflicts with the declarative style of the query language, in the absence of suitable optimizations. Experiments are underway to test the limits of the DLV implementation. The potential uses in the provenance setting of disjunctive Datalog, which is typically used in automated planning applications, is also left for future research.

Acknowledgements. The authors would like to thank the members of the Provenance Working Group at the W3C for their collective effort on the PROV specification, and in particular Prof. Luc Moreau for contributing the PROV-to-Datalog parser.

References

[ABC+10] Acar, U., Buneman, P., Cheney, J., Van Den Bussche, J., Kwasnikowska, N., Vansummeren, S.: A graph model of data and workflow provenance. In: Proceedings of the 2nd Conference on Theory and Practice of Provenance, TAPP 2010, p. 8. USENIX Association, Berkeley (2010)

[ABR10]   Arenas, M., Barceló, P., Reutter, J.L.: Datalog as a Query Language for Data Exchange Systems. In: de Moor, O., Gottlob, G., Furche, T., Sellers, A. (eds.) Datalog 2010. LNCS, vol. 6702, pp. 302–320. Springer, Heidelberg (2011)

[ACG07]   Atzeni, P., Cappellari, P., Gianforme, G.: Midst: model independent schema and data translation. In: SIGMOD Conference, pp. 1134–1136. ACM (2007)

[BET11]   Brewka, G., Eiter, T., Truszczyński, M.: Answer set programming at a glance. Commun. ACM 54(12), 92–103 (2011)

---

[14] http://bit.ly/HOYJA8
[15] http://bit.ly/HOY15T

[CBD06]   Cohen, S., Cohen-Boulakia, S., Davidson, S.B.: Towards a Model of Provenance and User Views in Scientific Workflows. In: Leser, U., Naumann, F., Eckman, B. (eds.) DILS 2006. LNCS (LNBI), vol. 4075, pp. 264–279. Springer, Heidelberg (2006)

[CGT89]   Ceri, S., Gottlob, G., Tanca, L.: What you always wanted to know about Datalog (and never dared to ask). IEEE Transactions on Knowledge and Data Engineering 1(1), 146–166 (1989)

[CGT90]   Ceri, S., Gottlob, G., Tanca, L.: Logic programming and databases. Springer-Verlag New York, Inc., New York (1990)

[DZL11]   Dey, S.C., Zinn, D., Ludäscher, B.: ProPub: Towards a Declarative Approach for Publishing Customized, Policy-Aware Provenance. In: Bayard Cushing, J., French, J., Bowers, S. (eds.) SSDBM 2011. LNCS, vol. 6809, pp. 225–243. Springer, Heidelberg (2011)

[EGM97]   Eiter, T., Gottlob, G., Mannila, H.: Disjunctive datalog. ACM Trans. Database Syst. 22(3), 364–418 (1997)

[Hal01]   Halevy, A.Y.: Answering queries using views: A survey. VLDB J. 10(4), 270–294 (2001)

[KMV10]   Kwasnikowska, N., Moreau, L., Van den Bussche, J.: A Formal Account of the Open Provenance Model. Technical report, University of Southampton (December 2010)

[Mor12a]   PROV-DM Part I: The PROV Data Model (March 2012), http://dvcs.w3.org/hg/prov/raw-file/default/model/prov-dm.html

[Mor12b]   PROV-DM Part II: Constraints of the Provenance Data Model (March 2012), http://dvcs.w3.org/hg/prov/raw-file/default/prov-dm-constraints.html

[Mor12c]   PROV-DM Part III: The PROV Notation (March 2012), http://dvcs.w3.org/hg/prov/raw-file/default/model/prov-n.html

[SDNR07]   Shen, W., Doan, A., Naughton, J.F., Ramakrishnan, R.: Declarative information extraction using datalog with embedded extraction predicates. In: VLDB, pp. 1033–1044. ACM (2007)

A   Excerpts of the EDB for the Running Example

```
entity(paper1,  nil).
entity(draftV1,  draftV1_attrs).
entity(draftComments,  nil).
entity(pubGuidelinesV2,  nil).
entity(wd1, wd1_attrs).

attrList(draftV1_attr, "distribution", "internal").
attrList(draftV2_attr, "distribution", "internal").
attrList(wd1_attrs, "distribution", "public").

activity(drafting, draft_start, draft_end, nil).
activity(reading, nil, nil, nil).
activity(commenting, comment_start, comment_end, nil).
activity(editing, edit_start, edit_end, nil).
activity(publication, pub_start, nil, nil).
activity(guideline_update, nil, gUpdate_end, nil).

used(drafting, paper1, nil, dr_p1_use).
wasGeneratedBy(draftV1, drafting, nil, dr_d1_gen).
used(commenting, draftV1, nil, comm_d1_use).
wasGeneratedBy(draftComments, commenting, nil, comm_dc_gen).

agent(alice, alice_attrs).
attrList(alice_attrs, "prov:type", "prov:Person").
agent(bob, bob_attrs).
attrList(bob_attrs, "prov:type", "prov:Person").
agent(bob_1, nil).
agent(bob_2, nil).
agent(charlie, charlie_attrs).
attrList(charlie_attrs, "prov:type", "prov:Person").
agent(w3c_consortium, w3c_attrs).
attrList(w3c_attrs, "prov:type", "institution").

wasDerivedFrom(draftV2, draftV1, nil, nil).
wasDerivedFrom( bob_2, bob_1, nil, nil).
wasDerivedFrom(pubGuidelinesV2, pubGuidelinesV1, nil, nil).

wasAssociatedWith(drafting, bob_1, nil, waw1_attrs).
attrList(waw1_attrs, "prov:role", "author").
wasAssociatedWith(commenting, alice, nil, waw2_attrs).
attrList(waw2_attrs, "prov:role", "editor").

wasAssociatedWith(editing, bob_2, nil, waw3_attrs).
attrList(waw3_attrs, "prov:role", "author").
actedOnBehalfOf(bob_1, alice, drafting, nil).
actedOnBehalfOf(charlie, alice, publication, nil).

specializationOf(bob_1, bob).
specializationOf(bob_2, bob).
```

B Summary of Datalog Rules Implemented for PROV

Constraint name	Datalog rule(s)
Activities and Entities are disjoint	:- activity(X,_,_,_,_), entity(X,_).
Event ordering interpretation constraints	
Start of activity precedes its end	precedes(T1, T2) :- activity(_, _, T1, T2, _).
The generation of an entity always precedes any of its usages	precedes(T2,T1) :- used(_, E, _,T1), wasGeneratedBy(E, _, _, T2).
Usage-within-activity	precedes(T2,T1) :- used(_, E, _,T1), wasGeneratedBy(E,_, _, T2).
	precedes(UT, T2) :- activity(A, _, T1, T2, _), used(A,_, _,UT).
Generation-within-activity	precedes(T1, UT) :- activity(A, _, T1, T2, _), used(A,_, _,UT).
	precedes(T1, GT) :- activity(A, _, T1, T2, _), wasGeneratedBy(_,A,_, GT).
Derivation-usage generation-ordering[16]	precedes(T1,T2) :- wasDerivedFrom(E2, E1, A,_), used(A,E1, _,T2), wasGeneratedBy(E2, A, _, T1).
Detection of extended derivation loops	:- derivable(E2, E1), derivable(E1, E2).
	derivable(E2, E1) :- wasDerivedFrom(E2, E1,_,_) , E1 != E2.
	derivable(E2, E1) :- derivable(E2, E0), derivable(E0, E1).
derivation-generation generation-ordering	precedes(T1,T2) :- wasDerivedFrom(E2, E1,_,_), wasGeneratedBy(E2,_,_, T2), wasGeneratedBy(E1,_,_, T1).
wasInformedBy-ordering	precedes(ST1, ET2) :- wasInformedBy(A2, A1,_), activity(A1, _, ST1, _, _), activity(A2, _, _, ET2, _).
wasStartedBy-ordering	precedes(ST1, ST2) :- wasStartedBy(E2,E1,_), activity(A1,_, ST1,_,_), activity(A2,_, ST2,_,_).
wasStartedByAgent-ordering, wasAssociatedWith-ordering	Not implemented because start and end events for entities (and agents in particular) are not clearly defined
Structural constraints	
Generation-uniqueness	:- activity(A1,_,_,_, _), activity(A2,_,_,_,_), wasGeneratedBy(E, A1,_,_), wasGeneratedBy(E, A2,_,_),A1 != A2.
derivation-use	used(A,E1, nil ,Attrs) :- wasDerivedFrom(E2, E1, _, Attrs), wasGeneratedBy(E2, A, Attrs, _).
Element-specific constraints	
Association-agent	agent(E, Attrs) :- entity(E, Attrs), wasAssociatedWith(_,E,_,Attrs).
Derivation-implication	wasDerivedFrom(E2, E1, A, Attrs) :- wasDerivedFrom(E2, E1, _, Attrs), wasGeneratedBy(E2, A, _, _), used(A,E1,_,_).
Transitivity of specialization	specializationOf(E3,E1) :- specializationOf(E3,E2), specializationOf(E2,E1).
Anti-symmetry of specialization	:- specializationOf(E1,E2), specializationOf(E2,E1), E2 != E1.
Symmetry of alternate	:- alternateOf(E1,E2), alternateOf (E2,E1), E2 != E1.
Derivation implies traceability	tracedTo(E2, E1) :-wasDerivedFrom(E2,E1,_,_).
Traceability of agent for a generating activity	tracedTo(E2, Agent) :-wasGeneratedBy(E2,A,_,_), wasAssociatedWith(A,Agent,_).
Traceability of a delegated agent for a generating activity	tracedTo(Ag2, Ag1) :- wasGeneratedBy(E2,A,_,_), wasAssociatedWith(A,Ag1,_,_), actedOnBehalfOf(Ag2,Ag1,A).
Traceability by starting and generating activities	tracedTo(E2, E1) :-wasStartedBy(A,E1,_), wasGeneratedBy(E2,A,_,_).
Transitivity of traceability	tracedTo(E2, E1) :-tracedTo(E3, E2), tracedTo(E2,E1).
wasStartedBy (only 'if' part is actionable')	wasStartedBy(A2,A1) :- wasGeneratedBy(E,A1,_), wasStartedBy(A2,E,_).

[16] Note that this rule only applies if both use and generation are specified.

Declarative Rules for Inferring Fine-Grained Data Provenance from Scientific Workflow Execution Traces

Shawn Bowers[1], Timothy McPhillips[2], and Bertram Ludäscher[3]

[1] Dept. of Computer Science, Gonzaga University
[2] Stanford Synchrotron Radiation Lightsource, SLAC National Accelerator Laboratory, Stanford University
[3] Dept. of Computer Science, University of California Davis

Abstract. Fine-grained dependencies within scientific workflow provenance specify lineage relationships between a workflow result and the input data, intermediate data, and computation steps used in the result's derivation. This information is often needed to determine the quality and validity of scientific data, and as such, plays a key role in both provenance standardization efforts and provenance query frameworks. While most scientific workflow systems can record basic information concerning the execution of a workflow, they typically fall into one of three categories with respect to recording dependencies: (1) they rely on workflow computation steps to declare dependency relationships at runtime; (2) they impose implicit assumptions concerning dependency patterns from which dependencies are automatically inferred; or (3) they do not assert any dependency information at all. We present an alternative approach that decouples dependency inference from workflow systems and underlying execution traces. In particular, we present a high-level declarative language for expressing explicit dependency rules that can be applied (at any time) to workflow trace events to generate fine-grained dependency information. This approach not only makes provenance dependency rules explicit, but allows rules to be specified and refined by different users as needed. We present our dependency rule language and implementation that rewrites dependency rules into relational queries over underlying workflow traces. We also demonstrate the language using common types of dependency patterns found within scientific workflows.

1 Introduction

A key feature of scientific workflow systems is their ability to record workflow execution events at runtime, which can be used to establish various types of provenance relationships. Common events that are observed and recorded by workflow systems include the computational steps that were invoked as part of a workflow run as well as the data that were input to and output by each step. Recording these types of events in most workflow systems is straightforward, however, recording detailed provenance dependency relationships presents a number of

P. Groth and J. Frew (Eds.): IPAW 2012, LNCS 7525, pp. 82–96, 2012.

challenges. For instance, determining the sequence of computations performed
to produce a data result requires understanding the fine-grained dependencies of
step outputs on step inputs, which generally requires an understanding of how
the underlying computation of the step is performed. While recent approaches [2]
have begun to incorporate so-called "white-box" components into workflows—
i.e., steps implemented in languages from which dependencies can be inferred,
such as SQL and other database manipulation languages—workflow systems typically treat computation steps as "black-boxes" in which very little is known or
assumed regarding the underlying implementation of steps.

Scientic workflow systems generally adopt one of three approaches for asserting provenance dependencies: (1) they rely on workflow computation steps
to *declare* dependency relationships at runtime (e.g., see [4]); (2) they impose
implicit assumptions concerning dependency patterns from which dependencies
are automatically inferred (e.g., see [9,1,8,13]); or (3) they do not assert any
dependency information at all. Relying on workflow steps to declare provenance
relationships can be problematic, e.g., it requires a well-defined API for recording dependencies and can add considerable overhead to each step (e.g., [3]). Also,
not all computational steps of interest may declare, or declare correctly, the dependencies introduced by executing the step. The use of implicit rules can be
equally problematic. For example, depending on the underlying model of computation employed by a workflow system and the complexity of workflow steps,
establishing implicit rules regarding dependency relationships can often lead to
incomplete and incorrect dependency assertions (e.g., see [3,13]).

Contributions. In this paper, we describe approaches for inferring data dependencies from workflow execution traces based on *explicit* user-defined rules
as opposed to implicit rules assumed by a workflow system or dependencies
declared by computation steps. We propose a high-level language for expressing user-defined dependency rules that can be applied (at any time) to workow
trace events to generate fine-grained dependency information. This approach
takes the burden of determining provenance dependencies off of workflow systems, and allows rules to be specified and refined by different users (such as
workflow developers) as needed. We present a dependency rule language and a
formal implementation that converts high-level dependency rules into relational
queries over an underlying workflow trace model. We also demonstrate the expressivity of the language by using the language to define common types of
dependency patterns found within scientific workflows. Our approach is compatible with existing provenance standardization efforts such as OPM [15] and the
W3C Prov effort [18]. In particular, both of these approaches focus on representing fine-grained data dependencies, and our approach can be used to compute
these dependencies from underlying workflow execution traces.

Organization. This paper is organized as follows. Section 2 describes an abstract, minimal model for describing workflows, workflow traces, and data dependencies. The model is used in Section 3 as the foundation for our declarative
provenance rule language. Section 3 also describes an implementation of our
approach that stores execution traces within a relational schema and converts

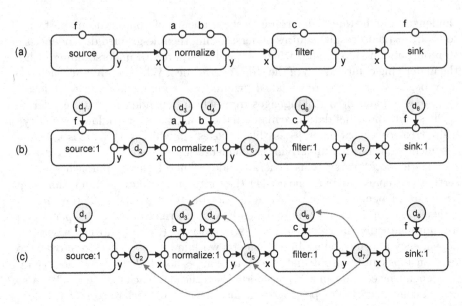

Fig. 1. (a) An example workflow specification, (b) an execution showing the first invocation step of each actor, and (c) the corresponding data dependencies

provenance rules into queries over schema instances. We also give examples of common dependency patterns and show how these patterns are captured using the declarative rule language of Section 3. Related work is presented in Section 4 and we summarize our contributions in Section 5.

2   Workflows, Traces, and Dependencies

This section describes a minimal set of observables that must be recorded by a workflow system to apply the user-defined dependency rules of Section 3. Observables are defined as part of an abstract model, and a specific (relational) implementation of the model is given in Section 3. The abstract model is divided into three distinct layers: workflow specifications, workflow traces, and fine-grained data dependencies.

Figure 1a shows a simple example workflow. In the abstract model, workflows consist of actors (which define types of steps), actor parameters, and actor channels. Actor parameters are designated as input, output, or state variables. Actor inputs receive (or read) data items, outputs produce (or write) data items, and state parameters maintain data across actor invocations (or "firings"). Actor channels define dataflow between two actors, connecting one output parameter of an actor to one input parameter of an actor. Workflow specifications in the abstract model are defined more formally as follows.

Definition 1. *A* workflow specification $W = (A, P, C, \sigma)$ *is a 4-tuple consisting of actor names A, parameter names P, dataflow channels C, and a signature* *function* $\sigma : A \to 2^{P \times \{\text{in,out,state}\}}$ *that maps actors to their corresponding input, output, and state parameters. Each parameter in the signature of an actor must have a unique name, i.e., for each actor* $a \in A$, *if* $(p, r_1) \in \sigma(a)$ *and* $(p, r_2) \in \sigma(a)$ *then* $r_1 = r_2$. *We often write* a.p *to refer to the (unique) parameter* p *of actor* a. *Let* A_{in} *and* A_{out} *be the input and output parameters, respectively, of actors in* W, *i.e.,* $A_{in} = \{a.p \mid a \in A \wedge (p, \text{in}) \in \sigma(a)\}$ *and* $A_{out} = \{a.p \mid a \in A \wedge (p, \text{out}) \in \sigma(a)\}$. *The (directed) dataflow channels are defined as the set* $C \subseteq A_{out} \times A_{in}$ *connecting output parameters of actors in* A *to input parameters of actors in* A.

For dependency inference rules, we only assume the presence of actor signatures (i.e., actor parameters and whether they represent inputs, outputs, or state). Channels are not required to apply the inference rules, and are included in the abstract model to provide a more complete view of a workflow specification. The following example describes the workflow in Figure 1a using the abstract model.

Example 1. Consider the workflow W of Figure 1a in which the first actor reads data from a file; the second actor produces a normalized value from each value read (where a and b are the min and max values, respectively); the third actor performs a low-pass filter (i.e., outputs items received if they are less than a given cutoff value); and the last actor writes data to a file. Using Definition 1, this workflow can be represented as follows.

$$W = (A, C, \sigma)$$
$$A = \{\text{source}, \text{normalize}, \text{filter}, \text{write}\}$$
$$C = \{(\text{source.y}, \text{normalize.x}), (\text{normalize.y}, \text{filter.x}),$$
$$(\text{filter.y}, \text{sink.x})\}$$
$$\sigma(\text{source}) = \{(\text{f}, \text{in}), (\text{y}, \text{out})\}$$
$$\sigma(\text{normalize}) = \{(\text{x}, \text{in}), (\text{y}, \text{out}), (\text{a}, \text{in}), (\text{b}, \text{in})\}$$
$$\sigma(\text{filter}) = \{(\text{x}, \text{in}), (\text{y}, \text{out}), (\text{c}, \text{in})\}$$
$$\sigma(\text{sink}) = \{(\text{x}, \text{in}), (\text{f}, \text{in})\}$$

Here, source.f gives the filename that data is to be read from, filter.c gives the cutoff value, and sink.f gives the filename that data is written to.

A trace of a workflow execution in the abstract model consists of a set of actor invocations, called *steps*, and their corresponding parameter *updates* (i.e., changes in parameter values). Thus workflow systems that conform to the model must be able to observe and must record both invocations and parameter updates, which are both recorded by the majority of provenance-aware workflow systems today [5,17,6]. In addition, we require only a relative order on parameter updates within actor invocations (i.e., order information across actor invocations is not required), and this information is typically provided by workflow systems using various forms of timestamps. Workflow execution traces in the abstract model are defined more formally as follows.

Definition 2. *A trace* $T = (S, U)$ *of a workflow* W *is a pair consisting of actor steps* S *and their corresponding parameter updates* U. *In particular,* $S \subseteq A \times \mathbb{N}$ *such that for a step* $s \in S$, $s = (a, i)$ *denotes an invocation step of actor* a, *which we typically write as* a:i. *No ordering constraints are placed on steps, i.e.,* a:i *may or may not have executed before* a:(i+1). *Similarly,* $U \subseteq S \times P \times D \times \mathbb{N}$ *is the set of parameter updates, where* D *is the set of data items produced by the workflow such that an update* $u = (s, p, d, j)$ *in* U *denotes the* j-*th update of step* $s = a{:}i$ *in which the parameter* $a.p$ *was set to data item* d. *Updates are partially ordered for a given step. Further, each update of a specific parameter in a step must have a unique order, i.e, if* $(s, p, d_1, i) \in U$ *and* $(s, p, d_2, i) \in U$, *then* $d_1 = d_2$.

The only constraints placed on an execution trace with respect to a workflow specification is that all actor updates are for actors and parameters defined in the corresponding actor signatures. While it is possible to add additional constraints, these would largely be based on the computation model employed by an underlying workflow system. While most workflow systems adopt computation models based on dataflow, they often have slight differences. Examples include whether the same data item is allowed to be "written" (i.e., part of an update to an output parameter) multiple times, the number of data items that can be passed between actor invocations, and whether workflow channels define "strict" constraints on data passing (for a non-strict approach see [11]). It may also be the case that a workflow is not fully specified, or can be adapted during workflow execution. Thus, for generality, the abstract model does not presuppose any particular model of computation. The following example demonstrates how an execution (shown in Figure 1b) of the example workflow in Figure 1a can be described in the abstract model.

Example 2. Consider the example workflow execution shown in Figure 1b. This execution can be represented according to Definition 2 using a trace T as follows.

$$T = (S, U)$$
$$S = \{\text{source:1}, \text{normalize:1}, \text{filter:1}, \text{sink:1}\}$$
$$U = \{(\text{source:1}, \text{f}, d_1, 1), (\text{source:1}, \text{y}, d_2, 2), (\text{normalize:1}, \text{x}, d_2, 1)$$
$$(\text{normalize:1}, \text{a}, d_3, 2), (\text{normalize:1}, \text{b}, d_4, 3), (\text{normalize:1}, \text{y}, d_5, 4)$$
$$(\text{filter:1}, \text{x}, d_5, 1), (\text{filter:1}, \text{c}, d_6, 2), (\text{filter:1}, \text{y}, d_7, 3)$$
$$(\text{sink:1}, \text{x}, d_7, 1), (\text{sink:1}, \text{f}, d_8, 2)\}.$$

Traces in the abstract model can be mapped to OPM provenance graphs [15]. In particular, actor invocations are similar to OPM `processes`, data items are similar to OPM `artifacts`, updates to input parameters define OPM `used` edges, and updates to output parameters define OPM `wasGeneratedBy` edges. OPM `wasTriggeredBy` edges can be obtained as follows. Assume a trace $T = (S, U)$ of a workflow $W = (A, C, \sigma)$ such that $a_1, a_2 \in A$, $(p_1, \text{out}) \in \sigma(a_1)$, and $(p_2, \text{in}) \in \sigma(a_2)$. A `wasTriggeredBy` edge exists between steps $a_1{:}i_1$ and $a_2{:}i_2$ whenever there exists updates $(a_1{:}i_1, p_1, d, j_1) \in U$ and $(a_2{:}i_2, p_2, d, j_2) \in U$.

Dependency inference rules are used to infer fine-grained lineage dependencies from a given workflow trace. A lineage dependency is represented in the abstract model as a directed edge over trace updates. Thus, a dependency graph can be viewed as a separate graph of lineage edges "superimposed" over a trace (e.g., see Figure 1c). Fine-grained dependency graphs in the abstract model are defined more formally as follows.

Definition 3. Data (lineage) dependencies $L \subseteq U \times U$ over a workflow trace $T = (S, U)$ form a directed acyclic dependency graph, where each $(u_2, u_1) \in L$ states that the update u_2 depended on the update u_1 (i.e., u_1 was a dependency of u_2). We often write $u_1 \xleftarrow{\text{ddep}} u_2$ to denote that u_2 depended on u_1, i.e., that $(u_2, u_1) \in L$. The following additional restrictions are placed on dependency edges in L. Given updates $u_1 = (s_1, p_1, d_1, t_1)$ and $u_2 = (s_2, p_2, d_2, t_2)$ in T, if $u_1 \xleftarrow{\text{ddep}} u_2$ then

1. u_1 and u_2 must be updates of the same step, i.e., $s_1 = s_2$;
2. update u_1 must occur before update u_2, i.e., $t_1 < t_2$; and
3. u_2 must be either an output or state parameter such that if u_2 is an output, u_1 must be an input or state parameter, and if u_2 is a state parameter then u_1 can be an input, output, or state parameter, i.e., if $W = (A, P, C, \sigma)$ is the workflow corresponding to T where $s_1 = a{:}i$, $(p_1, r_1) \in \sigma(a)$, and $(p_2, r_1) \in \sigma(a)$, one of the following must be true: $r_2 = \text{out}$ and $r_1 \in \{\text{in}, \text{state}\}$, or $r_2 = \text{state}$ and $r_1 \in \{\text{in}, \text{out}, \text{state}\}$.

Dependencies in L correspond to OPM's wasDerivedFrom edge. Specifically, a wasDerivedFrom edge exists from data item d_2 to data item d_1 whenever $u_1 \xleftarrow{\text{ddep}} u_2$ for $u_1 = (s, p_1, d_1, t_1)$ and $u_2 = (s, p_2, d_2, t_2)$. The following example demonstrates how the dependencies in Figure 1c can be represented within the abstract model.

Example 3. Figure 1c shows the data dependencies introduced by the workflow execution of Figure 1b. These dependencies can be represented using Definition 3 as follows:

$$
\begin{aligned}
L = \{ & (\texttt{normalize:1}, \texttt{x}, d_2, 1) \xleftarrow{\text{ddep}} (\texttt{normalize:1}, \texttt{y}, d_5, 4), \\
& (\texttt{normalize:1}, \texttt{a}, d_3, 2) \xleftarrow{\text{ddep}} (\texttt{normalize:1}, \texttt{y}, d_5, 4), \\
& (\texttt{normalize:1}, \texttt{b}, d_4, 3) \xleftarrow{\text{ddep}} (\texttt{normalize:1}, \texttt{y}, d_5, 4), \\
& (\texttt{filter:1}, \texttt{x}, d_5, 1) \xleftarrow{\text{ddep}} (\texttt{filter:1}, \texttt{y}, d_7, 3), \\
& (\texttt{filter:1}, \texttt{c}, d_6, 2) \xleftarrow{\text{ddep}} (\texttt{filter:1}, \texttt{y}, d_7, 3) \}.
\end{aligned}
$$

Finally, we expand the notion of dependency above to consider four different kinds of possible dependency relationships among updates. First, we define the set of data items $D = D_{val} \cup D_{id}$ to be the union of the disjoint sets of data values D_{val} and data *identifiers* D_{id} (where identifiers correspond, e.g., to OPM artifacts or "tokens" in the dataflow model [7] that wrap underlying values).

For each data identifier $d_{id} \in D_{id}$ the function $v : D_{id} \to D_{val}$ gives the value $v(d_{id})$ of d_{id}. We do not assume any additional constraints on the interpretation of values, where values can be primitive data elements (like numbers or strings) or references to external data items.

Definition 4. *Given a dependency set L, data derivations L_{der}, value-copy derivations L_{val}, and identifier-copy derivations L_{id} are subsets of L such that $L_{id} \subseteq L_{val} \subseteq L_{der} \subseteq L$. If $(u_2, u_1) \in L_{der}$ (denoted $u_1 \xleftarrow{\text{dder}} u_2$) then the data value of update u_1 was involved in the derivation of the data value of update u_2. Derivation is a stronger assertion of lineage than dependency alone: if $(u_2, u_1) \in L$ but $(u_2, u_1) \notin L_{der}$ then the presence of u_1 led to the presence of u_2, but the value of u_1 was not used in this process. If $(u_2, u_1) \in L_{val}$ (denoted $u_1 \xleftarrow{\text{dval}} u_2$) then the value of update u_2 was copied from the value of update u_1. Similarly, if $(u_2, u_1) \in L_{id}$ (denoted $u_1 \xleftarrow{\text{did}} u_2$) then the identifier of update u_2 was copied from the identifier of update u_1. Thus, if $u_1 \xleftarrow{\text{dval}} u_2$ such that $u_1 = (s, p_1, d_1, t_1)$ and $u_2 = (s, p_2, d_2, t_2)$ then $v(d_1) = v(d_2)$. Further, if $u_1 \xleftarrow{\text{did}} u_2$ then $d_1 = d_2$.*

The following example further refines the fine-grained data depenencies shown in Figure 1c in terms of the types of dependencies they represent.

Example 4. Consider again the dependencies shown in in Figure 1c. In the case of `normalize:1`, the update of parameter y was derived from the x, a, and b values giving:

$$(\texttt{normalize:1}, \text{x}, d_2, 1) \xleftarrow{\text{dder}} (\texttt{normalize:1}, \text{y}, d_5, 4),$$
$$(\texttt{normalize:1}, \text{a}, d_3, 2) \xleftarrow{\text{dder}} (\texttt{normalize:1}, \text{y}, d_5, 4), \text{ and}$$
$$(\texttt{normalize:1}, \text{b}, d_4, 3) \xleftarrow{\text{dder}} (\texttt{normalize:1}, \text{y}, d_5, 4).$$

Similarly, for `filter:1` while the value of y was copied directly from the x value, it was not derived from (i.e., only depended on) the c value, thus:

$$(\texttt{filter:1}, \text{x}, d_5, 1) \xleftarrow{\text{dval}} (\texttt{filter:1}, \text{y}, d_7, 3), \text{ and}$$
$$(\texttt{filter:1}, \text{c}, d_6, 2) \xleftarrow{\text{ddep}} (\texttt{filter:1}, \text{y}, d_7, 3).$$

3   Fine-Grained Data Dependency Rules

This section defines a set of high-level, declarative rules for specifying fine-grained data dependency patterns. Rules are expressed over actor signatures, and can be executed over traces to generate dependencies. We first describe the rule language, then describe a relational implementation of the abstract model in which Datalog queries are used to implement the patterns defined by the high-level dependency rules. We then demonstrate the dependency rules using commonly found types of dataflow actors.

Table 1. High-level rule language for specifying fine-grained dependencies of actors

Dependency Rule	Rule Definition
y depends_on x in a	If $u_1 = (a{:}i, x, d_1, t_1)$, $u_2 = (a{:}i, y, d_2, t_2)$, and $t_1 < t_2$, then assert $u_1 \xleftarrow{\text{ddep}} u_2$.
y derives_from x in a	If $u_1 = (a{:}i, x, d_1, t_1)$, $u_2 = (a{:}i, y, d_2, t_2)$, and $t_1 < t_2$, then assert $u_1 \xleftarrow{\text{dder}} u_2$.
y derives_from_value x in a	If $u_1 = (a{:}i, x, d_1, t_1)$, $u_2 = (a{:}i, y, d_2, t_2)$, $t_1 < t_2$, and $v(d_1) = v(d_2)$, then assert $u_2 \xleftarrow{\text{dval}} u_1$.
y derives_from_id x in a	If $u_1 = (a{:}i, x, d_1, t_1)$, $u_2 = (a{:}i, y, d_2, t_2)$, $t_1 < t_2$, and $d_1 = d_2$, then assert $u_2 \xleftarrow{\text{did}} u_1$.
y depends_on_prev x in a	If $u_1 = (a{:}i, x, d_1, t_1)$, $u_2 = (a{:}i, y, d_2, t_2)$, $t_1 < t_2$, and there does not exists a $u_3 = (a{:}i, x, d, t)$ such that $t_1 < t < t_2$, then assert $u_2 \xleftarrow{\text{did}} u_1$.
y derives_from_prev x in a	If $u_1 = (a{:}i, x, d_1, t_1)$, $u_2 = (a{:}i, y, d_2, t_2)$, $t_1 < t_2$, and there does not exists a $u_3 = (a{:}i, x, d, t)$ such that $t_1 < t < t_2$, then assert $u_2 \xleftarrow{\text{dder}} u_1$.
y derives_from_value_prev x in a	If $u_1 = (a{:}i, x, d_1, t_1)$, $u_2 = (a{:}i, y, d_2, t_2)$, $t_1 < t_2$, $v(d_1) = v(d_2)$, and there does not exists a $u_3 = (a{:}i, x, d, t)$ such that $t_1 < t < t_2$, then assert $u_2 \xleftarrow{\text{dval}} u_1$.
y derives_from_id_prev x in a	If $u_1 = (a{:}i, x, d_1, t_1)$, $u_2 = (a{:}i, y, d_2, t_2)$, $t_1 < t_2$, $d_1 = d_2$, and there does not exists a $u_3 = (a{:}i, x, d, t)$ such that $t_1 < t < t_2$, then assert $u_2 \xleftarrow{\text{dval}} u_1$.

3.1 Dependency Rule Language

The dependency rule language is based on the eight high-level patterns described in Table 1. Each dependency rule takes the form "$s\ d\ t$ in a", where s is a source parameter, d is a dependency type, t is a target, and a is an actor. Given a source y and target x for an actor a, a rule asserts dependencies from updates of parameters $a.y$ to updates of parameters $a.x$. We consider four basic types of dependencies, namely, depends_on which establishes a basic dependency, derives_from which establishes a derivation, derives_from_value which establishes a value-copy derivation, and derives_from_id which establishes an identifier-copy derivation. We also consider two dependency qualifiers. The default qualifier all states that each update of a parameter $a.y$ depended on every previous update of a parameter $a.x$ within an actor step. The first four dependency rules shown in Table 1 (implicitly) use the all qualifier. Alternatively, the prev qualifier states that only the most recent update of $a.x$ is a dependency of $a.y$ for a particular step. The last two rules in Table 1 use the prev qualifier.

3.2 Abstract Model and Dependency Rule Implementation

Here we briefly describe a relational implementation of the abstract model and an approach for applying dependency rules. In general, dependency rules would be provided as part of the actor definitions of a workflow or possibly specified and refined by a workflow developer or end-user. As shown later in this section, each actor may have multiple dependency rules, in which case each rule is applied (i.e., the union of the rules is taken, instead of their intersection). Dependency rules are used to define a corresponding data-dependency *view* (or query) over a given workflow trace, and thus dependencies are decoupled from, i.e., not specified as part of, the trace itself.

Actor parameter specifications (signatures) are represented using the relation $\mathrm{param}(x_a, x_p, x_t)$, which states that the parameter name x_p is defined for the actor x_a and has the type $x_t \in \{\mathtt{in}, \mathtt{out}, \mathtt{state}\}$. Here we do not consider channels since only actor signatures are required for workflow specifications in the abstract model.

A workflow trace consists of parameter updates and value definitions. Parameter updates are represented using the relation $\mathrm{update}(x_u, x_a, x_s, x_p, x_d, x_k, x_t)$, where x_u is a unique update identifier, x_a is the actor and x_s is the actor invocation id (together denoting the step), x_p is the parameter being updated, x_d is a data item where x_k is the item type such that $x_k \in \{\mathtt{id}, \mathtt{val}\}$, and x_t is the relative update order (with respect to the step). Data values are represented using the relation $\mathrm{value}(x_d, x_v)$, where x_d is the data identifier and x_v is the value. As an example, the updates for the $\mathtt{filter}$ actor in the trace of Figure 1b would be represented as the following facts, assuming $\mathrm{d_5}$ and $\mathrm{d_7}$ are both represented as the same value v.

> $\mathrm{update}(7, \mathtt{filter}, 1, \mathrm{x}, \mathrm{v}, \mathtt{val}, 1)$,
> $\mathrm{update}(8, \mathtt{filter}, 1, \mathrm{c}, \mathrm{d_6}, \mathtt{val}, 2)$,
> $\mathrm{update}(9, \mathtt{filter}, 1, \mathrm{y}, \mathrm{v}, \mathtt{val}, 3)$.

We consider four separate relations for representing dependencies: $\mathrm{ddep}(u_2, u_1)$, $\mathrm{dder}(u_2, u_1)$, $\mathrm{dval}(u_2, u_1)$ and $\mathrm{did}(u_2, u_1)$, together with the following Datalog rules for capturing the subsumption hierarchy between the different dependency types.

$$\mathrm{ddep}(u_2, u_1) :- \mathrm{dder}(u_2, u_1).$$
$$\mathrm{dder}(u_2, u_1) :- \mathrm{dval}(u_2, u_1).$$
$$\mathrm{dval}(u_2, u_1) :- \mathrm{did}(u_2, u_1).$$

Each provenance rule is represented as a fact in the relation $\mathrm{prov\_rule}(x_a, x_{p2}, x_{p1}, x_t)$, where x_a denotes the actor, x_{p2} specifies the target parameter, x_{p1} specifies the source parameter, and x_t is the type of the dependency. Given a set of $\mathrm{prov\_rule}$ facts, the following Datalog rules define a program for inferring all explicitly defined dependencies of a trace. Dependencies are inferred for rules of the form "y depends_on x in a" using the Datalog query:

$$\mathrm{ddep}(u_2, u_1) :- \mathrm{prov\_rule}(a, y, x, \mathtt{depends\_on}), \mathrm{update}(u_1, a, s, x, d_1, k_1, t_1),$$
$$\mathrm{update}(u_2, a, s, y, d_2, k_2, t_2), t_1 < t_2.$$

A similar query with $\mathtt{depends\_on}$ replaced by $\mathtt{derives\_from}$ and $\mathtt{ddep}$ replaced by $\mathtt{dder}$ is used for the case of "y $\mathtt{derives\_from}$ x in a". For rules of the form "y $\mathtt{derives\_from\_value}$ x in a", we have three separate cases depending on the type of data item:

$\mathtt{dval}(u_2, u_1) :- \mathtt{prov\_rule}(a, y, x, \mathtt{derives\_from\_value}),$
$\quad\quad\quad \mathtt{update}(u_1, a, s, x, v, \mathtt{val}, t_1), \mathtt{update}(u_2, a, s, y, v, \mathtt{val}, t_2), t_1 < t_2.$

$\mathtt{dval}(u_2, u_1) :- \mathtt{prov\_rule}(a, y, x, \mathtt{derives\_from\_value}),$
$\quad\quad\quad \mathtt{update}(u_1, a, s, x, d_1, \mathtt{id}, t_1), \mathtt{update}(u_2, a, s, y, d_2, \mathtt{id}, t_2),$
$\quad\quad\quad \mathtt{value}(d_1, v), \mathtt{value}(d_2, v), t_1 < t_2.$

$\mathtt{dval}(u_2, u_1) :- \mathtt{prov\_rule}(a, y, x, \mathtt{derives\_from\_value}),$
$\quad\quad\quad \mathtt{update}(u_1, a, s, x, v, \mathtt{val}, t_1), \mathtt{update}(u_2, a, s, y, d, \mathtt{id}, t_2),$
$\quad\quad\quad \mathtt{value}(d, v), t_1 < t_2.$

$\mathtt{dval}(u_2, u_1) :- \mathtt{prov\_rule}(a, y, x, \mathtt{derives\_from\_value}),$
$\quad\quad\quad \mathtt{update}(u_1, a, s, x, d, \mathtt{val}, t_1), \mathtt{update}(u_2, a, s, y, v, \mathtt{id}, t_2),$
$\quad\quad\quad \mathtt{value}(d, v), t_1 < t_2.$

For rules of the form "y $\mathtt{derives\_from\_id}$ x in a" we use the query:

$\mathtt{did}(u_2, u_1) :- \mathtt{prov\_rule}(a, y, x, \mathtt{derives\_from\_id}),$
$\quad\quad\quad \mathtt{update}(u_1, a, s, x, d, \mathtt{id}, t_1), \mathtt{update}(u_2, a, s, y, d, \mathtt{id}, t_2), t_1 < t_2.$

Finally, for rules of the form "y $\mathtt{depends\_on\_prev}$ x in a" we define the following two queries:

$\mathtt{ddep}(u_2, u_1) :- \mathtt{prov\_rule}(a, y, x, \mathtt{depends\_on\_prev}),$
$\quad\quad\quad \mathtt{update}(u_1, a, s, x, d_1, k_1, t_1), \mathtt{update}(u_2, a, s, y, d_2, k_2, t_2),$
$\quad\quad\quad t_1 < t_2, \neg\mathtt{after}(u_1, t_2).$

$\mathtt{after}(u, t) :- \mathtt{update}(u, a, s, p, d, k, t_1), \mathtt{update}(u_2, a, s, p, d_2, k_2, t_2),$
$\quad\quad\quad \mathtt{update}(u_3, a, s, p_3, d_3, k_3, t), t_1 < t_2, t_2 < t.$

where $\mathtt{after}(u, t)$ states that an update occurred in the same step and on the same parameter after u but before t. A similar query is used for rules of the form "y $\mathtt{derives\_from\_prev}$ x in a", again, where $\mathtt{depends\_on}$ is replaced by $\mathtt{derives\_from}$ and $\mathtt{ddep}$ is replaced by $\mathtt{dder}$.

3.3   Dependency Rules for Common Actor Invocation Patterns

Here we provide examples of different types of actor dependency patterns found within scientific workflow systems (and in particular, those systems supporting dataflow models of computation [7] such as Kepler [10] and Taverna [14], among others). For each type of actor we give the corresponding rules for describing the data dependencies generated by each actor invocation. Our goal is to highlight the benefits of our approach by showing that for these common types of patterns, the high-level rules both capture the dependency patterns and are easier (more concise) to specify than, e.g., the underlying queries implementing the rules.

Transform and Filter. The `normalize` actor in Figure 1 is an example of a basic transformer. The following provenance rules capture the dependencies for the `normalize` actor, in which each output y is derived from each corresponding input parameter x, a, and b.

```
y derives_from x in normalize,
y derives_from a in normalize,
y derives_from b in normalize.
```

Similarly the `filter` actor in Figure 1 is an example of a (low-pass) filter. The provenance rules for `filter` are

```
y derives_from_value x in filter,
y depends_on c in filter.
```

We note that the first rule could also be defined using `derives_from_id` if the actor implementation copies the input identifier to the output parameter (assuming this is also supported by the underlying workflow system).

As a simple example of the relational implementation, the above inference rules for the `filter` actor would result in the following two facts being asserted within the `prov_rule` relation.

```
prov_rule(filter, y, x, derives_from),
prov_rule(filter, y, c, depends_on).
```

Using the example updates of Figure 1b, the queries for `dder` and `ddep` given in the previous subsection together with the above rules would infer the following dependencies, where in update 7 parameter x was written to (as input to the invocation), in update 8 parameter c was written to (as input to the invocation), and in update 9 parameter y was written to (as output to the invocation such that y receives the value given to x, implying the value satisfied the conditional value in c).

```
dval(9, 7),
ddep(9, 8).
```

Delay. A typical `delay` actor consists of three parameters: an input x, a state parameter s, and an output y. The state parameter is set to a default value at the beginning of the initial invocation. At each invocation, the state value is copied to the output y, and the input value in x is then copied to the state parameter s. The current input is output on the *next* invocation (which, e.g., make approaches based on implicit dependency rules problematic). Delay actors are often used to initiate a loop. The dependency rules for a typical `delay` actor are as follows.

```
y derives_from_value s in delay,
s derives_from_value x in delay.
```

A similar pattern is to perform a transformation of x at each step. In this case, the second rule above would be changed from `derives_from_value` to `derives_from`.

Sliding Window. A sliding window performs an aggregate operation over an overlapping, fixed size number of input elements. For each window, an output is produced. For instance, consider the simple case of a sliding window actor `swp` that performs a product over a window size of two (see Figure 2). This actor has an input parameter x, a state parameter s, and an output parameter y. On each invocation, s contains the last element of the previous window, x is updated to the next value, y is then computed from x and s, and then s is updated to the new value of x. The dependency rules for `swp` are the following.

```
y derives_from x in swp,
y derives_from s in swp,
s derives_from x in swp.
```

Figure 2 shows an example trace and the dependencies inferred from the above rules.

Monotonic Integer Stream Merge. Often, two dataflow paths within a work-flow must be merged, and various strategies have been developed for performing merge operations (e.g., depending on whether order must be preserved, only unique data items should be output, and so on). Here we consider a simple case of an order-preserving merge operation, which takes two input data streams represented by parameters x and y, and produces one output stream represented by parameter z. The data items arriving on each respective parameter x and y are assumed to be ordered. On the first invocation of the actor, data items are read into both x and y, with the smallest value being copied to output parameter z and the larger value copied to a state variable s. The actor also records the input parameter having the smallest value. On subsequent invocations, the parameter with the smallest previous value is read into, if this value is smaller than the current state parameter value, its value is copied to z, otherwise the state value is copied to z (and the next execution will read from the other input parameter). Assuming that data identifiers are copied between parameters by the merge actor, the dependency rules can be expressed as follows.

```
s derives_from_id x in merge,
s derives_from_id y in merge,
z derives_from_id x in merge,
z derives_from_id y in merge,
z derives_from_id s in merge,
z depends_on x in merge,
z depends_on y in merge,
z depends_on s in merge.
```

The depends_on rules state that the particular output depended on each parameter update (but was derived via a copy from only one of the parameters). If only data values are copied (as opposed to identifiers), the above rules can be modified to use derives_from_value, however, two parameters with the same value will result in multiple derivations (i.e., either the initial x and y or subsequent updates of s with x or y).

List Transformer. A list transformer is an instance of a standard map operation. In particular, given a sequence of tokens on an input parameter x a list transformer outputs corresponding values on an output parameter y. Consider the simple case of an add1 actor, which adds one to each element of an input list, and outputs a list with the modified values. Thus, on a single invocation, add1 reads multiple values from x and produces multiple values on y. However, each output value on y is dependent only on the most recently read data item on x. Thus, the dependency rule for add1 is the following.

    y derives_from_prev x in add1.

List sum. An invocation of the list sum actor computes the sum of a given list of data items. The actor can be implemented with an input parameter x, state parameter s, and output parameter y. At the start of an invocation, s is updated with the default value 0. The actor then reads a value on x, adds it to s, and stores the result back in s. When all values have been read, the latest value of s is output on y. Thus, each s value is derived from the previous s value, and the final output is a copy of the value on s. The dependency rules for list sum are the following.

    s derives_from_prev s in sum,
    s derives_from_prev x in sum,
    y derives_from_value_prev s in sum.

List sum is an instance of a fold function, and the same rules can be used for list sum implemented via scan, i.e., with intermediate state values also output on y.

4   Related Work

While many workflow systems provide support for recording workflow trace information [5,6], systems that provide support for fine-grained data dependencies employ either implicit rules (e.g., [1,8,14,9]) or rely on actors to declare dependencies (e.g., [11]). Our approach allows for expressing explicit rules (high-level view definitions) that are independent of the underlying workflow system and layered over standard execution traces. In [12], explicit rules are also used for efficiently tracking the provenance of stream-based continuous queries. Three types of rules are defined: two for specifying sliding windows (via time intervals and window element size), and another based on data selection queries (e.g.,

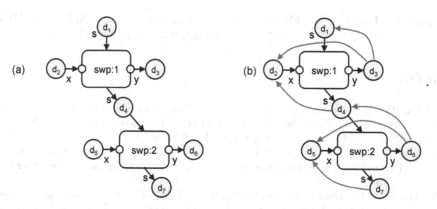

Fig. 2. Example sliding window product actor `swp` (with window size 2): (a) two invocations with data items d_i for i the update order, and (b) inferred dependencies

to assert that certain outputs depend on all inputs having specific attribute values). Our rules are more generic in that they do not rely on specific data values and cover a larger class of components than those designed for sliding window operators. Finally, fine-grained dependencies are automatically inferred from workflows composed of white-box components in [2] (based on the Pig Latin language). While we do not assume the presence of white-box actors, our rules could be used within such an approach to support cases where white-box and user-defined, black-box functions are used together.

5 Summary

This paper has presented an approach for addressing the problem of determining fine-grained data dependencies within scientific workflows by decoupling the specification of dependencies from the "observables" recorded within workflow execution traces. Our approach defines both an abstract model of observables and a high-level declarative rule language for specifying detailed dependency patterns. We also demonstrated how the abstract model and rule patterns can be implemented within a relational framework and provided examples of common dataflow actors expressed using our rule language. Inferring fine-grained dependencies from workflow execution traces is complementary to existing provenance standardization efforts such as OPM [15] and the W3C Prov model [18], which serve as general-purpose representing schemes for provenance information. Our basic model of provenance assumed and the dependencies generated from the inference rules presented here are compatible with both the OPM and Prov models. In this way, our framework could easily be used to produce detailed provenance information from workflow traces that conforms to the OPM and Prov representation schemes. Finally, both the model and the inference rule language described here are currently being implemented as part of the provenance framework supported by the RestFlow scientific workflow system [16].

Acknowledgements. This work supported in part through NSF grants IIS-1118088, DBI-0743429, DBI-0753144, DBI-0960535, and OCI-0722079.

References

1. Altintas, I., Barney, O., Jaeger-Frank, E.: Provenance Collection Support in the Kepler Scientific Workflow System. In: Moreau, L., Foster, I. (eds.) IPAW 2006. LNCS, vol. 4145, pp. 118–132. Springer, Heidelberg (2006)
2. Amsterdamer, Y., Davidson, S.B., Deutch, D., Milo, T., Stoyanovich, J., Tannen, V.: Putting lipstick on pig: Enabling database-style workflow provenance. PVLDB 5(4) (2011)
3. Anand, M.K., Bowers, S., McPhillips, T.M., Ludäscher, B.: Efficient provenance storage over nested data collections. In: EDBT (2009)
4. Bowers, S., McPhillips, T., Riddle, S., Anand, M.K., Ludäscher, B.: Kepler/pPOD: Scientific Workflow and Provenance Support for Assembling the Tree of Life. In: Freire, J., Koop, D., Moreau, L. (eds.) IPAW 2008. LNCS, vol. 5272, pp. 70–77. Springer, Heidelberg (2008)
5. Davidson, S.B., Freire, J.: Provenance and scientific workflows: challenges and opportunities. In: SIGMOD (2008)
6. Gil, Y., et al.: Examining the challenges of scientific workflows. IEEE Computer 40(12), 24–32 (2007)
7. Lee, E., Parks, T.: Dataflow process networks. Proc. of the IEEE 83(5), 773–799 (1995)
8. Lim, C., Lu, S., Chebotko, A., Fotouhi, F.: Prospective and retrospective provenance collection in scientific workflow environments. In: IEEE SCC, pp. 449–456 (2010)
9. Ludäscher, B., Podhorszki, N., Altintas, I., Bowers, S., McPhillips, T.M.: From computation models to models of provenance: the rws approach. Concurrency and Computation: Practice and Experience 20(5), 507–518 (2008)
10. Ludäscher, B., et al.: Scientific workflow management and the Kepler system. Concurrency and Computation: Practice and Experience 18(10) (2006)
11. McPhillips, T., Bowers, S., Zinn, D., Ludäscher, B.: Scientific workflow design for mere mortals. Future Generation Computer Systems 25(5) (2009)
12. Misra, A., Blount, M., Kementsietsidis, A., Sow, D., Wang, M.: Advances and Challenges for Scalable Provenance in Stream Processing Systems. In: Freire, J., Koop, D., Moreau, L. (eds.) IPAW 2008. LNCS, vol. 5272, pp. 253–265. Springer, Heidelberg (2008)
13. Missier, P., Paton, N., Belhajjame, K.: Fine-grained and efficient lineage querying of collection-based workflow provenance. In: EDBT (2010)
14. Missier, P., Soiland-Reyes, S., Owen, S., Tan, W., Nenadic, A., Dunlop, I., Williams, A., Oinn, T., Goble, C.: Taverna, Reloaded. In: Gertz, M., Ludäscher, B. (eds.) SSDBM 2010. LNCS, vol. 6187, pp. 471–481. Springer, Heidelberg (2010)
15. Moreau, L., et al.: The open provenance model core specification (v1.1). Future Generation Computer Systems 27(6), 743–756 (2011)
16. RestFlow, https://sites.google.com/site/restflowdocs/
17. Simmhan, Y.L., et al.: A survey of data provenance in e-science. SIGMOD Record 34(3) (2005)
18. The W3C Provenance Working Group, http://www.w3.org/2011/prov

Automatic Discovery of High-Level Provenance Using Semantic Similarity

Tom De Nies, Sam Coppens, Davy Van Deursen,
Erik Mannens, and Rik Van de Walle

Ghent University - IBBT
Department of Electronics and Information Systems, Multimedia Lab
Gaston Crommenlaan 8 bus 201
B-9050 Ledeberg-Ghent, Belgium
{tom.denies,sam.coppens,davy.vandeursen,erik.mannens,
rik.vandewalle}@ugent.be

Abstract. As interest in provenance grows among the Semantic Web community, it is recognized as a useful tool across many domains. However, existing automatic provenance collection techniques are not universally applicable. Most existing methods either rely on (low-level) observed provenance, or require that the user discloses formal workflows. In this paper, we propose a new approach for automatic discovery of provenance, at multiple levels of granularity. To accomplish this, we detect entity derivations, relying on clustering algorithms, linked data and semantic similarity. The resulting derivations are structured in compliance with the Provenance Data Model (PROV-DM). While the proposed approach is purposely kept general, allowing adaptation in many use cases, we provide an implementation for one of these use cases, namely discovering the sources of news articles. With this implementation, we were able to detect 73% of the original sources of 410 news stories, at 68% precision. Lastly, we discuss possible improvements and future work.

Keywords: Provenance, Data Model, Semantic Web, Linked Data, Similarity, News.

1 Introduction

Nowadays, as interest in provenance grows among the Semantic Web community [1], media content authors are faced with a dilemma. While they clearly see the advantages of providing provenance information with their data, the process of manual annotation is labor intensive and dull work, especially for those without a technical background [2]. Clearly, there is a need for automated ways to add provenance to produced content.

Most existing automatic provenance collection techniques in literature either observe all activity on the target resources (so called *observed* provenance), or require that the users specify formal workflows which are used to create and modify the resources (*disclosed* provenance) [3]. The first approach often results

P. Groth and J. Frew (Eds.): IPAW 2012, LNCS 7525, pp. 97–110, 2012.

in a low-level view of the provenance associated with a resource, which is not always suitable (e.g., in the use case described in this paper). The latter approach requires significant effort from the user, and is not always applicable, since many creative processes are difficult, if not impossible, to formally describe.

In this paper, we propose a new approach for automatic discovery of provenance from limited information, at multiple levels of granularity. Whereas low-level provenance denotes the exact change at the finest granularity (e.g., at the character level), higher-level provenance denotes changes at a coarser granularity (e.g., at the document level). To achieve this, we detect inter-document derivations, using clustering methods based on semantic similarity, resulting in provenance complementary to the observed and disclosed kind. We apply the approach to a specific use case, originated from the news sector. We will attempt to reconstruct missing provenance, solely based on the content and timing information, allowing us to track down the original source of an article.

The paper is structured as follows: first, we explain our interpretation of high-level provenance, and how this fits into the ongoing standardization efforts of the W3C Provenance Working Group[1]. Next, we provide an in-depth explanation of the proposed approach and describe our use case implementation, which we then use to evaluate our approach. Before concluding, we discuss the results, followed by the related and future work.

2   Terminology and Key Concepts

Before describing our proposed approach, we explain our view on high-level provenance. We also provide a summary of the relevant features of the Provenance Data Model (PROV-DM), currently under development by the W3C Provenance Working Group.

2.1   High-Level Provenance

In our research, we make the distinction between low-level and high-level provenance. Low-level provenance is the sort of provenance expected from capturing systems and versioning systems. A typical example is that of a programmer's versioning system, where the provenance of each document is stored as a list of characters that where changed, together with their position in the document. An example of high-level provenance, at the *document level* might be: "Document A is a revision of document B".

While these types of provenance are certainly important in many cases, for our research, we aim for a more conceptualized form of provenance, and propose an intermediary approach. For example: "Document A is a derivation of document B, with concept 'Magistrate' in document A narrowed down to 'Prosecutor' in document B". We will label this as provenance at the *semantic level*, providing more details than at the document level, but remaining high-level, at a coarser granularity than low-level systems.

---

[1] http://www.w3.org/2011/prov/

In this paper, we will investigate ways to generate high-level provenance, both at the document level and the semantic level.

2.2 PROV-DM: The Provenance Data Model

Currently, the W3C Provenance Working Group is composing a standard data model for provenance. In our research, we aim to comply with the latest working draft of PROV-DM, at the time of writing (WD6, [4]). For a full description of the data model, we refer to [4]. Below, we provide a brief overview of the concepts needed for our research.

PROV-DM provides us with 3 essential (core) elements: *entities, activities* and *agents*. Entities can be related to each other, and to activities acting upon them. For our research, the most important entity-entity relations are **derivation**, **alternate** and **specialization**. Entity-activity relations are limited to usage and generation. Throughout this paper, in all figures and examples, the standard notation specified in [4] is used to specify these relations.

According to PROV-DM, a **derivation** is anything that transforms an entity into another, that constructs an entity from another, or that updates an entity, resulting in a new one. However, the underpinning activities and their associated details are not always known. Therefore, we will make the distinction between *precise* and *imprecise* derivations. When two entities are linked by a **precise-1** derivation, it means they are connected by a single, known activity, which uses (consumes) one of the entities and generates the other. When the activity connecting two entities is unknown, but it is certain that they are connected by a single activity, we obtain an **imprecise-1** derivation. For an **imprecise-n** derivation, the number of activities interconnecting the two entities is unknown. Note that while the formal distinction between imprecise and precise provenance was removed from PROV-DM since the fifth working draft, the informal distinction is still relevant to the work in this paper, and remains supported by PROV-DM (all parameters of derivation regarding the involved activity are optional).

The **alternate** relation connects two entities that refer to the same thing in the world, in different environments. For example, 'fbase:Magistrate'[2] is an alternate entity of 'dbpedia:Magistrate'[3]. The **specialization** relation connects two entities that refer to the same thing in the world, at different levels of abstraction. For example, 'dbpedia:Prosecutor'[4] is a specialization of 'dbpedia:Magistrate'.

In additional to these relations, PROV-DM allows to provide provenance of provenance. Concretely, this means that all provenance entities, activities, agents and relations can be organized in *bundles*. A bundle holds the provenance of a resource, and can have, in turn, its own provenance. This way, it becomes possible to provide provenance of the provenance, explaining how it was obtained.

A final method that we use to provide organization among entities, is the *collection* entity. According to PROV-DM, this is an entity that provides a

---

[2] http://rdf.freebase.com/ns/Magistrate
[3] http://dbpedia.org/resource/Magistrate
[4] http://dbpedia.org/resource/Prosecutor

structure to some constituents, which are themselves entities, and connected to the collection by the **memberOf** relation.

3   Proposed Approach

In this section, we provide an in-depth description of how we aim to discover provenance derivations, using semantic similarity. While we want to keep our approach as general as possible, it is necessary to make some assumptions about the data we will be providing provenance for.

We will assume that the data essentially consists of two types of entities. We define a *document* as an entity that is characterized by multiple other entities, which we will refer to as *semantic properties*. Both documents and semantic properties can be modeled as a prov:Entity[5], and thus can be connected through activities and/or entity-entity relations. In our news use case, an example of a document would be a news article, whereas examples of semantic properties would be the descriptive metadata annotations of this article. We also assume that timing information (i.e., date of creation) is available for all documents.

The general goal of our research is to analyze documents to automatically discover provenance information about them. Since this is very general, we will narrow it down to 3 subgoals. Starting from a set of documents S, we aim to:

1. Discover high-level **imprecise-n** and **imprecise-1** derivations at a *coarse granularity*.
2. Convert these imprecise derivations to high-level **precise-1** derivations.
3. Discover additional **precise-1** derivations at a *finer granularity*.

Below, we describe how we achieve these goals.

3.1   Discovering Imprecise Derivations

To discover provenance at the coarsest granularity, we rely on the semantic similarity of documents. Since it is safe to assume that revisions of the same document are semantically similar to each other, we can assume that in many cases (unfortunately, not always), the inverse also holds: if documents are very similar to each other, it is likely that they are also a revision of the same document.

First, we group (or *cluster*) all semantically similar documents into clusters S_i, so that for all documents $doc_a \in S_i$:

$$doc_a \in S_i \Leftrightarrow \forall doc_b \in S_i : sim_D(doc_a, doc_b) > T_s \qquad (1)$$

with T_s an empirically determined *similarity threshold*, and $i \in \{1, 2, ..., N\}$ with N the number of clusters[6]. Sim_D is a similarity metric, which enables semantic comparison of documents. Note that this similarity metric is interchangeable, and a more accurate similarity metric will result in better clustering (in our

---

[5] http://www.w3.org/ns/prov-dm/Entity
[6] Note that overlap between clusters is possible.

implementation, semantic similarity of documents is based on the comparison of their semantic properties). To avoid clusters becoming too large, resulting in poor derivations, all clusters larger than a *clustering threshold* T_c, are re-clustered with a higher similarity threshold T_s.

Next, we order all documents in each cluster according to their date of creation. For each cluster, we assume that the document doc_1 that was created first is the original source of all other documents in the cluster. This means that we can now connect each document of the cluster to doc_1 by an **imprecise-n** derivation, as illustrated by Fig. 1(a).

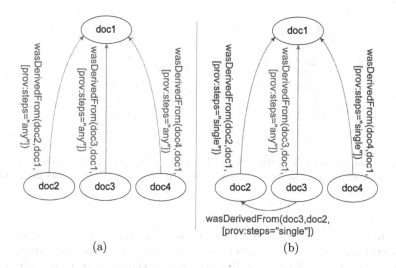

(a)   (b)

Fig. 1. Example of how documents doc_2, doc_3 and doc_4 within one cluster are related (a) to the original source doc_1 by imprecise-n derivations, and (b) to each other by imprecise-1 derivations. We assume that $time(doc_i) < time(doc_j) \Leftrightarrow i < j$. Here, doc_2 is most similar to doc_1, doc_3 most similar to doc_2 and doc_4 most similar to doc_1. Even though doc_4 was created after doc_3, it was directly derived from doc_1.

In order to create **imprecise-1** derivations, we take both the inter-document similarity and timing information into account[7]. In each set S_i, for each document $doc_a \in S_i$ (with $a \neq 1$), we find the semantically most similar document doc_b, and connect them by an imprecise-1 derivation, following Formula 2.

$$\exists doc_b \in S_i : (\forall k \neq a : sim_D(doc_a, doc_b) \geq sim_D(doc_a, doc_k))$$
$$\wedge$$
$$time(doc_b) < time(doc_a)$$
$$\Rightarrow wasDerivedFrom(doc_a, doc_b, [prov : steps = \text{``single''}]) \qquad (2)$$

---

[7] Note that simply considering the timing and connecting successive documents with imprecise-1 derivations is not a correct approach, since multiple revisions can be based on a single document, regardless of timing.

The direction of this derivation depends on which document was created first. In Fig. 1(b), we apply this method to the example from Fig. 1(a).

3.2   High-Level Precise Derivations

Precise-1 derivations need to specify an *activity*, responsible for using the original entity, and generating the derived entity. Converting the imprecise-1 derivations from Sect. 3.1 to precise-1 is done by defining a *revision* activity for each imprecise-1 derivation, as illustrated by Fig. 2.

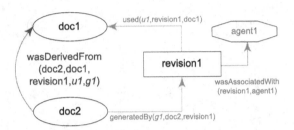

Fig. 2. The imprecise-1 derivation of doc_2 from doc_1 is converted into a precise-1 derivation by specifying an activity $revision_1$, which uses doc_1 and generates doc_2, and is associated with an agent $agent_1$

Specifying this activity enables us to vary the granularity of the obtained provenance (see Sect. 3.3), and to model *responsibility* for the revision, by specifying an agent, if available. In the best case scenario, this agent is found in the document's metadata, as the annotated author or editor. In the worst case, when no agent can be found, the provenance of the revision can still be asserted, without an agent. In other cases it might be possible to find the correct agent by querying other data sources and finding a matching document, with author information available. However, for this paper, reconstructing this missing author information would lead us too far.

3.3   Precise Derivations at Finer Granularity

To obtain provenance at a finer granularity, we will use the semantic properties characterizing the documents. As a document is revised, some of its semantic properties will change, and others will remain the same. Changes might imply *replacements, generalizations* or *specializations*. Some properties might be *omitted* from the document, whereas new ones may be *added*. All of these changes can be modeled with the PROV-DM model. We start from the coarse-grained provenance bundle associated with a set of related documents, as generated in the previous steps, and create a new, fine-grained bundle, enclosing it.

How the semantic properties of a document are identified is dependent on the type of data, and may vary for each use case. In our use case (as can be seen in Sect. 4), this is achieved by applying a named entity extraction technique to the documents. Once the properties are identified, we define a *usage* activity for each of them, linking the properties to the document they are used by.

Next, the properties of each document pair related by a precise-1 derivation are semantically compared. Once again, this comparison is dependent of the type of data and use case. However, it is important that the comparison can model **replacements, generalizations** and **specializations**. Additionally, we will model **additions** and **omissions**.

In PROV-DM, **replacements** or synonyms are modeled by the *alternateOf* relation. The replaced property p_i is *used* by the revision activity, which *generates* the new property p_j. **Specialization** is modeled by the PROV-DM *specializationOf* relation. The more general property p_i is *used* by the revision activity, which *generates* the specialized property p_j. **Generalization** is modeled as an inverse specialization. **Addition** is modeled by a revision activity that *generates* a property p_i, but does not use a replaced, specialized or generalized property. Similarly, **omission** is modeled by a revision activity that *uses* a property p_i, but does not generate a replacing, specializing or generalizing property.

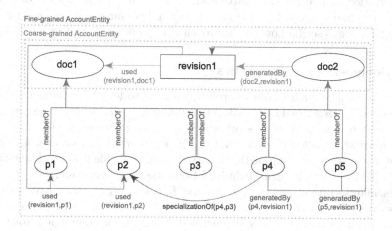

Fig. 3. Finer-Grained Precise Derivations (some usage and generation arguments omitted for clarity)

As an example, we consider the coarse-grained bundle associated with two documents doc_1 and doc_2, as illustrated by Fig. 2. Suppose we were able to identify three properties p_1, p_2, p_3 of doc_1 and three properties p_3, p_4, p_5 of doc_2. Figure 3 shows the usage activities linking these properties with doc_1 and doc_2. When comparing the properties, it was discovered that p_4 is a specialized concept of p_2. This is modeled by the usage of p_2 and generation of p_4 by $revision_1$, and the specialization relation between p_4 and p_2. p_1 was omitted from the revised document, which is modeled by the usage of p_1 by $revision_1$ and the lack of a generation of a related property. p_5 was added to the revised document, which is modeled by the generation of p_5 by $revision_1$ and the lack of a usage of a related property. Storing these assertions into a new, fine-grained bundle, encompassing the original, coarse-grained bundle, provides us with a multi-level view of the provenance of doc_1 and doc_2.

4   Use Case: News Versioning

We kept our description of the proposed approach as general as possible, since it is applicable in many use cases. However, for clarification and evaluation purposes, we will describe a particular use case, originating from the news sector. In today's news industry, specification and justification of sources are key factors for producing high quality journalism. Unfortunately, due to the strong time constraints inherent to news production, provenance information is often incomplete or omitted. The consumers' need for near-immediate reporting also results in an abundance of very similar publications by all leading news organizations, often slightly modified versions of the same article, with limited to no possibility to determine the original source, or to determine which modifications were made to the content. This is exactly where our approach fills the gap. By detecting the derivation of one revision into another, our approach makes it possible to find the original source of an article, as well as the intermediary revisions. In this section, we describe how our approach is implemented for this use case.

4.1   Documents and Properties

For the implementation of our approach, we need to identify "documents" and "properties", as described in Sect. 3. As documents, we use *news stories*, provided in different *revisions*. A news story starts as an *alert*, which is then expanded into a *short story*, a *brief article*, and finally a *full article* (in some cases one or more of these stages are skipped). The articles are available in several languages, so multiple brief articles can be derived from one short story, etc.

As semantic properties, we use *Named Entities* (NEs) associated with the news stories. These can be manually added, or automatically extracted from the content. In either case, the NEs are enriched, linking them to unique resources in the Linked Open Data (LOD) Cloud[8]. For the implementation of our approach, the named entities are also modeled as entities in PROV-DM, with each news article linked to the entities corresponding to the metadata by a *usage* activity.

4.2   Extracting Properties through Named Entity Recognition

When news articles are not annotated with sufficient descriptive metadata, as is often the case in real-world scenarios, we need to automatically generate this metadata ourselves. The availability of accurate metadata associated with the documents will be beneficial to the resulting provenance.

To achieve this, we use publicly available Named Entity Recognition(NER) services. These services accept regular text as input, and output a list of linked

---

[8] http://linkeddata.org

NEs, detected in the text. The NERD [5] comparison tools allow us to evaluate the services and select the most fitting one for our work. For our implementation, we choose to use OpenCalais[9], a well-established, thoroughly tested [6] and freely available NER service. Note that as OpenCalais does not support Dutch, nor French at the time of writing, an automatic translation step is performed before sending the data, using the Microsoft Bing API[10].

4.3   Similarity Measure

Traditionally, document similarity is calculated using the Vector Space Model (VSM), also known as the "bag of words" model. When using this method, documents are viewed as vectors of *Term Frequency - Inverse Document Frequency (TF-IDF)* weights, signifying the importance of each term in the document. We adapt this approach to work with Named Entities (NEs) instead of words. This will allow two documents containing similar concepts, but of significantly varying length, to receive a high similarity score, whereas the classic TF-IDF approach would yield a lower score, due to the difference in text length.

The similarity measure is calculated as follows. When comparing two documents A and B, we create two vectors representations a and b of their NEs, where a_i is the weight of NE i in document A (analogous for B), as determined during the NER step. The similarity between the documents is then calculated as the *cosine similarity* of the vectors, given by Formula 3.

$$Sim_{VSM}(A,B) = \frac{\sum_i a_i b_i}{\sqrt{\sum_i a_i^2} \sqrt{\sum_i b_i^2}} \tag{3}$$

When no NEs were detected, we revert to the classic "bag of words" approach, using TF-IDF weights for every word in the text. Note that the semantic awareness of this similarity metric can be improved (see discussion, Sect. 7).

4.4   Coarse-Grained Provenance through Clustering

As described in Sect. 3.1 and Sect. 3.2, we obtain the first, coarse-grained provenance by clustering sufficiently similar documents together. Using the similarity-measure in Sect. 4.3, we cluster the total set of news articles into sets of closely related articles. As shown in [7], clustering with a lower bound on similarity is an NP-Hard optimization problem. Fortunately, the authors of [7] also provide a greedy heuristic, SimClus, which we choose to use to cluster our dataset.

The applied algorithm is summarized as follows. The set of possible cluster centers S_{pc} initially contains all elements (with at least three NE's, to ensure accuracy of the similarity measure) of S. We compute the complete similarity matrix of the dataset S, which is then used to determine a *cover-set* S_u for each item $u \in S$. S_u contains all elements of S *covered* by u, which means their similarity to u is above an empirically determined threshold T_s. We now choose the cluster centers as follows:

---

[9] http://www.opencalais.com
[10] http://www.microsofttranslator.com/dev/

1. Choose the item $u \in S_{pc}$ with the largest cover-set S_u as the next cluster center (if multiple items are tied, choose the one with the most properties; if there is still a tie, choose arbitrarily).
2. Remove all elements of S_u from S_{pc}.
3. Repeat step 1.

The algorithm terminates when there are no items left to choose as cluster center. The dataset is now divided into (possibly overlapping) clusters, corresponding to the cover-sets of each cluster center. As an optimization, clusters with more items than a predetermined upper bound T_c are clustered again with a higher similarity threshold T_s. In our implementation, we choose $T_c = 10$, since news items rarely have more than ten revisions. For each cluster, we now add the imprecise-n and imprecise-1 derivations according to the method described in Sect. 3.1. Next, we construct the activities as in Sect. 3.2, resulting in precise-1 derivations.

4.5 Finer-Grained Provenance

Starting from the coarse-grained provenance bundle from Sect. 4.4, we can create a finer-grained bundle in the manner described in Sect. 3.3. Note that the semantic properties are already identified in the NER step (see Sect. 4.2). Since these properties are linked to the LOD Cloud, information regarding synonyms, specializations and generalizations is available by following (or dereferencing) these links to popular datasets such as DBPedia, WordNet, Freebase, etc. Synonym relationships include *owl:sameAs* and *skos:exactMatch*, whereas examples of links specifying generalization and specialization are (respectively) *skos:broader* and *skos:narrower*. Using the methods in Sect. 3.3, we create the correct derivations, usages and generations linked to the revision activities from the coarse-grained provenance, and create a new, finer-grained provenance bundle, encompassing the original. In Fig. 4, this is illustrated for one news item.

5   Evaluation

Our evaluation data consists of a set of 410 news stories, corresponding to 100 news items, in up to two different languages (Dutch and French), acquired from Belga[11], a professional Belgian news agency, over the course of one week.

The originally available provenance for the news stories, as specified by the content provider, is limited to the *revision types, original sources* and *imprecise-n derivations.* The source of a news item is always the earliest news story associated with that news item (usually an alert or short story). All following stories about that news item are (directly or indirectly) derived from its source (as an imprecise-n derivation).

Since there is no formal workflow to describe the creative process of news production, indisputably correct imprecise-1 derivations are nearly impossible

---

[11] http://www.belga.be

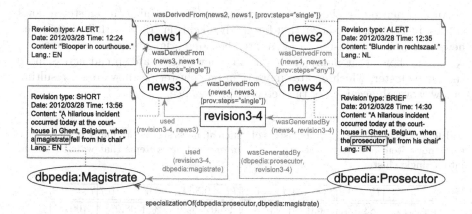

Fig. 4. Example of discovered provenance in the news use case. The news item starts as an English alert $news_1$, which is then translated into a Dutch alert $news_2$. Soon after that, a short story $news_3$ is written based on the English alert. Finally, the short story is revised to a brief story $news_4$, replacing the word "magistrate" with "prosecutor".

to determine, even for the content providers (which is why our approach is so useful to them). Therefore, we restrict the evaluation to imprecise-n derivations.

We constructed coarse-grained provenance using the approach described in Sect. 4, based only on the (enriched) content and timing information of the news stories in our dataset. We can now compare the detected clusters, sources and imprecise-n derivations to the original information provided by the news agency. In Table 1, the results are shown for different initial similarity thresholds T_s. In the optimal case, with $T_s = 0.5$, we were able to detect 73% of the original news sources, with 68.2% precision. The imprecise-n derivations constructed from these sources have a precision of 72.3% and a recall of 44.5%.

Table 1. Accuracy of provenance discovery with similarity threshold $T_s \in \{0.2, 0.3, 0.4, 0.5, 0.6, 0.7, 0.8\}$ and cluster threshold $T_c = 10$. p_{source} and r_{source} represent the precision and recall of the detected news sources, compared to original derivations from the dataset

	$T_s = 0.2$	$T_s = 0.3$	$T_s = 0.4$	$T_s = 0.5$	$T_s = 0.6$	$T_s = 0.7$	$T_s = 0.8$
p_{source}	68.0%	67.3%	**69.2%**	68.2%	64.3%	59.3%	57.7%
r_{source}	70.0%	68.0%	72.0%	**73.0%**	72.0%	70.0%	71.0%
$p_{imprecise-n}$	56.3%	61.6%	67.6%	**72.3%**	71.5%	57.1%	57.9%
$r_{imprecise-n}$	45.8%	**48.1%**	45.2%	44.5%	41.3%	28.4%	26.1%

An explanation for these figures is found when examining the clustered news stories. In Table 2, it is shown that for nearly all clusters (96% with $T_s = 0.5$), the news stories in the cluster all belong to the same original news item. However, $r_{newsitem}$ shows that many of the original news items are spread across more than one cluster, which creates more than one cluster per news item, resulting in lower overall accuracy of the detected provenance.

Table 2. Percentage $p_{cluster}$ of clusters of which all news stories originally belong to the same news item and percentage $r_{newsitem}$ of original news items that were cataloged into a single cluster

	$T_s = 0.2$	$T_s = 0.3$	$T_s = 0.4$	$T_s = 0.5$	$T_s = 0.6$	$T_s = 0.7$	$T_s = 0.8$
$p_{cluster}$	83.8%	86.0%	93.3%	96.0%	97.7%	98.0%	100%
$r_{newsitem}$	30.0%	37.0%	32.0%	31.0%	26.0%	11.0%	8.0%

The accuracy of the fine-grained provenance depends strongly on the correctness of the detected named entities, and the quality of their links to ontologies that describe alternates, specializations and generalizations. When processing the 410 news stories, OpenCalais extracted 722 distinct named entities. Upon manual evaluation of these NEs we labeled 20 of them as incorrectly detected, resulting in 97.2% precision. Criteria for labeling a property as incorrectly detected were *non-existence* (no such concept exists) and *incorrect disambiguation* (linked to the wrong resource). These results are consistent with those of a larger performance analysis of OpenCalais, described in [6]. Of the 722 Named Entities, 47 were automatically linked to a resource in the LOD Cloud by OpenCalais.

6   Related Work

When it comes to automated production of provenance information, several methods exist. These techniques mostly focus on either *observed provenance*, or *disclosed provenance*[8]. In [3], it is noted that these systems need to capture all activities, since they do not necessarily understand the semantics of their observations. Although domain-specific techniques used to reconstruct lost or missing provenance information do exist, such as in [9] and [10], no generic solution is available to date.

As shown in [2], provenance produced by these methods is often low-level and/or too complex for a domain expert (e.g., a journalist) with limited knowledge of computer science. In [11], the need for high level provenance is motivated, and a conceptualization is proposed, namely as a combination of interconnected elements including *"what"*, *"when"*, *"where"*, *"how"*, *"who"*, *"which"*, *and "why"*. However, a recent survey, [12], shows that high-level knowledge provenance is still a sparsely researched topic.

7   Discussion and Future Work

The results of our evaluation clearly show that our approach to discover provenance of resources, solely based on their (enriched) content and timing information, is feasible and provides the foundations for future work. A better, more semantically aware similarity measure, such as the one described in [13], is likely to have a significant impact on the overall accuracy. To accommodate such a metric, the extracted semantic properties need to be accurately linked to the Semantic Web. To achieve this in future implementations, additional disambiguation and enrichment techniques are being developed to combine with the available NER services. Finally, even though it would make the approach less general, it might prove worthwhile considering domain specific information, as it may significantly improve accuracy and levels of granularity of the discovered provenance.

In this paper, we illustrated our approach with one specific use case: news versioning. However, thanks to the general nature of the proposed provenance discovery method, several other use cases are feasible. Examples of possible applications include plagiarism detection, provenance of code snippets and the tracing of information sources used for quotes in online content, such as blogs. Implementation of one or more of these use cases will allow us to further evaluate the approach, and provide more meaningful fine-grained provenance assertions.

8   Conclusions

We developed an approach that succeeds in creating provenance derivations for a large dataset, discovered from a limited amount of information (content and timing information). Our approach is general enough for adaptation in several domains, and is compliant with the current standard, the Provenance Data Model (PROV-DM). When adapted to the use case of news versioning, our approach detected the original source of a news item with 68% precision and 73% recall. These results are promising, considering that there are several potential improvements to be made to the current implementation. Implementing these improvements is the key to future research in this field, in which additional links to the Semantic Web and a more semantically aware similarity measure will further improve the accuracy of the discovered provenance.

Acknowledgments. The research activities in this paper were funded by Ghent University, the Interdisciplinary Institute for Broadband Technology (IBBT, a research institute founded by the Flemish Government), the Institute for Promotion of Innovation by Science and Technology in Flanders (IWT), the FWO-Flanders, and the European Union, in the context of the IBBT project Smarter Media in Flanders (SMIF). Companies involved are Belga, Concentra, VRT and Roularta, with project support of IWT.

References

1. Gil, Y., Cheney, J., Groth, P., Hartig, O., Miles, S., Moreau, L., Da Silva, P.P.: Provenance XG final report. Final Incubator Group Report (2010)
2. Gómez-Pérez, J.M., Corcho, O.: Problem-solving methods for understanding process executions. IEEE Computing in Science & Engineering 10, 47–52 (2008)
3. Braun, U., Garfinkel, S., Holland, D.A., Muniswamy-Reddy, K.-K., Seltzer, M.I.: Issues in Automatic Provenance Collection. In: Moreau, L., Foster, I. (eds.) IPAW 2006. LNCS, vol. 4145, pp. 171–183. Springer, Heidelberg (2006)
4. PROV-DM Part 1: The Provenance Data Model, W3C Editor's Draft (May 29, 2012), http://dvcs.w3.org/hg/prov/raw-file/default/model/prov-dm.html
5. Rizzo, G., Troncy, R.: NERD: Evaluating Named Entity Recognition Tools in the Web of Data. In: Workshop on Web Scale Knowledge Extraction, WEKEX 2011 (2011)
6. Iacobelli, F., Nichols, N., Birnbaum, L., Hammond, K.: Finding new information via robust entity detection. In: Proactive Assistant Agents AAAI Fall Symposium (2010)
7. Hasan, M.A., Salem, S., Pupacdi, B., Zaki, M.J.: Clustering with Lower Bound on Similarity. In: Theeramunkong, T., Kijsirikul, B., Cercone, N., Ho, T.-B. (eds.) PAKDD 2009. LNCS, vol. 5476, pp. 122–133. Springer, Heidelberg (2009)
8. Zhao, J., Sahoo, S.S., Missier, P., Sheth, A., Goble, C.: Extending semantic provenance into the web of data. IEEE Internet Computing, 40–48 (2011)
9. Zhao, J., Gomadam, K., Prasanna, V.: Predicting Missing Provenance using Semantic Associations in Reservoir Engineering. In: 2011 Fifth IEEE International Conference on Semantic Computing, ICSC (2011)
10. Zhang, J., Jagadish, H.V.: Lost source provenance. In: Proceedings of the 13th International Conference on Extending Database Technology. ACM (2010)
11. Ram, S., Liu, J.: A new perspective on Semantics of Data Provenance. In: First International Workshop on the Role of Semantic Web in Provenance Management, SWPM (2009)
12. Moreau, L.: The foundations for provenance on the web. Now Publishers (2010)
13. Hliaoutakis, A., Varelas, G., Voutsakis, E., Petrakis, E.G.M., Milios, E.: Information retrieval by semantic similarity. International Journal on Semantic Web and Information Systems (IJSWIS), 55–73 (2006)

Transparent Provenance Derivation for User Decisions

Ingrid Nunes[1,2], Yuhui Chen[2], Simon Miles[2], Michael Luck[2], and Carlos Lucena[1]

[1] LES, Departamento de Informática, PUC-Rio, Rio de Janeiro, Brazil
{ionunes,lucena}@inf.puc-rio.br
[2] Department of Informatics, King's College London, London, WC2R 2LS, United Kingdom
{yuhui.chen,simon.miles,michael.luck}@kcl.ac.uk

Abstract. It is rare for data's history to include computational processes alone. Even when software generates data, users ultimately decide to execute software procedures, choose their configuration and inputs, reconfigure, halt and restart processes, and so on. Understanding the provenance of data thus involves understanding the reasoning of users behind these decisions, but demanding that users explicitly document decisions could be intrusive if implemented naively, and impractical in some cases. In this paper, therefore, we explore an approach to transparently deriving the provenance of user decisions at query time. The user reasoning is simulated, and if the result of the simulation matches the documented decision, the simulation is taken to approximate the actual reasoning. The plausibility of this approach requires that the simulation mirror human decision-making, so we adopt an automated process explicitly modelled on human psychology. The provenance of the decision is modelled in Open Provenance Model (OPM), allowing it to be queried as part of a larger provenance graph, and an OPM profile is provided to allow consistent querying of provenance across user decisions.

Keywords: Decision making, explanation, OPM profile, inference.

1 Introduction

Humans are involved somewhere in most software processes, and the decisions they take are part of an explanation of the processes' effects. Therefore, as part of provenance information, it would be helpful to know the reasons why decisions were made as they were, including why a particular option was chosen and why others were not. While it is plausible to elicit something about a user's preferences over time, in many circumstances it is unrealistic to expect them to record the reasons behind every individual decision. If a decision is between many alternatives, each with pros and cons, and is influenced by a combination of different factors, it will not be apparent, just by knowing the user's preferences, why the decision was made. Moreover, a complex decision is influenced not just by what a user prefers, but also how they reason over the alternatives, i.e. psychological processes.

For example, when looking back at the total budget spent attending conferences by a group in a year, and considering how it might be reduced in subsequent years, it is relevant to consider why members of the group have chosen particular travel and accommodation options. The preferences of an individual may be apparent by looking across records from multiple years, but the choices made on a specific trip may be

P. Groth and J. Frew (Eds.): IPAW 2012, LNCS 7525, pp. 111–125, 2012.

based on many attributes of the options available such as price, duration, location and facilities, and on preferences that do not consistently indicate one option, e.g. desire to spend little versus preference to share a hotel with a colleague with expensive tastes. The provenance of the budget spent can be seen as a process involving decisions drawing on many factors, and may be the result of heuristics that do not correspond exactly with 'rational' economic choices.

We wish to answer queries about the provenance of data where that provenance includes user decisions and the query relates to the reasons for those decisions. We are concerned with cases where the reasons for a decision are not immediately obvious as they require a choice between options with multiple attributes with pros and cons. We assume that, at recording time, the human reasoning is not captured, and instead derive a plausible explanation as part of the provenance query execution. This explanation is determined through simulating the user decision process using an automated decision making technique tailored to account for human psychological heuristics, e.g. preferring an option with uniformly acceptable attributes to one very good in some regard and very poor in another. The provenance of the simulated process is recorded. If the outcome of the decision-making process is the same as happened in reality, then the simulation provenance provides a plausible explanation of the user reasoning.

This problem is not one that has been tackled in depth in the literature, with notable exceptions. Naja et al. [10] consider a similar problem of the reasons behind decisions in a multi-agent simulation of an emergency response domain. They look at how the states a software agent transitioned through led to the decisions that were made. This is a comparable but not equivalent problem to our own. That is, they consider how the agent perceptions and prior actions influenced the decision rather than the reasoning on that decision itself. Moreover, they track the provenance of the software agent as developed for the response simulation, rather than trying to create a psychologically-realistic simulation of the decision reasoning. They construct an Open Provenance Model (OPM) [9] profile for the provenance, but this is specific to the emergency response domain rather than about decisions in general. Other work concerns the provenance of decisions, but again concern the gathering of data to inform the decision rather than the decision itself. For example, Kifor et al. [5] investigate the provenance of organ transplant decisions, but the decision itself is not modelled, only the observable factors used as input, while Missier et al. [8] record the quality of inputs to an automated decision, based on user criteria, to interpret the trustworthiness of the result. In the following sections, we first define the problem and provide a motivating example, before presenting the overall approach and its components: an *automated decision maker* and an *OPM profile for user decisions*, to later detail questions that can be answered regarding the human decisions.

2   Explaining User Decisions

We start by articulating the problem to be solved. Broadly, we aim to infer the provenance of user decisions, i.e. what reasoning led to those decisions, that take place within larger processes for which provenance is recorded. The decisions are choices between *options* based on criteria for making that decision, *preferences*. We assume some knowledge of those options and preferences in inferring the reasoning. The provenance is to be used to explain the effects of those decisions later in the larger processes.

2.1 Motivating Example

We will take a use case from the healthcare domain as our a running example.

Background. As part of the drug development process, clinical trials are conducted with patients by clinical researchers from, for example, pharmaceutical companies. Where the process of recruiting these patients has traditionally been carried out through personal meetings between researchers and doctors, automation is being brought to each stage. Projects such as Electronic Health Records for Clinical Research (EHR4CR) [3] or Translational Medicine and Patient Safety in Europe (TRANSFoRm) [2] aim to provide clinical research (CR) platforms that allow researchers to identify and recruit patients, querying their data from hospitals and other clinical data sites in multiple countries. The trial recruitment process is becoming one in which software processes are intermingled with human decisions (by researchers, patients, doctors, hospital auditors, etc.). Verified provenance data is critical in this context, due to the regulatory requirements applied to drug development and clinical trials. However, less strictly defined provenance information is also valuable in helping to refine trial recruitment. New clinical trials often have to face difficulties recruiting an adequate number of patients within a limited budget and timescale. A CR platform allows clinical researchers to design protocol feasibility studies with a set of patient eligibility criteria, send study queries to distributed clinical information systems, and rapidly get feedback on patient population numbers at each site and the geographic distribution of eligible patients. Understanding why a trial has not recruited enough patients means understanding what decisions were made during the studies and how.

Process. Alex is a clinical researcher with a pharmaceutical company. He is currently planning a clinical trial for a new drug that targets *Haemophilia A*. He needs to find sites for conducting the trial. He designs a study and composes a set of eligibility criteria for identifying suitable patients. For instance, he specifies inclusion criteria, such as *"male aged between 12 and 65," "immunocompetent with a CD4+ lymphocyte count >$200/mm^3$,"* and exclusion criteria, such as *"platelet count < 75,000/mm^3."* He submits the query to the a CR platform which in turn tries to discover eligible patients in the UK. After some time, the query result is ready, containing a list of feasible sites and important site-specific information, such as the number of eligible patients at the site, per-patient cost, and estimated local R&D approval time (Table 1).

Decision. Alex decides which sites, if any, to recruit from. We assume that deciding to recruit patients from a site means that all eligible patients are recruited from that site, e.g. due to an agreement with sites to help them recoup admin costs. It is the provenance of this decision that we focus on.

Table 1. CR query result example (illustrative only)

Site	Number of eligible patients	Per-patient cost	Approximate local approval time (days)
A	30	£25,000	70
B	27	£22,000	60
C	22	£27,000	45

Preferences. From past experience and the specification of an individual study, the researcher will have preferences on how to choose trial sites. For instance, if Alex needs at least 20 patients and accepts up to £600,000 trial cost and up to 80 days approval time, and is more concerned to reduce approval time than cost, then C is the ideal choice. If he instead prioritised number of patients recruited, B is preferable. A is discounted as it exceeds acceptable costs (30 patients x £25,000 = £750,000).

Options. There are eight options given the sites above: none (0), A only (A), B only (B), C only (C), A and B (AB), A and C (AC), B and C (BC), or all three (ABC).

2.2 Explanations

In order to justify a decision, different granularities of explanation can be given. High-level explanations either (i) highlight the positive and negatives aspects of chosen and rejected options [6,7], giving arguments for or against options, or (ii) briefly indicate how the choice was made, as is typical in Recommender Systems (RSs) [17], e.g. "people who bought this product also bought..." However, for complex decisions, it can be unclear how the decision follows from the preferences known and options available. In such cases, more of the reasoning process must be exposed. Where option i was chosen over option j (amongst others), users ask questions such as the following.

- **Q1.** Are there preferences that compare i and j but did not affect the decision?
- **Q2.** Were any implicit (unstated) preferences considered?
- **Q3.** Do the positive aspects of i relative to j compensate its negative aspects?
- **Q4.** How much better is i to j relative to the trade-offs between i and other options?

3 Overall Approach and Background

In this section, we describe the components and methodology that comprise our approach, and provide a brief background on two works, which our approach is based on: the Open Provenance Model (OPM) [9] and a psychologically-inspired decision maker. The components required to realise our approach are the following.

System-independent provenance model. To form a connected account of provenance, including user decisions and software processes, we require a model that is system-independent. Here, we use the OPM.

Decision provenance pattern. We wish our solution to be generic and re-usable, allowing queries of a repeatable form over different decisions. Therefore, the provenance of a user decision should follow an application-independent pattern, expressed in this paper as a profile of OPM.

Human decision simulator. Most existing automated decision-makers do not attempt to reflect human decision making, but search for the choice that best matches the stated preferences. For our simulation, we use an existing decision making approach [14,15] that explicitly applies heuristics observed in studies of human psychology.

Explanation from provenance queries. The results of the provenance recording and decision simulation should be a connected provenance graph. Finally, we need to provide some means to ask the provenance queries over this graph.

Our overall methodology is composed of six steps, detailed next.

1. As an application executes, an OPM graph is recorded documenting what has occurred in observable software processes.
2. A data item (OPM artifact) denotes a decision made by a user.
3. An automated decision-maker processes the known preferences potentially influencing the decision and set of options chosen between.
4. As the automated decision-maker executes, it documents its operations in OPM following a pre-defined profile for the provenance of a user decision.
5. If the outcome of the decision maker is the same as the actual decision, the graphs from steps 1 and 4 are combined to form a single graph.
6. Provenance queries that concern the reasons behind the decision can be executed.

3.1   Open Provenance Model

The Open Provenance Model (OPM) [9] is an abstract provenance model that describes past occurrences in terms of *artifacts*, immutable states of data items or physical objects, *processes*, actions performed on, using or generating artifacts, and *agents*, contextual entities acting as catalysts for processes. These entities are connected into graphs with edges from effect to cause, e.g. that a process used an artifact or an artifact was generated by a process. When depicted visually, as in Figures 1, 2 and 3, ovals denote artifacts and rectangles denote processes. An edge between an artifact and a process can include a *role* identifier, stating the artifact's function in the process, denoted by brackets after the edge type. Artifacts and processes can be *typed* by giving an annotation opm:type=X, where X is a unique type identifier.

To execute a query over an OPM graph, you need to know its structure. Ideally, queries can be re-used across similar applications, and so OPM *profiles* are used to give domain-specific extensions for OPM, allowing the graph structures to be common within that domain. An OPM profile is defined by *(i)* a unique global identifier; *(ii)* an optional controlled vocabulary for annotations; *(iii)* optional general guidance to express OPM graphs; and *(iv)* optional profile expansion rules. In the following sections, we describe the key elements of our method: the automated decision maker, and the OPM profile for user decisions. We then describe how the combined graph would be queried to answer questions about the reasons behind decisions.

3.2   Psychologically-Inspired Automated Decision Making

The automated decision maker used to simulate the user decisions is described in prior work [14,15]. As described in the published work, it has been evaluated to ensure it reflects the decisions that users would make given adequate information on the options. Here we summarise the key aspects, which are illustrated with a scenario in which a researcher is looking for an apartment to stay at, and each apartment is described in terms of the city zone that it is located, distance from university and price. The decision maker inputs are the user *preferences*, and the *options* available, specified in terms of their *attributes*. Derived from studies of how users express preferences in practice, there are seven kinds that can be specified, shown in Table 2. Preferences may apply only conditionally, where the condition is an expression in terms of attribute values. In addition, *priorities* can be expressed either between attributes or between preferences, so that the attribute/preference is given more weight in the decision making.

Two primary models are then constructed. The Preference Satisfaction Model (PSM) is a mapping of each attribute of each option to a rating of how much that option is individually desired, e.g. considering preferences 4 and 5, an apartment in zone 1 is mapped to *best*, while one in zone 2 to *prefer* (w.r.t. zone). The Options-Attribute Preference Model (OAPM) states, for each attribute of each option, how it compares to the same attribute of each other option, either better $(+)$, worse, $(-)$, similar $(\sim)$ or inconclusive $(?)$, e.g. if Ap_A is cheaper than Ap_B then $OAPM[Ap\_A, Ap\_B, price] = +$. Where the explicitly stated preferences are insufficient for building these models, the decision maker will look for preferences *implied* by those stated. For example, if an upper bound is given as in preference 1, a goal to minimise this attribute is derived from it.

The relative benefits of options across all attributes are then calculated using preferences to derive *how much* an attribute value is better then another, and this cost-benefit analysis is combined with two principles from psychology on how humans make decisions [16]. The first, *extremeness aversion*, states that people avoid options that compromise one attribute too much to improve another. For example, an Ap_A is 2Km away from the university and costs £125 per week, Ap_B is 2.5Km away and costs £100, and Ap_C is 3Km away and costs £75. The costs of each option is compensated by its benefits, but people tend to choose Ap_B because its attributes are less extreme. The second, *trade-off contrast*, indicates that people consider the whole set of options when evaluating the trade-off between two options, i.e. the scale of differences across available options influences individual comparisons. Comparing only Ap_A and Ap_B, it is difficult to know if paying more £25 compensates being 0.5Km closer to the university, so people look at this relationship among all the other options to evaluate this particular one.

Many decision making systems have been proposed over the years, including Expert Systems (ESs), which capture domain knowledge to make decisions like a domain expert [11], Recommender Systems (RSs), which recommend options from a (huge) set based on statistical models [17], and Decision Support Systems (DSSs), which use decision making models, commonly inspired in economy [4], to make choices [6,7].

Table 2. Preference types

Preference	Description	Example	#
Constraint	Specifies the values that attributes must (not) have	$uni < 4Km$	1
Goal	Specifies which attributes should be minimised or maximised	*minimise price*	2
Order	Specifies where one attribute value is preferred to another	$zone = 1 > zone = 2$	3
Qualifying Preference	States how much an attribute value is wanted or needed	$prefer\ zone = 1 \lor 2$	4
Rating Preference	Specifies which values are best or worst	$zone = 1\ best$	5
Indifference	Specify where there is no preference between two attribute values	$zone = 1 \sim zone = 2$	6
Don't care	Specifies where an attribute is irrelevant to the decision	*don't care price*	7

For several use cases, it is important to explain how decisions made by these processes came about. For RS and DSS, explanations focus on indicating the general idea underlying the recommendation ("people that bought this product also bought...") or indicating positive and negative aspects of options. While enough in some situations, users sometimes need details to understand why and how an option should be chosen, and merely exposing the software process or its inputs may be not helpful. ESs typically present the chain of rules fired to produce a given output. This approach is limited by its specificity: rules are domain-specific and a huge amount of them are elicited for each ES, and thus there is no reuse across applications. As we will show in the next section, we present a generic OPM profile to try to capture the reasoning process enabling detailed questions to be answered.

4   An OPM Profile for Decision Making

As the decision is simulated by the above decision maker, it records the reasoning in OPM following a profile. The profile ensures consistency of OPM graphs for decision reasoning, so allowing reusable queries to be created. We refer to the profile as the User-Centric Preference-Based Decision (UCPB) profile. A base URI is used for all types defined, `http://www.les.inf.puc-rio.br/`, referred to with prefix `ucpb`. The profile's unique identifier is `ucbp:Profile`. The profile has all optional elements listed in Section 3 except for expansion rules.

The profile includes a graph template for the provenance of a decision, depicted in Figures 1 and 2 (split into parts for space reasons). Each artifact or process is given a URI type annotation, defined in Table 3, so that queries can identify what part of the reasoning process it represents. Where a subgraph is specific to one option and/or attribute, that subgraph will be repeated for each option and/or attribute considered, and the artifact/process type is shown as parametrised, e.g. `Extremeness(i)`.

Note that part of the provenance graph's value comes from connecting a decision with only those preferences that were taken into account, i.e. filtering for relevance. The provenance graph excludes preferences, priorities and weightings that did not influence the decision, and so a subset of those known of the user.

Figure 1 presents the part of the provenance graph that describes how an option was selected based on the decision values of options compared to the others. The decision making process finishes when an option i is selected from a set of options, based on the decision values of this option with respect to the others and vice-versa. A decision value, in turn, is the result of the weighted sum of the relative benefits between options, the trade-off contrast, and the extremeness aversion, the three human processes components that the technique simulates. Initially, individual attribute values are analysed and their differences are evaluated. But, according to the importance of particular attributes, a small difference may be considered very significant. Then, people observe two other factors, which look at the relationship among attribute values. First, when an option compromise too much an attribute to compensate another, it is considered an extreme option, which is in general avoided by people (extremeness aversion). Second, as people often are not sure when a positive aspect of an option compensates a negative aspect, they look at this trade-off relationship of all options to make this evaluation,

Table 3. Term definitions

ApplyImplicitPreferences	Applies preferences implicitly derived from known user preferences.
AssessAttributeBenefit	Assesses the benefit of attribute a of option i w.r.t. option j.
AssessAttributeImportance	Builds a partial order of attributes, based on priorities.
AssessAvgTradeOff	Assesses the average of the cost-benefit relationship (trade-off) among all options.
AssessDistanceFromBest	Calculates the disadvantage of an option attribute w.r.t. the best possible value.
AssessExtremeness	Assesses option extremeness (standard deviation of the distance from best of each attribute).
AssessOptionAttribute	Assesses the preference for an option attribute value based on monadic preferences.
AssessOptionDecisionValue	Assesses a value that represents how an option is better than another.
Attribute	Criterion used to describe an option, which is associated with a attribute domain.
AttributeBenefit	Advantage (in percentage points) of the attribute value of option i w.r.t. option j.
AttributeDomain	Range of all possible values that can be assigned to an attribute.
AttributeFunction	WeightFunction parameterised to calculate attribute weights given an AttributePartialOrder.
AttributeIndifference	Priority that states that an attribute a is as important as attribute b.
AttributePartialOrder	Partial order among attributes, establishing an importance relationship.
AttributePriority	Priority that states that an attribute a is more important than attribute b.
AttributeWeight	Weight specified for an attribute, representing its importance.
AVPO	Partial order of values of a particular attribute, stands for attribute value partial order.
BuildAttributeValuePartialOrder	Builds a partial order of the values of an attribute, based on order preferences.
CalculateAttributeWeight	Calculates an attribute weight based on a function and the attribute importance.
CalculateFunctionParameters	Calculates the parameters of the WeightFunction based on the AttributePartialOrder.
CompareOptionsAttribute	Compares the attribute values of two options, establishing a preference order or indifference.
DecisionValue	Value (in percentage points) that represents how much an option is preferred w.r.t. another.
DistanceFromBest	Distance from an option attribute value (in percentage points) to the best possible value.
DontCare	Preference that specifies an attribute whose values are irrelevant for the decision.
EvaluateAllOptionBenefits	Evaluates the overall benefits of option i w.r.t. option j.
EvaluateExtremenessAversion	Evaluates the difference between the extremeness of two options.
EvaluateTradeOffContrast	Evaluates the difference between the trade-off of two options and the trade-off average.
Extremeness	Value that indicates (in percentage points) how extremeness an option is.
ExtremenessAversion	Value that indicates the benefit of an option for being less extreme than another.
Goal	Preference that states the desire of maximising or minimising an attribute value.
Indifference	Preference that indicates attribute values that are equally preferred.
ModifierScale	Scale that establishes a partial order of the strength of modifiers (performatives or rates).
MonadicPreference	Preference that refers to a single target, and evaluates it with modifiers.
OAPM	Options-attribute preference model, states preference between option attribute values.
OrderPreference	Preference that indicates that an attribute value is preferred to another.
PreferencePriority	Priority that states that a preference is preferred to another.
RelativeBenefit	Values that indicates (in percentage points) the advantage of an attribute value w.r.t. another.
PSM	Preference Satisfaction model, associates attribute values of options with a modifier.
SelectOption	Selects an option from those available based on decision values.
SelectedOption	Option selected from a set.
TradeOffContrast	Value that indicates the benefit of an option for having a good trade-off w.r.t another.
TO	Trade-off (cost-benefit relationship) between two options.
TOAvg	Average of the trade-offs among all options.
WeightEA	Weight of the extremeness aversion used in the decision function.
WeightTO	Weight of the trade-off contrast used in the decision function.
WeightFunction	Parameterised function (e.g. $f(x) = log_a x + b$) that is used to calculate attribute weights.

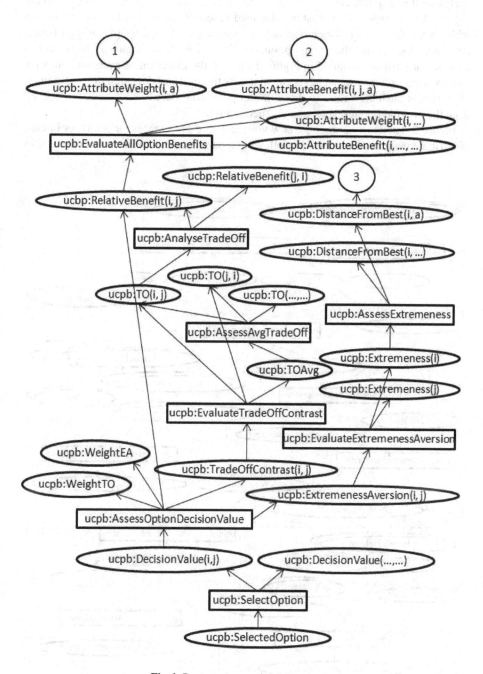

Fig. 1. Provenance graph I (prototype)

analysing the trade-off contrast. Options that have a good cost-benefit relationship are preferred. The trade-off contrast is calculated based on the benefit between an option with respect to another, which depends on two factors: (i) the weight of a particular attribute, which is specific for an option, detailed in Figure 2(1); and (ii) the benefit of a particular attribute, detailed in Figure 2(2). And the extremeness aversion compares how extreme options are, which is calculated as the standard deviation of the distances of an option attribute values to those of an option considered best — this is obtained from the provided preferences, and detailed in Figure 2(3).

Figure 2 details these three parts, whose leafs are preferences, or priorities in case of attribute weights. Therefore, by following a particular path of the tree beginning in

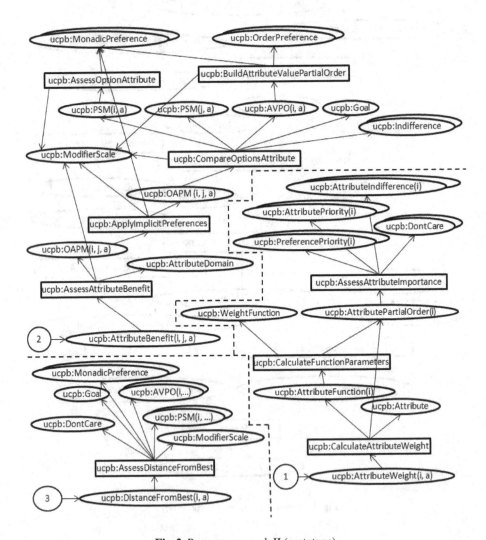

Fig. 2. Provenance graph II (prototype)

the selected option one can understand the preference(s) that caused calculated values, which lead to the choice for that option. Different preferences are treated differently. Monadic preferences are first used to build the PSM, which in turn is used together with the remaining preferences to construct the OAPM. This model is later refined by considering implicit preferences in the explication process.

Returning to our example, as part of the scenario, Alex chose sites B and C (BC). We simulate the decision based on preferences we believe him to have. Specifically, Alex has the following goals: (P_1) maximise the number of eligible patients recruited; (P_2) minimise costs; (P_3) minimise approval time. He further has some qualifying preferences: (P_4) want around 50 patients; (P_5) accept spending between £1M and £1.2M. Finally, Alex has a priority: (P_6) prioritise number of patients over other attributes. Taking the eight options and the latter preferences, the decision maker simulates the decision, recording an OPM graph, an extract of which is shown in Figure 3.

5   Decision Provenance Queries

Given a provenance graph following our profile, queries can be made about the reasoning behind a decision. The following are examples, illustrated with our case study. They make reference to the chosen option i and another option j. To make the queries more precise, we will use an XPath-like notation, where each step in the path is the type of an artifact, process or edge, and a parent-child relation denotes that an edge links into or from an artifact or process. For example, //ucpb:SelectOption/opm:used/* returns all artifacts used by a ucpb:SelectOption process. The language is for illustration and is only semi-formal, but is similar to real provenance query languages [1].

Q1. Are there preferences that compare i and j but did not affect the decision? Alex chose option BC, recruiting 49 patients in total and not, for example, AB, recruiting 57. Querying the graph will tell us that BC was preferred to AB specifically with regard to the number of patients, recorded as artifact ucpb:OAPM having value "+". The graph further tells us the preference that was the reason for this decision, P_4, through a was-DerivedFrom OPM edge. Preference P_1 also concerns this attribute, and was an input to the process generating the ucpb:OAPM, but was not the reason, so no wasDerivedFrom edge exists. This query can be executed by first retrieving all preferences used in comparing options, //ucpb:CompareOptionsAttribute/opm:used/*, and then removing all those having a positive result on the chosen option //ucpb:OAPM [opm:value='[BC]=+']/opm:wasDerivedFrom/*. Those remaining cannot have influenced the final choice.

Q2. Were any implicit preferences considered? In our example, Alex had preference P_5 stating that a cost higher than £1M and lower than £1.2M is 'acceptable.' This is not necessarily a hard constraint, i.e. a cost lower or higher may still be a valid option, but values in that range fit in the 'acceptable' range of the modifier scale. This explicit preference also implies a further preference, P_7, that values outside of the interval are more acceptable if closer to it, e.g. £0.9M is closer to being acceptable than £0.8M. However, in this example, the explicitly stated preferences, including P_2, are adequate for making a comparison of options, so the implicit preference has no effect. This can be seen in the

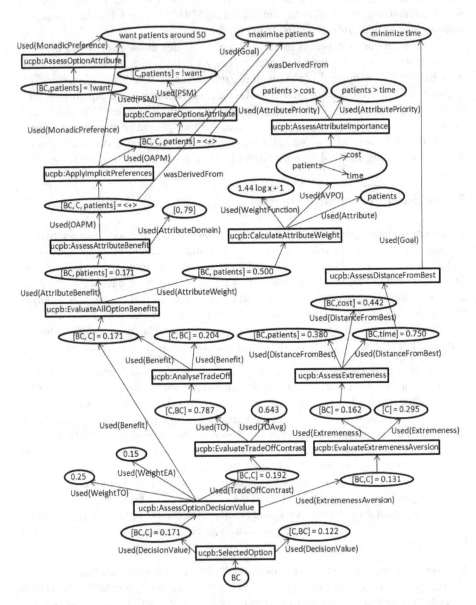

Fig. 3. CR Provenance Graph (partial)

provenance graph where `ucpb:InferImplicitPreferences` does not alter the comparison value ('[B,C,patients]=<+>'), B is preferable to C with regards to number of patients, before and after the process). This query can be executed by detecting any instances where the OAPM output and input of the implicit preference step are different, `//ucpb:OAPM[opm:value!=opm:wasGeneratedBy/ //ucpb:Apply ImplicitPreferences/opm:used/ ucpb:OAPM/opm:value]`.

Q3. Do the positive aspects of option i relative to option j compensate its negative aspects? Alex's decision making was not necessarily a pure reflection of the positive and negative attribute differences, but will have been influenced by human psychological processes. Here we model two known effects described earlier, trade-off evaluation and extremeness aversion. The influence of these on the eventual decision is weighted in the simulation (0.25 and 0.15 respectively). The weights may be derived from observations of Alex, or based on averages across a wider population. We can then ask whether these psychological processes affected the particular decision. In this case, the benefit of option BC over C, given value 0.171, was lower than the benefit of C over BC (given value 0.204, shown in Figure 3 as an artifact used by `ucpb:AnalyseTradeOff`). However, the difference between the options is small relative to the differences across the set (trade-off) and C has a higher rating primarily because one attribute, approval time, is very good but at the expense of another, eligible patients (extremeness aversion). Because of this, the eventual decision chooses BC. This query can be executed by checking whether the benefits comparison without trade-off and extremeness aversion, `//opm:wasGeneratedBy/ucpb:EvaluateAllOptionBenefits`, results in one option being preferred to another while the inputs to the final selection `//ucpb:SelectedOption/opm:used` show the reverse.

Q4. How much better is i to j relative to the trade-offs between i and other options? The trade-off between two options is always evaluated based on its comparison with other trade-offs, i.e. what is taken into account is the trade-off *contrast*. Therefore, in order to understand the trade-off between two options it is important to allow users to verify the average of the trade-offs. In Figure 3, it can be observed that the trade-off (cost-benefit ratio) between options site C only and sites B and C together is 0.787, which is higher (worse) than the average 0.643. This query can by comparing the particular trade-off measures, `//opm:wasGeneratedBy/ucpb:AnalyseTradeOff`, with the average of those values.

Answers to Q1 and Q2 will refer to attributes, leading to further questions such as "Why was i's value for attribute a considered better than j's?" or "Why was attribute a more important than b?"

Recording the decision making process that matches a user choice using our profile also allows generating high-level explanations, mentioned before. Even though they may not be enough in some cases, mainly when there is the need for a detailed explanation between pros and cons of individual attributes, which is the case of the queries above, giving an initial high-level explanation may be useful. However, in order to do so, existing approaches [6,7] need as input attribute weights and values, and therefore a provenance graph is also needed to generate such explanations. We are currently working on this direction as well. In order to identify the explanations users expect to receive as a justification for a choice, we have performed a study on how people justify their choices [12,13], assuming that given explanations are those they expect to receive. As a result of this study, we derived guidelines and patterns of explanations, providing guidance on explanations to be generated and the context in which each of them should be provided. Given this study, we are developing a technique that generates explanations following derived patterns, taking as inputs a provenance graph built using our proposed profile.

6 Conclusion

Knowing the reasoning of decisions taken by humans in the context of partially automated systems is crucial in many domains, such as those that involve design decisions: clinical trials, software development and civil construction. Nevertheless, it is unrealistic to expect that all decisions are justified by users given the time and effort that this activity requires. Therefore, we presented in this paper an approach that aims at automating the process of recording humans decisions.

Our approach consists of observing user's choices in the context of software applications that support people to manage tasks that involve decision making. With an automated decision-maker whose goal is to simulate human reasoning, we detect situations in which a human choice matches that of the decision-maker, whose reasoning process can be used to justify a human decision. In order to record such explanations, we based our approach on the Open Provenance Model (OPM), which is a generic model to represent the provenance of data (or physical objects, ...) and is being adopted as a pattern to allow the interoperability of systems. We proposed an OPM profile, which is an extension of this generic model to accommodate the specific artifacts of the automated decision-maker, and the processes associated with it. Moreover, we showed how to query provenance graphs built with our profile in order to obtain explanations to justify choices made based on preferences. Human decision making is very complex, and therefore there are many decisions that our human decision simulator still cannot reproduce. Our future work is thus to incorporate to our automated decision-maker other principles of psychology that can help to explain human decisions.

References

1. Anand, M.K., Bowers, S., Altintas, I., Ludäscher, B.: Approaches for Exploring and Querying Scientific Workflow Provenance Graphs. In: McGuinness, D.L., Michaelis, J.R., Moreau, L. (eds.) IPAW 2010. LNCS, vol. 6378, pp. 17–26. Springer, Heidelberg (2010)
2. Delaney, B., Taweel, A., et al.: Transform: translational medicine and patient safety in Europe. In: Proceedings of the AMIA 2010 Annual Symposium (2010)
3. Kalra, D., Schmidt, A., Potts, H.W.W., Dupont, D., Sundgren, M., De Moor, G.: Case report from the ehr4cr project— a european survey on electronic health records systems for clinical research. iHealth Connections (2011)
4. Keeney, R.L., Raiffa, H.: Decisions with Multiple Objectives: Preferences and Value Tradeoffs. John Wiley & Sons, Inc., New York (1976)
5. Kifor, T., Varga, L., Vazquez-Salceda, J., Alvarez, S., Willmott, S., Miles, S., Moreau, L.: Provenance in agent-mediated healthcare systems. IEEE Intelligent Systems 21(6), 38–46

6. Klein, D.A., Shortliffe, E.H.: A framework for explaining decision-theoretic advice. Artif. Intell. 67, 201–243 (1994)

7. Labreuche, C.: A general framework for explaining the results of a multi-attribute preference model. Artif. Intell. 175, 1410–1448 (2011)

8. Missier, P., Embury, S., Stapenhurst, R.: Exploiting Provenance to Make Sense of Automated Decisions in Scientific Workflows. In: Freire, J., Koop, D., Moreau, L. (eds.) IPAW 2008. LNCS, vol. 5272, pp. 174–185. Springer, Heidelberg (2008)

9. Moreau, L., Clifford, B., Freire, J., Futrelle, J., Gil, Y., Groth, P., Kwasnikowska, N., Miles, S., Missier, P., Myers, J., Plale, B., Simmhan, Y., Stephan, E., den Bussche, J.V.: The Open Provenance Model core specification (v1.1). Future Gener. Comput. Syst. 27(6), 743–756 (2011)

10. Naja, I., Moreau, L., Rogers, A.: Provenance of Decisions in Emergency Response Environments. In: McGuinness, D.L., Michaelis, J.R., Moreau, L. (eds.) IPAW 2010. LNCS, vol. 6378, pp. 221–230. Springer, Heidelberg (2010)

11. Nakatsu, R.T.: Explanatory power of intelligent systems. In: Gupta, J.N.D., Forgionne, G.A., Mora T., M. (eds.) Intelligent Decision-making Support Systems. Decision Engineering, pp. 123–143. Springer, London (2006)

12. Nunes, I., Miles, S., Luck, M., de Lucena, C.J.P.: Investigating Explanations to Justify Choice. In: Masthoff, J., Mobasher, B., Desmarais, M.C., Nkambou, R. (eds.) UMAP 2012. LNCS, vol. 7379, pp. 212–224. Springer, Heidelberg (2012)

13. Nunes, I., Miles, S., Luck, M., Lucena, C.: A study on justifications for choices: Explanation patterns and guidelines. Tech. Report CS-2012-03, University of Waterloo, Canada (2012)

14. Nunes, I., Miles, S., Luck, M., Lucena, C.: User-centric preference-based decision making. In: AAMAS 2012 (to appear, 2012)

15. Nunes, I., Miles, S., Luck, M., Lucena, C.: User-centric principles in automated decision making. In: 21st Brazilian Symposium on Artificial Intelligence (SBIA 2012) (to appear, 2012)

16. Simonson, I., Tversky, A.: Choice in context: Tradeoff contrast and extremeness aversion. Journal of Marketing Research 29(3), 281–295 (1992)

17. Tintarev, N., Masthoff, J.: A survey of explanations in recommender systems. In: 23rd International Conference on Data Engineering Workshop, pp. 801–810. IEEE (2007)

Detecting Duplicate Records in Scientific Workflow Results

Khalid Belhajjame[1], Paolo Missier[2], and Carole A. Goble[1]

[1] School of Computer Science
University of Manchester
Oxford Road, Manchester, UK
{Khalid.Belhajjame,Carole.Goble}@cs.man.ac.uk
[2] School of Computer Science
Newcastle University,
Newcastle upon Tyne, UK
Paolo.Missier@ncl.ac.uk

Abstract. Scientific workflows are often data intensive. The data sets obtained by enacting scientific workflows have several applications, e.g., they can be used to identify data correlations or to understand phenomena, and therefore are worth storing in repositories for future analyzes. Our experience suggests that such datasets often contain duplicate records. Indeed, scientists tend to enact the same workflow multiple times using the same or overlapping datasets, which gives rise to duplicates in workflow results. The presence of duplicates may increase the complexity of workflow results interpretation and analyzes. Moreover, it unnecessarily increases the size of datasets within workflow results repositories. In this paper, we present an approach whereby duplicates detection is guided by workflow provenance trace. The hypothesis that we explore and exploit is that the operations that compose a workflow are likely to produce the same (or overlapping) dataset given the same (or overlapping) dataset. A preliminary analytic and empirical validation shows the effectiveness and applicability of the method proposed.

1 Introduction

Scientific workflows are increasingly used by scientists as a means for specifying and enacting their experiments. Such workflows are often data intensive [6]. The data sets obtained by their enactment have several applications, e.g., they can be used to understand new phenomena or confirm known facts, and therefore are worth storing (preserving) for future analyzes. For example, such datasets can be stored in public repositories, and made available from within the linked data cloud [18], to be browsed, queried, analyzed and used to feed the execution of other workflows.

Because of the exploratory nature of research investigations, the datasets obtained by workflow executions often contain duplicate data records. (By record, we mean an instance that is used to feed an input parameter or is generated by an output parameter.) Indeed, scientists tend to enact the same workflow several times using the same or overlapping datasets, which gives rise to duplicates

P. Groth and J. Frew (Eds.): IPAW 2012, LNCS 7525, pp. 126–138, 2012.

in workflow results. Typically, the duplicate records generated as a result are assigned different identifiers by the workflow engine. This yields the following undesirable outcomes: *i)-* The analysis and interpretation of workflow results may become cumbersome and tedious, as it is up to the scientist to identify the data records that are semantically identical, to eventually draw scientific conclusions. *ii)-* Moreover, the presence of duplicate records unnecessarily increases the size of datasets within workflow results repositories.

Existing record linkage techniques [9] can be used to detect duplicates in workflow results. Consider a workflow wf that has been enacted for many times over a given period of time, and that the results of the workflow and its constituent operations were stored. To identify duplicates that were used or generated by the operations that compose the workflow wf, record linkage techniques can be applied to those records. Specifically, given the set of records R_i (resp. R_o) that were used (resp. generated) by a constituent operation op of wf, the records in R_i (resp. R_o) are compared to detect duplicate records. Comparing all possible pairs to identify duplicate records in a set R can be expensive when R is large: the number of record pair comparisons grows quadratically with the number of records to be matched.

To overcome the above problem, a number of researchers have investigated the use of blocking methods [1] to reduce the number of record pair comparisons. The underlying idea of blocking methods is to split the set of records to be compared into subsets, known as *blocks*. Two records are compared only if they belong to the same block. While their effectiveness have been proven, blocking methods are highly domain dependent. They require some detective work from the part of a domain expert who identifies the subset of attributes that can be used for forming blocks or provides training data that can be used to learn blocking criteria [14,3].

In this paper, we explore and exploit an additional and different source of information, namely provenance traces collected when enacting workflows, to guide the detection of duplicates in workflow results. Specifically, we make the following contributions:

- **A method for guiding duplicates detection in workflow results.** Rather than comparing pairwise the data records bound to every operation parameter within a workflow, we show how the results of record pair comparisons can be reduced to a subset of operation parameters based on provenance trace.
- **Extension of the method proposed to support collection-based workflows.** We show how the method proposed can be extended to support duplicate detection in the context of collection-based workflows in which operation parameters can use and/or generate a set of records within a single operation invocation.
- **Validation of the method proposed.** We report on the results of an analytical and empirical validation that shows the effectiveness and applicability of the method proposed.

The paper is structured as follows. We begin by analyzing and comparing related work to ours (in Section 2). We present the model that we use, for the purposes of this paper, to define scientific workflows and the provenance trace obtained by their enactment (in Section 3). We then present the algorithm that we propose for detecting duplicate records in workflow results (in Section 4). We report on the results of a preliminary evaluation (in Section 5), and close the paper discussing our ongoing and future work (in Section 6).

2   Related Work

Research in duplicate record detection has been active for more than three decades. Elmagarmid *et al.* [9] conducted a thorough analysis of the literature in this field. They covered the similarity metrics used for matching individual record fields, the techniques for comparing records, as well as the systems providing such capabilities.

As mentioned earlier, the number of record pair comparisons grows quadratically with the number of records to be matched $O(n^2)$. To improve the efficiency of duplicate detection, several blocking techniques [1] have been devised. Using such techniques, the set of records to be compared is subdivided into a set of mutually exclusive blocks. Two records are compared only if they belong to the same block. Typically, blocking techniques reduces the number of record pair comparisons to $O(\frac{n^2}{b})$, where b is to the number of blocks [7]. As well as blocking, other techniques have been proposed to improve the efficiency of duplicate detection. Using the Sorted Neighbourhood, for example, the records are sorted based on a sorting key. Two records are then compared only if they are within a window of a fixed size w. As a result, the total number of record comparisons using the Sorted Neighbourhood is $O(wn)$ [1].

The above techniques require user inputs. For example, to use blocking techniques, the user, or domain expert, needs to identify the attributes that can be used to split the set of records into blocks. Often, this is a trail-and-error task [17], in which the user examines records attributes, and select the ones that will (or are expected to) yield *good* partitioning of the set of records.

To reduce the complexity of this task, some researchers investigated the use of machine learning techniques [16,10,12]. Generally speaking, using such techniques, the attributes to be used in blocking are selected based on training data, which take the form of records that are known to be duplicates and other that are known not to be duplicates, and which are provided by the domain expert.

As well as supervised machine learning techniques, some researchers have investigated the use of unsupervised machine learning techniques for record linkage. For example, Michalowski *et al.* [11] showed how duplicates can be identified by using secondary sources such as location, phone number, etc. Elfeky *et al.* [8] proposed an algorithm that combines both supervised and unsupervised machine learning techniques to detect duplicate records. Specifically, they use a two-step process whereby record classes are first identified using clustering, then supervised machine learning techniques are applied to classify the records within the classes identified.

The method that we present in this paper is not an alternative to the above techniques. Rather it is complementary: it is meant to further improve the efficiency of the above duplicate detection methods in the context of workflow results by exploiting provenance traces to propagate the results of record pair comparison along the operations parameters that are connected within the workflow.

The method we present in this paper can also be useful when the number of records to be compared is small, as it reduces the need for data preparation [9] to few operation parameters within the workflow. Indeed, the (raw) records instances of a given operation parameter are often long complex strings. Consider for example the *SearchSimple* service operation provided by the DNA Data Bank of Japan[1]. The records used as input to such operation are biological entries, which takes the form of long strings containing complex information specifying the accession of the biological entry, its accession number, organism, motif, cross-references to biological data sources, etc. Moreover, such entries may be formatted using different representations, e.g., Uniprot, Fasta, IPR. Therefore, comparing such records based on their textual content may lead to detecting false duplicates and missing true ones. For example, two records that represent the same biological entry may be found to be different because they are formatted using different representations. On the other hand, two different records may be found to be identical because they have similar content. To avoid the above issues, duplicate detection is often preceded by a data preparation phase stage [9] during which the raw records are parsed to identify individual data elements and then transformed into structured, uniformly formatted, and therefore comparable, records. Since the parameters of the operations that compose a workflow can be (and are typically) semantically and syntactically different, data preparation may turn out to be expensive as it potentially requires building a parser for every operation parameter. The method that we describe in this paper eases this problem, since data preparation is required only for a subset of operation parameters within the workflow.

3   Data-Driven Workflows and Provenance Trace

We focus in this paper on the problem of identifying duplicate records that are used or generated by data-driven workflows. A data driven workflow is a directed acyclic graph $wf = \langle N, E \rangle$. A node $\langle op, I_{op}, O_{op} \rangle \in N$ represents an analysis operation op, which can be implemented as a Java program, a Perl script or provided by a third party web service, has a set of ordered input parameters I_{op}, and has a set of ordered output parameters O_{op}. The edges are data flow dependencies specifying how the data records generated by a given operation are used by the succeeding operation(s) within the workflow. Therefore, an edge $\langle\langle op, o \rangle, \langle op', i \rangle\rangle \in E$ is a pair that connects the output o of the op operation to the input i' of another operation op'.

---

[1] www.ddbj.nig.ac.jp

The execution of workflows gives rise to provenance trace, which we capture using two relations: transformation and transfer [13]. Consider an operation op that has n input parameters $I_{op} = \langle i_1, \ldots, i_n \rangle$, and m output parameters $O_{op} = \langle o_1, \ldots, o_m \rangle$, we use

$$\langle op, \langle o_1, r_{o_1} \rangle \rangle, \ldots, \langle op, \langle o_m, r_{o_m} \rangle \rangle \;\rightsquigarrow\; \langle op, \langle i_1, r_{i_1} \rangle \rangle, \ldots, \langle op, \langle i_n, r_{i_n} \rangle \rangle \quad (1)$$

to denote the transformation relation specifying that the execution of the op operation within a workflow took as input the ordered set of records $\langle r_{i_1}, \ldots, r_{i_n} \rangle$, and generated the ordered set of records $\langle r_{o_1}, \ldots, r_{o_m} \rangle$, where r_{x_i} denotes a record that is instance of the input or output parameter x_i. For exposition sake, we use in what follows $OutB_{op} \rightsquigarrow InB_{op}$ to denote the transformation relation in (1), where InB_{op} denotes the set of input bindings $\langle op, \langle i_1, r_{i_1} \rangle \rangle, \ldots, \langle op, \langle i_n, r_{i_n} \rangle \rangle$, and $OutB_{op}$ denotes the set of output bindings $\langle op, \langle o_1, r_{o_1} \rangle \rangle, \ldots, \langle op, \langle o_m, r_{o_m} \rangle \rangle$.

As well as transformation relations connecting output records to input records of an operation execution, provenance trace also caters for transfer relations which specify transfer of records along the edges of the workflow between different operations. Specifically, we use:

$$\langle op', \langle i', r \rangle \rangle \leftarrow \langle op, \langle o, r \rangle \rangle \quad (2)$$

to denote the transfer relation specifying that the record r generated by the output parameter o of the operation op was used to feed the input i' of the operation op'.

Together, the transformation and transfer relations defined above, are used to encode provenance trace $\mathcal{T}$ obtained by the execution of workflows.

4 Provenance-Guided Detection of Duplicates

In this section, we present a method for identifying duplicate records in workflow results.

To guide the detection of duplicates, we exploit the following observation. Consider op an operation that is used within a workflow, and consider that i and o are respectively an input parameter and output parameter of op. If the operation op is known to be deterministic, then two records r and r' instances of the output o are identical if they are generated using the same set of input bindings, i.e.:

$$deterministic(op) \wedge (\exists \; (OutB_{op} \rightsquigarrow InB_{op} \in \mathcal{T}) \wedge (OutB'_{op} \rightsquigarrow InB_{op} \in \mathcal{T})$$
$$s.t. \; (\langle op, \langle o, r \rangle \rangle \in OutB_{op}) \wedge (\langle op, \langle o, r' \rangle \rangle \in OutB'_{op}))$$
$$\Rightarrow id(r, r') \quad (3)$$

$id(r, r')$ denotes that two records r and r' are identical.

If the operation op is known to be injective, then two records r and r' that are instances of the input i are identical if they yield the same set of output bindings, i.e.:

$$injective(op) \land (\exists \ (OutB_{op} \rightsquigarrow InB_{op} \in \mathcal{T}) \land (OutB_{op} \rightsquigarrow InB'_{op} \in \mathcal{T})$$
$$s.t. \ (\langle op, \langle i, r \rangle \rangle \in InB_{op}) \land (\langle op, \langle i, r' \rangle \rangle \in InB'_{op}))$$
$$\Rightarrow id(r, r') \qquad (4)$$

The above rules can be used to substantially reduce the number of records that need to be compared for detecting duplicates in workflow results. In particular, if the operations that compose the workflows are known to be deterministic, then the records used as input to the workflow as a whole, i.e., those used to feed the starting operation(s) within the workflow, can be compared. Rule 3 can then be applied transitively to identify duplicates generated by other operations in the workflow. On the other hand, if the operations that compose the workflow are known to be injective, then the records generated by the workflow as a whole, i.e., those generated by the last operation(s) w.r.t. to the dataflow, can be compared. Rule 4 can then be applied transitively to records that are used as input to the operations within the workflow.

The method that we present in this paper for detecting duplicates assumes that operations are deterministic. In other words, workflow containing non deterministic operations are outside the scope of this paper. Generally, the operations that constitute a workflow may not be deterministic. It is nevertheless important to study the special case where operation determinism holds, especially that the empirical evaluation that we will report on in Section 5 suggests that most analysis operations are deterministic. Note, also, that we will present, later on in Section 4.1, a technique that can be used to check if a given analysis operation is deterministic, and therefore can be used to identify the workflows on which the method we present in this section can be safely applied.

Given the above discussion, we present in what follow an algorithm in which operations are assumed to be deterministic. The algorithm for detecting duplicates operates as illustrated in Figure 1. In what follow, we present in details the phases outlines in Figure 1.

Phase 1. Given a workflow wf and the provenance trace $\mathcal{T}$ obtained by executing the workflow wf multiple times, in the first phase the records that are bound to the input parameters of each of the starting operations are compared to identify duplicate records. To illustrate this, consider that op_s is a starting operation of the workflow wf, i.e., the input parameters of op_s are not associated with any data links within the workflow wf, consider that i is an input of op_s, and consider that $R_i^{op_s}$ is the set of records that are bound with the input i in the provenance trace $\mathcal{T}$. In the first phase, we compare the records in $R_i^{op_s}$ to identify duplicate records. The techniques used for matching the records are outside the scope of this paper. Matching techniques such as those provided by the Tailor [7] and Febrl [4] systems can be used for this purpose. The result of this phase is a partition of disjoint sets $R_i^{op_s} = R_1 \cup \cdots \cup R_n$ where R_i, $1 \leqslant i \leqslant n$ is a set of duplicate records.

Phase 2. The sets of input bindings that are used to feed each starting operation of the workflow wf in the provenance trace $\mathcal{T}$ are compared and clustered into groups of identical sets of input bindings. To illustrate this, consider that the

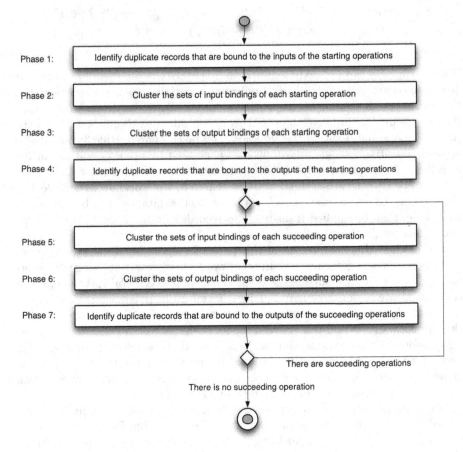

Fig. 1. Process for provenance-guided duplicates detection

starting operation op_s has the following input parameters $I_{op_s} = \{i_1, \ldots, i_n\}$, and consider that $\mathcal{IB}_{op_s}$ is the sets of input bindings that are associated with the operation op_s in the provenance trace $\mathcal{T}$. Two sets of input bindings $\langle op_s, \langle i_1, r_{i_1} \rangle \rangle, \ldots, \langle op_s, \langle i_n, r_{i_n} \rangle \rangle$ and $\langle op_s, \langle i_1, r'_{i_1} \rangle \rangle, \ldots, \langle op_s, \langle i_n, r'_{i_n} \rangle \rangle$ in $\mathcal{IB}_{op_s}$ are identical iff:

$$\forall \, 1 \leqslant k \leqslant n, \; id(r_{i_k}, r'_{i_k})$$

After comparing the sets of input bindings in $\mathcal{IB}_{op_s}$, they are clustered into groups of identical sets of bindings. For example, consider that $\mathcal{IB}_{op_s}$ contains the following 5 sets of input bindings: $\mathcal{IB}_{op_s} = \{InB_1, \ldots, InB_5\}$. The following clustering $\{\{InB_1, InB_2, InB_4\}, \{InB_2, InB_5\}\}$ specifies that the bindings InB_1, InB_3 and InB_4 are identical, and that the bindings InB_2 and InB_5 are identical.

Phase 3. Given the clustering of the input bindings of the starting operation op_s of the workflow wf, provenance trace $\mathcal{T}$ is used to cluster the sets of outputs bindings of op_s into groups of identical sets of output bindings. To do so, we exploit the clustering of sets of input binding obtained in *phase 1*. Specifically, two sets of output bindings $OutB_{op}$ and $OutB'_{op}$ are identical, and therefore clustered together if they are obtained using identical input bindings. In other words, two sets of output binding $OutB_{op_s}$ and $OutB'_{op_s}$ of the operation op_s are identical, and therefore grouped into the same cluster, if:

$$\exists \, InB_{op_s}, InB'_{op_s} \in \mathcal{T}$$
$$s.t. \; OutB_{op} \leftrightsquigarrow InB_{op} \land OutB'_{op} \leftrightsquigarrow InB'_{op} \land id(InB_{op_s}, InB'_{op_s})$$

where $id(InB_{op_s}, InB'_{op_s})$ denotes that the sets of bindings InB_{op_s} and InB'_{op_s} are identical.

Phase 4. In this phase, the records that are bound to the output parameters of each starting operation op_s are identified given the clustering obtained in *phase 3*. As an example, consider two sets of output bindings of the operation op_s: $OutB_{op_s} = \langle op_s, \langle o_1, r_{o_1} \rangle \rangle, \ldots, \langle op_s, \langle o_m, r_{o_m} \rangle \rangle$ and $OutB'_{op_s} = \langle op_s, \langle o_1, r'_{o_1} \rangle \rangle, \ldots, \langle op_s, \langle o_m, r'_{o_m} \rangle \rangle$. If $OutB_{op_s}$ and $OutB_{op_s}$ are in the same group according to the clustering obtained in *phase 3*, then the records r_{o_i} and r'_{o_i} are identical for $1 \leqslant i \leqslant m$.

Phase 5. The sets of input bindings that are associated with each operation op that succeeds the starting operations in the workflow wf are clustered into groups of identical sets of input bindings. To illustrate this, consider that $InB_{op} = \langle op, \langle i_1, r_{i_1} \rangle \rangle, \ldots, \langle op, \langle i_n, r_{i_n} \rangle \rangle$ and $InB'_{op} = \langle op, \langle i_1, r'_{i_1} \rangle \rangle, \ldots, \langle op, \langle i_n, r'_{i_n} \rangle \rangle$ are two sets of input bindings of the operation op. InB_{op} and InB'_{op} are identical, and therefore grouped into the same cluster, if the records r_{i_k} and r'_{i_k}, $1 \leqslant k \leqslant n$ are identical, i.e., $\forall \, 1 \leqslant k \leqslant n, \; id(r_{i_k}, r'_{i_k})$.

Phase 6. Just like with the starting operation op_s, the sets of output bindings associated with each of the operations that succeed the operation op_s are clustered into groups of identical sets of bindings (see *phase 3*).

Phase 7. The set R_o^{op} of records that are bound to each output parameter o of a succeeding operation op are partitioned into disjoint sets of identical records. This phase is similar to *phase 4*.

   Phases 5, 6 and 7 are repeated until treating, i.e., identifying duplicates, in records that are bound to the output parameters of each of the termination operations in the workflow wf. By termination operations, we mean operations with output parameters that are not associated with any data links in the workflow wf.

   In the above algorithm, we make use of rule 3 (in *phase 3* and *phase 6*), which assumes that operations are deterministic. We can also identify duplicates by using rule 4 instead, which can be used when the operations that compose the workflow wf are known to be injective. To do so, the algorithm presented above needs to be modified. Specifically, the algorithm starts by comparing the records that are produced by the outputs of the termination operations within the workflow. Then using transitively rule 4, we identify the records that are bound to the remaining operation parameters in the workflow.

4.1 Verifying the Determinism of Analysis Operations

As mentioned earlier, the algorithm presented assumes that the operations that compose the workflow are known to be deterministic. If the source code of analysis operations is available, then program analysis techniques [5] can be employed to verify whether they are deterministic. In practice, analysis operations that are supplied by third parties often come without source code. For those operations, we can use the following approach to check whether they are deterministic. Given an operation op, we select examples values that can be used by the inputs of op, and invoke op using those values multiple times. We then examine the values produced by the operation. If the operation produces identical output values given identical input values, then it is likely to be deterministic, otherwise, it is not deterministic. Note that we say *likely to be deterministic*, since an operation may, in certain corner cases, be deterministic for the examples we selected but not for the whole space of legal input values. Note that such tests should be performed continuously over time. Indeed, as we shall explain later on in Section 5.2, many analysis operations use underlying data sources in their computation, and, as a result, updates to those sources may break the determinism of those operations. Therefore, tests performed for checking the determinism of operations should be performed over time to determine the window of time during which the operations in a given workflow remain deterministic.

4.2 Collection-Based Workflows

So far we have considered workflows in which operations take as input an ordered set of records each instance of a given input parameter and produce a set of ordered records each is an instance of a given output parameter. In practice, however, an important class of scientific workflows are collection-based workflows [13]. The analysis operations that constitute such workflows can have inputs (resp. outputs) that consume (resp. generate) a set of records instead of a single record within a single operation invocation.

The algorithm presented in Section 4 needs to be slightly modified to be able to cater for collection-based workflows. In particular, we need to be able to identify when two sets are identical *(phase 1)*, and to identify duplicates records between two sets that are known to be identical *(phases 4,7)*. To illustrate this consider an operation op with an input i that takes a set of records. Given two sets of records R_i and R_j that are bound to the operation op in two different invocations within the provenance trace $\mathcal{T}$, we need to determine whether the two sets R_i and R_j are identical. To do so, we need to compare the records in R_i to the records in R_j. The sets R_i and R_j are identical if they are of the same size, and there is a bijective mapping $map : R_i \rightarrow R_j$ that maps each record r_i in R_i to a record r_j in R_j such that r_i and r_j are identical, i.e., $id(r_i, map(r_j))$.

Inversely, in *phases 4* and *7*, given two sets R_i and R_j that are known to be identical, we need to compare the records in R_i with the records in R_j to find a bijective mapping $map : R_i \rightarrow R_j$ that maps each record r_i in R_i to an identical record r_j in R_j.

5   Validation

To assess the effectiveness of the method presented in this paper, we performed two kinds of validation: analytical and empirical.

5.1   What Is the Benefit in Terms of Reducing the Number of Record Pair Comparisons?

We performed an an analytical analysis to understand the benefit that the method we described in this paper presents in terms of reducing the search space that needs to be explored to detect duplicate records. Consider a workflow wf, the operations of which are known to be deterministic. For simplicity sake, and without loss of generality, consider that the operations of wf have one input and one output, and that they are connected in sequence using data links. Let $\mathcal{T}$ be the provenance trace obtained by multiple executions of the workflow wf, and consider that n is the number of records that are bound to the input i of the starting operation op_s in the provenance trace $\mathcal{T}$. Consider that the workflow is composed of n_{op} operations. The number of record pair comparisons needed without using provenance trace is $(n_{op} + 1) \times N$, where N is the number of of record pair comparisons needed for a single operation parameter. For example, if the workflow is composed of two operations op_1 and op_2 that are connected in sequence, then we need $3 \times N$ record pair comparisons: N for comparing the records bound to the input of op_1, N for comparing the records bound to the output of op_1 and N for comparing the records bound to the output of op_2. Note that we do not need to compare the records bound to the input of op_2, since this input is connected to the output of op_2 by a data link, and therefore the set of records bound to the input of op_2 is the same set of records bound to the output of op_1.

Using the method we described in this paper, we need to identify duplicates only for the starting operations in the workflow. In other words, the number of record pair comparisons is N. Using blocking techniques N is $\frac{n^2}{b}$, where b denotes the number of blocks. Notice that that number does not depend on the number of operations that compose the workflow. To illustrate the benefit our method can provide, consider the case in which the workflow is composed of 10 operations that have one input and one output, and are connected in sequence. And consider that 100 records are bound to each operation parameter, and that blocking techniques split the records associated with each operation parameter to 5 blocks. Using blocking techniques, without relying on provenance trace, requires 22000 record pair comparisons. This number is reduced to 2000 using the method presented in this paper. Notice that, the greater the number of operations that compose the workflow, the greater the reduction in terms of number of record pair comparisons.

5.2   Are Real-World Analysis Operations Deterministic?

The method we presented in this paper relies on the assumption that the operations that compose the workflow are deterministic. To have an insight on the degree to which this assumption holds in practice, we run an experiment using real world scientific workflows from the myExperiment repository [15]. Specifically, we selected 15 bioinformatics workflows that cover a wide range of analyzes, namely biological pathway analysis, sequence alignment, molecular interaction analysis. (Note that the myExperiment repository contains a large number of workflows, however, most of the workflows cannot be enacted for several reasons, notably the unavailability of the services that compose the workflows.) Together, the workflows we selected are composed of 151 operations. To identify which of these operations are deterministic, we run each of them 3 times using example values that were found either within myExperiment or Biocatalogue [2]. We then manually analyzed the output values of each operation. This analysis revealed that a small number of operations, namely 5 of 151 are not deterministic. After examining these 5 operations, it transpires they output URLs of files that contain the actual results of the computation. Note that although the URLs of the files generated by such operations were different between runs, the contents of the files were the same. The remaining operations, i.e., 146, generated the same output given the same input in the 3 invocations, and therefore are likely to be deterministic. We say *likely to be deterministic*, since an operation may, be deterministic for the examples we selected but not for the whole space of legal input values.

The results of the above experiment are encouraging, as it implies a broad applicability of the method described in this paper for propagating record pair comparison results. Note, however, that many of the operations that we analyzed access and use underlying data sources in their computation. For example, operations that perform sequence alignment use underlying sequences data sources. Therefore updates to such sources may break the determinism assumption. This suggests that the determinism holds within a window of time during which the underlying sources remain the same, and that there is a need for monitoring techniques to identify such windows.

6   Conclusions and Future Work

The presence of duplicates in workflow results can hinder the analysis of the results, specially when the number of workflow executions is large. In this paper, we described a method that can be used to reduce the number of record pair comparisons and the need for data preparation to a subset of the parameters within the workflow. Preliminary validation of the proposed method is encouraging.

Our ongoing and future work includes further evaluation. As mentioned in the previous section, operation determinism may break because of updates to underlying data sources. In this respect, we are investigating new techniques for monitoring the determinism of analysis operations over time using test suites designed for this purpose. The monitoring results can be used to identify the cases in which the method described in this paper can be safely applied. We are also investigating ways to deal with the issue of false matches propagation. If two different records are identified as duplicates, then this may lead to detecting false matches using provenance trace. The same observation applies to false negatives propagation. If two identical records r and r' are not detected, then using provenance trace, we will fail in detecting identical records generated using r and r'. Note also that some true matches may not be identified using the method we described. In particular, a deterministic, yet not injective, operation within the workflow may output identical records given different input bindings. Using the algorithm described in Section 4 will not allow detecting those duplicates. We intend to conduct further evaluation to assess the scale at which false matches are propagated and true matches are missed. We are also investigating ways whereby our method can be adapted to alleviate the above issues, e.g., by running our method multiple times, not only once. Each time different parameters, not only the inputs of the starting operations, are selected as a starting point, and then cross-validating duplicate detection results obtained by the different runs. As well as the above, we are investigating ways in which the method presented can be adapted to identify duplicates across workflows, and conducting a user study to assess the usefulness of the method in practice.

Acknowledgment. We would like to thank the anonymous reviewers for their detailed and constructive comments.

References

1. Baxter, R., Christen, P., Churches, T.: A comparison of fast blocking methods for record linkage. In: Proceedings of the KDD 2003 Workshop on Data Cleaning, Record Linkage, and Object Consolidation, Washington, DC, pp. 25–27 (2003)
2. Belhajjame, K., Goble, C., Tanoh, F., Bhagat, J., Wolstencroft, K., Stevens, R., Nzuobontane, E., McWilliam, H., Laurent, T., Lopez, R.: BioCatalogue: A Curated Web Service Registry for the Life Science Community. In: Proceedings of the Microsoft eScience Conference (2008)
3. Bilenko, M., Kamath, B., Mooney, R.J.: Adaptive blocking: Learning to scale up record linkage. In: ICDM, pp. 87–96. IEEE Computer Society (2006)
4. Christen, P.: Febrl -: an open source data cleaning, deduplication and record linkage system with a graphical user interface. In: KDD, pp. 1065–1068. ACM (2008)
5. Cousot, P., Cousot, R.: Systematic design of program analysis frameworks. In: Proceedings of the 6th ACM SIGACT-SIGPLAN Symposium on Principles of Programming Languages, POPL 1979, pp. 269–282. ACM, New York (1979)
6. Deelman, E., Chervenak, A.L.: Data management challenges of data-intensive scientific workflows. In: CCGRID, pp. 687–692. IEEE Computer Society (2008)

7. Elfeky, M.G., Elmagarmid, A.K., Verykios, V.S.: Tailor: A record linkage tool box. In: ICDE, pp. 17–28. IEEE Computer Society (2002)
8. Elfeky, M.G., Ghanem, T.M., Verykios, V.S., Huwait, A.R., Elmagarmid, A.K.: Record linkage: A machine learning approach, a toolbox, and a digital government web service (2003)
9. Elmagarmid, A.K., Ipeirotis, P.G., Verykios, V.S.: Duplicate record detection: A survey. IEEE Trans. Knowl. Data Eng. 19(1), 1–16 (2007)
10. Hernández, M.A., Stolfo, S.J.: Real-world data is dirty: Data cleansing and the merge/purge problem. Data Min. Knowl. Discov. 2(1), 9–37 (1998)
11. Michalowski, M., Thakkar, S., Knoblock, C.: Exploiting secondary sources for automatic object consolidation. In: Proceedings of the KDD 2003 Workshop on Data Cleaning, Record Linkage, and Object Consolidation, Washington, DC, pp. 34–36 (2003)
12. Michelson, M., Knoblock, C.A.: Learning blocking schemes for record linkage. In: AAAI. AAAI Press (2006)
13. Missier, P., Paton, N.W., Belhajjame, K.: Fine-grained and efficient lineage querying of collection-based workflow provenance. In: EDBT, pp. 299–310. ACM (2010)
14. Parag, Domingos, P.: Multi-relational record linkage. In: Proceedings of the KDD 2004 Workshop on Multi-Relational Data Mining, pp. 31–48 (August 2004)
15. De Roure, D., Goble, C.A., Stevens, R.: The design and realisation of the my-Experiment virtual research environment for social sharing of workflows. Future Generation Comp. Syst. 25(5), 561–567 (2009)
16. Sarawagi, S., Bhamidipaty, A.: Interactive deduplication using active learning. In: KDD, pp. 269–278. ACM (2002)
17. Winkler, W.E.: Approximate string comparator search strategies for very large administrative lists. Technical report, Statistical Research Report Series, US Census Bureau (2005)
18. Zhao, J., Sahoo, S.S., Missier, P., Sheth, A.P., Goble, C.A.: Extending semantic provenance into the web of data. IEEE Internet Computing 15(1), 40–48 (2011)

The Xeros Data Model: Tracking Interpretations of Archaeological Finds

Michael O. Jewell[1], Enrico Costanza[1], Tom Frankland[2], Graeme Earl[2], and Luc Moreau[1]

[1] School of Electronics & Computer Science, University of Southampton, Southampton, United Kingdom, SO17 1BJ
[2] Faculty of Humanities, University of Southampton, Southampton, United Kingdom, SO17 1BF

Abstract. At an archaeological dig, interpretations are built around discovered artifacts based on measurements and informed intuition. These interpretations are semi-structured and organic, yet existing tools do not capture their creation or evolution. Patina of Notes (PoN) is an application designed to tackle this, and is underpinned by the Xeros data model. Xeros is a graph structure and a set of operations that can deal with the addition, edition, and removal of interpretations. This data model is a specialisation of the W3C PROV provenance data model, tracking the evolution of interpretations. The model is presented, with operations defined formally, and characteristics of the representation that are beneficial to implementations are discussed.

1 Introduction

Archaeological practice is focused on the aggregation and interpretation of knowledge. The process begins with the excavation of multiple regions within a trench, known as 'contexts'. The finds discovered during excavation are tagged with an ID and placed into find bags, thus grouping them according to the context in which they were found. These 'Find IDs' are usually unique to sites, with larger sites sometimes prefixing a non-unique ID with an area code to ensure uniqueness. Archaeologists also use symbols for different purposes: contexts are circled, smaller finds are in triangles, soil samples are in diamonds, etc.

The find bags and their contents then become the subject of interpretation by specialists of different areas of archaeology. For example, skeletal material may be examined by an osteoarchaeologist, while an environmental archaeologist may glean information from charcoal and plant remains found at the site. Measurements by each specialist are recorded and associated with the individual finds by use of a recording sheet, which is associated with the unique ID on the find bag. Finally, an expert will examine the aggregated data for the site, and produce a report based on an interpretation of the data.

During the whole process, individual archaeologists also produce personal interpretations of their work. These may be in the form of handwritten notes,

P. Groth and J. Frew (Eds.): IPAW 2012, LNCS 7525, pp. 139–151, 2012.

diary entries, photographs, or multimedia recordings. At present, there is a divide between this 'unstructured data' and the 'structured data' recorded by the specialists on recording sheets. While both types of data may inform the excavation process, the unstructured data is not usually included in the dissemination of the findings from the site, whereas the structured data is recorded directly and preserved for analysis. At commercial sites, structured data is of a higher priority, but the interpretation is still dependent on the prior experience of the archaeologist.

Structured and unstructured data may influence the recording of structured data: if, for example, an excavator posits or determines via measurement that a shard may be part of a larger item, they are likely to take this into consideration when analysing further shards found in the same context. The excavation approach is also strongly influenced by preliminary examination techniques, including geophysics, survey methods, field walking, and the digging of trial pits.

Given the amount of recording that takes place at a dig, it is valuable to preserve both the structured and unstructured data as interpretations of finds. This is of use both to students, who could explore how conclusions were reached, and to other archaeologists, who may reach hypotheses that were not previously considered. By opening this data up to all of the archaeologists at a dig site, multiple viewpoints can be created and knowledge accumulated.

Some technologies already exist with the ability to capture finds and notes, but these have shortcomings. Existing 'find databases' (such as ARK[5] and IADB[9]) let archaeologists record the structured data mentioned earlier, but do not allow for the creation of interpretations of this data and do not visualise how knowledge has been built up or altered over time. Wikis provide for the creation of the unstructured data, and preserve edits, but do not model the fact that a note may be expanding on knowledge from another note. Users would have to write the structure into the wiki pages using wiki markup, but this is not readily exploitable as it is not explicitly designed into the software. There are also parallels to version control systems, such as SVN and CVS, but these operate on a per-directory level: several files in a folder that is then committed to a repository would be seen as having been created at the same time as the directory.

PoN (Patina of Notes), a web application that allows for the creation and organisation of structured and unstructured data about archaeological finds, was designed to address the above issues. Finds are extended with notes in a manner akin to attaching Post-it notes to an item. This results in a new 'state of knowledge': the original find has had extra information added, and the overall information in the system has grown. Notes can be stacked, thereby extending prior states of knowledge; alternative stacks can be created; and notes can be placed bridging multiple entities. By preserving the state of the system as notes are added, it is possible to see how knowledge has accrued over time, how structures have grown, and how and why edits have taken place.

This paper describes the Xeros data model that underpins PoN. The model consists of a graph structure that extends the PROV[8] Provenance Data Model;

and a set of operations defined to act upon it. This research is detailed in three contributions:

1. A formal specification of the fundamental operations: extension, edition, and reduction. Extension allows for the 'stacking' of knowledge onto an existing state of knowledge, or onto a find itself. Edition models a change of content between two versions of a note or a find. Reduction removes a state from the data model, but ensures that entities are still preserved when exploring prior system states.
2. Several properties are required for the PoN system, including the ability to record asynchronously and the avoidance of locks (to allow a single entity to be edited by more than one party). These properties are effected in the data model by commutativity operations (cross-entity completion, post-fact merging, and pre-fact recall) and idempotence rules.
3. The commutativity operations incur some storage and computation costs. These are in part unavoidable, to ensure the integrity of the model, but some may be avoided in order to ease efficiency. An approach to optimisation is disussed.

2   Related Work

As mentioned previously, some popular archaeological systems already exist. IADB[9], the Integrated Archaeological Database, manages data throughout the lifespan of excavation projects, including recording, analysis, and dissemination. Unique URIs are provided for Finds, Contexts, etc, and these are stored in the system's database. ARK[5] provides similar facilities for the collection of archaeological data, but allows for more flexible interface control. As the PoN implementation of Xeros uses URIs, it can augment the IADB software very easily, while leaving the more specialised data entry to this purpose-built software.

There are also some approaches to add meaning to wikis: Semantic MediaWiki[6] lets users embed triples into wiki pages, which is especially useful with templated pages (e.g. a Country template may contain a hasCapital predicate). Alternatively, DBWiki[1] combines the schemas present in existing databases with wiki functionality, providing versioning on the data entry process. It is possible to query for information on a country, and then retrieve the history and provenance of that data. Neither of these approaches address the issue of interpretation building, however: to create a new note in these systems would require the user to explicitly add links to the states of knowledge to which they were referring.

Some ontologies already address areas of this research: CIDOC CRM[3], an ontology for concepts and relationships used in cultural heritage documentation, has been extended to capture the modeling and query requirements regarding the provenance of digital objects[10]; and the Annotation Ontology[2] is a vocabulary for annotating electronic documents with various forms of annotations. Xeros does not intend to replace these approaches: CIDOC artifacts could be treated as entities, and Annotation Ontology annotations could be used to extend them.

Existing provenance models, such as OPM[7] and PROV, offer a very generic model of provenance. While these are powerful due to their versatility, the models must be specialised if they are to fit the archaeology representation.

Finally, there are also existing annotation systems for other domains: The Distributed Annotation System (DAS)[4] allows for the exchange of biological sequence annotations, and many bioinformatic applications and websites support the DAS communication protocol.

3   Xeros: Representation and Operations

Xeros allows for the building of interpretations, the edition of entities, and for the non-destructive removal of states of knowledge using a reduction process. Users can navigate through the evolution of this knowledge, using completion operations to suggest interpretations that have not been explicitly created. The non-destructive nature of the operations means that the processes that have led to a state of knowledge can always be seen: hence the extension of the PROV data model.

The data model is defined as a graph structure, consisting of a set of entities (V) connected by edges (E). All entities have both a positional co-ordinate $\bar{c}$ with components (x, e, r) and an index i, allowing them to be uniquely identified in the model. The positional co-ordinate places the entity in a 3 dimensional space, with x, e, and r respectively corresponding to the eXtension, Edition, and Reduction operations that the entity has undergone: hence the name 'Xeros'. The displacement vectors for the three operations are shown in Figure 1.

$$\bar{x} = (1, 0, 0)$$
$$\bar{e} = (0, 1, 0)$$
$$\bar{r} = (0, 0, 1)$$

Fig. 1. Displacement vectors for extension, edition, and reduction.

$$new(V, \bar{c}_n) = m : \forall p, 0 \leq p < m,$$
$$V(\bar{c}_n, p) \neq \perp$$
$$V(\bar{c}_n, m) = \perp$$

Fig. 2. $new(V, \bar{c}_n)$. Produces a valid index i for a co-ordinate that does not conflict with an existing co-ordinate.

The index i is required when multiple entities occupy the same positional co-ordinate. For example, if an entity at position $\bar{a}$ is edited twice, the two resultant entities will have the same position $\bar{a} + \bar{e}$. As a result, the index i is incremented: the first entity would be at $(\bar{a} + \bar{e}, 0)$ and the second at $(\bar{a} + \bar{e}, 1)$. A formalization of this, given a set of vertices V, is provided in Figure 2.

Three Xeros-specific edges may be created by operations on the data model: $isX(\bar{a})$, $isE(\bar{a})$, and $isR(\bar{a})$. These correspond to the three main operations that can be performed on entities within the data model: extension, edition, and reduction ($\bar{a}$ being a displacement vector). These edges are subproperties of wasDerivedFrom in the PROV data model. An s edge is also used, which indicates that there is some other relationship between one entity and another (e.g. 'hasNote' between a find entity and a note entity). s must not be one of the Xeros edges, and it follows that for all s, $source(s) \neq dest(s)$. The following operations focus on the Xeros-specific edges, rather than the s relationship.

3.1 Extension

Extension, denoted by $\xrightarrow{isX}$, suggests an addition of information to the system: the accumulation of knowledge. Figure 3 shows the building up of knowledge via extension: an entity (in this case, a surface) is extended with a note; this state of knowledge is then extended with a further note; and later an alternative is added via an extension to the original entity.

Given an initial entity (e_0) and the entity by which it should be extended (e_1), the operation creates an extension entity e_n that represents the state of knowledge in which e_0 has relationship s with e_1. An $isX(\bar{x})$ edge is added from e_n to e_0, indicating that e_n is an extension of e_0 with displacement vector $\bar{x}$, and the s edge is added from e_n to e_1. The case described above would be achieved by extending the find entity with a note; extending the resultant e_n with another note; then later extending the find entity with a note.

(a) An entity is extended with Note 1.

(b) The state of knowledge is extended with Note 2.

(c) An alternate interpretation is added.

Fig. 3. The evolution of a state of knowledge via extensions

3.2 Edition

Edition, denoted by $\xrightarrow{isE}$, indicates that there has been an alteration of an entity's content. In an archaeological context this could be a correction to a find's weight, or an alteration to a note's content. The *edit* operation (Figure 5) creates an edition entity e_n that has an $isE(\bar{e})$ edge to the edited e_0.

When a sequence of operations could indicate that the resultant entity is the same as the original (such as an edit followed by a reversal of that edit), the fact that the entity has been through two processes is preserved. A link is not created between the two entities: partly as the more recent entity was created via

$$V(\bar{c}_0, i_0) = e_0$$
$$V(\bar{c}_1, i_1) = e_1$$
$$Type(e_0) = source(s)$$
$$\underline{Type(e_1) = dest(s)}$$
$$\bar{c}_n = \bar{c}_0 + \bar{x}$$
$$i_n = new(V, \bar{c}_n)$$
$$V' = V[(\bar{c}_n, i_n) \to e_n]$$
$$E' = E[[((\bar{c}_n, i_n), (\bar{c}_0, i_0)) \to isX(\bar{x})]]$$
$$[((\bar{c}_n, i_n), (\bar{c}_1, i_1)) \to s]$$
$$Type' = Type[e_n \to Type(e_0)]$$

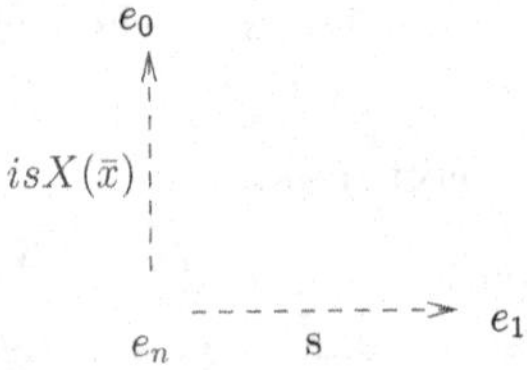

Fig. 4. $\langle V', E', e_n \rangle = extend(V, E, e_0, e_1, s, \bar{x})$. Extend e_0 with e_1, creating e_n. Dashed edges are created as a consequence of this operation.

$$\underline{V(\bar{c}_0, i_0) = e_0}$$
$$\bar{c}_n = \bar{c}_0 + \bar{e}$$
$$i_n = new(V, \bar{c}_n)$$
$$V' = V[(\bar{c}_n, i_n) \to e_n]$$
$$E' = E[[((\bar{c}_n, i_n), (\bar{c}_0, i_0)) \to isE(\bar{e})]]$$
$$Type' = Type[e_n \to Type(e_0)]$$

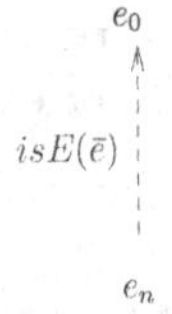

Fig. 5. $\langle V', E', e_n \rangle = edit(V, E, e_0, \bar{e})$. Edit e_0 to e_n.

a different process, and partly as detecting the match is not a simple automatic operation.

The edit operation only takes place on a non-extension entity: the x position in its positional co-ordinate must be zero. Edits of extension entities indicate that the target of either its s or isX edges have been altered, and so the original must be edited to point this edge to a new version. This results in an 'internal edit': these indicate that an edge has been retargeted. For example, cross-entity completion uses this to show that the s edge has to be retargeted; post-fact merging and pre-fact recall use this to show that the isX edge has to be retargeted. Internal edits therefore occur as a side-effect of completion operations, rather than directly via an edit operation.

3.3   Reduction

Reduction, denoted by $\xrightarrow{isR}$, indicates the removal of a state of knowledge (see Figure 6). Thus, if a measurement is found to be unnecessary or incorrect, the state of knowledge indicating that it extended the find can be removed. The state of knowledge is not deleted from the model: instead, new entities are created to omit the reduced entity.

$$V(\bar{c}_x, i_x) = e_x$$
$$V(\bar{c}_y, i_y) = e_y$$
$$V(\bar{c}_z, i_z) = e_z$$
$$V(\bar{c}_0, i_0) = e_0$$
$$V(\bar{c}_1, i_1) = e_1$$
$$E((\bar{c}_y, i_y), (\bar{c}_x, i_x)) = isX(\delta\bar{a})$$
$$E((\bar{c}_z, i_z), (\bar{c}_y, i_y)) = isX(\delta\bar{b})$$
$$E((\bar{c}_y, i_y), (\bar{c}_0, i_0)) = s$$
$$\underline{E((\bar{c}_z, i_z), (\bar{c}_1, i_1)) = t}$$
$$\bar{c}_n = \bar{c}_z + \bar{r}$$
$$i_n = new(V, \bar{c}_n)$$
$$\bar{d} = \delta\bar{a} + \delta\bar{b} + \bar{r}$$
$$V' = V[(\bar{c}_n, i_n) \rightarrow e_n]$$
$$E' = E[[((\bar{c}_n, i_n), (\bar{c}_z, i_z)) \rightarrow isR(\bar{r})]]$$
$$[((\bar{c}_n, i_n), (\bar{c}_x, i_x)) \rightarrow isX(\bar{d})]$$
$$[((\bar{c}_n, i_n), (\bar{c}_1, i_1)) \rightarrow t]$$
$$Type' = Type[e_n \rightarrow Type(e_z)]$$

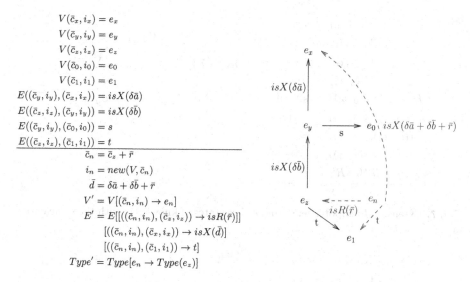

Fig. 6. $\langle V', E', e_n \rangle = reduce(V, E, e_y, s, e_0, e_z, t, e_1, e_x, \bar{x}, \bar{r}, \delta\bar{a}, \delta\bar{b})$. Removes the state of knowledge e_y and its associated entity e_0 from the knowledge graph.

To achieve this, the reduction operation requires two consecutive extension entities: the first of these (e_y) is removed by reducing the second (e_z). After the operation has been performed the state of knowledge of e_y is skipped, as the reduction of e_z (e_n) extends the root e_x directly. The isX weighting is a sum of the two original extension edges plus a reduction.

Due to the requirement of a second extension, reduction guarantees that the state of knowledge e_y is removed non-destructively. To remove e_z needs a slightly different approach, discussed as future work in Section 6.

3.4   Idempotence

While other systems make use of locking to prevent simultaneous operations on an entity, these represent alternatives in the Xeros model. If two archaeologists re-measure a vase, they may get two different measurements, so the two editions should be preserved. However, there are instances where an extension or edition may duplicate knowledge already present. Extension and edition idempotence rules (shown in Figure 7 and 8 respectively) are used to detect these situations and resolve them. The former holds when two extensions of an entity refer to the same entity via the same relation: two users adding the same note to the same find; the latter when two edits of the same entity have the same value: two users fixing the same spelling mistake in a note.

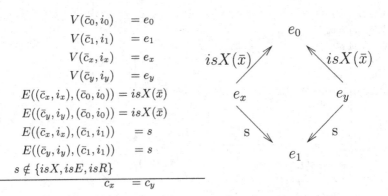

$$
\begin{aligned}
V(\bar{c}_0, i_0) &= e_0 \\
V(\bar{c}_1, i_1) &= e_1 \\
V(\bar{c}_x, i_x) &= e_x \\
V(\bar{c}_y, i_y) &= e_y \\
E((\bar{c}_x, i_x), (\bar{c}_0, i_0)) &= isX(\bar{x}) \\
E((\bar{c}_y, i_y), (\bar{c}_0, i_0)) &= isX(\bar{x}) \\
E((\bar{c}_x, i_x), (\bar{c}_1, i_1)) &= s \\
E((\bar{c}_y, i_y), (\bar{c}_1, i_1)) &= s \\
s &\notin \{isX, isE, isR\} \\
\hline
c_x &= c_y
\end{aligned}
$$

Fig. 7. Extension Idempotence: e_x and e_y are states of knowledge with the same entity e_1.

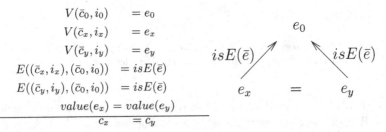

$$
\begin{aligned}
V(\bar{c}_0, i_0) &= e_0 \\
V(\bar{c}_x, i_x) &= e_x \\
V(\bar{c}_y, i_y) &= e_y \\
E((\bar{c}_x, i_x), (\bar{c}_0, i_0)) &= isE(\bar{e}) \\
E((\bar{c}_y, i_y), (\bar{c}_0, i_0)) &= isE(\bar{e}) \\
value(e_x) &= value(e_y) \\
\hline
c_x &= c_y
\end{aligned}
$$

Fig. 8. Edition Idempotence: e_x and e_y are edits of e_0 that have the same value

4   Completion

The operations formalized above can be used as is, especially in a single-user scenario. However, knowledge structures are not shared: if a find has a note added and that note is then edited, the find will still refer to the old version of the note; if a find with a note is edited, the updated entity will no longer have its extension.

To address this, three 'completion' operations are defined: cross-entity completion ensures that an entity is brought up to date if an attached entity is edited; post-fact merging ensures that prior operations are performed on a newly-edited entity; pre-fact recall provides a way to infer states of knowledge that may not have been explicitly stored. These operations can be applied iteratively to the graph structure.

4.1   Cross-Entity Completion

It is possible that an edited entity may originally have been associated with another entity via extension. If a find is extended with a note, and that note is edited, the find should be updated so that it is extended with the new entity

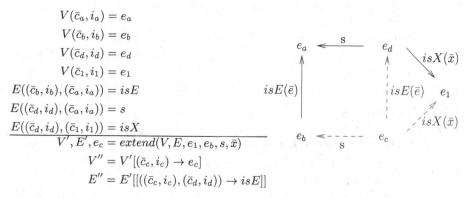

$$V(\bar{c}_a, i_a) = e_a$$
$$V(\bar{c}_b, i_b) = e_b$$
$$V(\bar{c}_d, i_d) = e_d$$
$$V(\bar{c}_1, i_1) = e_1$$
$$E((\bar{c}_b, i_b), (\bar{c}_a, i_a)) = isE$$
$$E((\bar{c}_d, i_d), (\bar{c}_a, i_a)) = s$$
$$\underline{E((\bar{c}_d, i_d), (\bar{c}_1, i_1)) = isX}$$
$$V', E', e_c = extend(V, E, e_1, e_b, s, \bar{x})$$
$$V'' = V'[(\bar{c}_c, i_c) \to e_c]$$
$$E'' = E'[[((\bar{c}_c, i_c), (\bar{c}_d, i_d)) \to isE]]$$

Fig. 9. $\langle V'', E'', e_c \rangle = cross(V, E, e_a, e_b, e_d, e_1, s, \bar{x}, \bar{e})$. Given the edit of e_a to e_b, where e_a is referred to by extension entity e_d, create e_c to bring the extension up to date.

rather than the original. Semantic and syntactic edits are treated as equal in this situation: in both cases, the associated entities must be updated to refer to the edited entity.

Cross-entity completion (see Figure 9) performs this process: assume that there is an entity e_1 that was extended with e_a via relationship s, resulting in an extension entity e_d, and that e_a was then edited to e_b. A completion entity e_c is created via an extension operation on e_1 that refers to the edited entity e_b via the same relationship s. Finally, an internal edit is created between the new extension entity e_c and the old e_d. As such it is shown that e_c is the state of knowledge in which e_1 is extended with the edited entity e_b.

4.2   Post-fact Merging

Post-fact merging ensures that the structures in the system are always representative of the latest operations to have occurred. A simple case is where a find has had some notes added, and is then edited: without a post-fact merge, the edited find would not retain the extensions performed earlier. The merge replicates the extensions onto the edited entity, thus bringing the graph up to date.

The process is also essential for asynchronous operations: it cannot be assumed that a user will perform an operation on the latest edition of an entity. A find may have been edited while a user was adding a note, or conversely a note may have been added while the user was editing the find. As such, any changes need to be performed on the updates that have occurred between the retrieval of the graph and the execution of an operation.

Given an entity e_a that is edited to e_b: if e_a is then extended, it follows that e_b may also be extended with the same extension entity. Alternatively, given an entity e_a that is extended and subsequently also edited, it follows that the edited version should also be extended with the same extension entity. Figure 10 shows the merging operation performing square completion given that an edit

$$V(\bar{c}_a, i_a) = e_a$$
$$V(\bar{c}_b, i_b) = e_b$$
$$V(\bar{c}_d, i_d) = e_d$$
$$V(\bar{c}_1, i_1) = e_1$$
$$E((\bar{c}_b, i_b), (\bar{c}_a, i_a)) = isE$$
$$E((\bar{c}_d, i_d), (\bar{c}_a, i_a)) = isX$$
$$\frac{E((\bar{c}_d, i_d), (\bar{c}_1, i_1)) = s}{V', E', e_c = extend(V, E, e_b, e_1, s, \bar{x})}$$
$$V'' = V'[(\bar{c}_c, i_c) \to e_c]$$
$$E'' = E'[[((\bar{c}_c, i_c), (\bar{c}_d, i_d)) \to isE]]$$

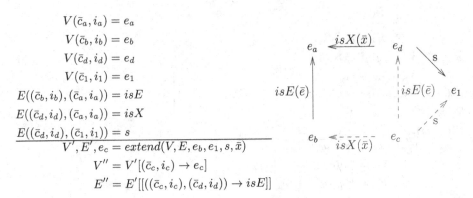

Fig. 10. $\langle V'', E'', e_c \rangle = merge(V, E, e_a, e_b, e_d, e_1, s, \bar{x}, \bar{e})$. Given the extension of e_a, where e_a has previously been edited, apply the extension to the edited entity e_b.

and extension have occurred on e_a (in any order). e_c is created as an extension of the edit entity e_b and an edit of the extension entity e_d. The merge performs an extension operation, ensuring that e_c also has the correct relation s to e_1.

Post-fact merging is most appropriate after edits where semantics are not altered, as the extensions will likely still apply. In cases where the meaning of an entity is altered, it may be prudent to either skip the post-fact merging step (i.e. requiring the user to re-extend the find with any notes) or to allow for the user to select any entities that should be added via the merge operation. It may, however, be more interesting to apply all existing extensions, so any interpretations that are no longer valid become apparent and provoke further annotations.

4.3   Pre-fact Recall

Pre-fact recall is complementary to post-fact merging: Where post-fact merging operates on the outer edges of the graph, pre-fact recall works on the inner structure. If a find is edited and then extended with a note, the structure suggests that there could be a state where the find was extended but not edited. This allows for the navigation of the graph through different permutations of operations - valuable for gaining new insights. In contrast to post-fact merging, pre-fact recall is a non-essential process and so can be determined post hoc. Pre-fact recall and post-fact merging result in the same graph: only the antecedent and consequent differ.

Given an entity e_c that has been produced as a result of an extension of e_b, which is in turn an edit of e_a, a completion entity e_d is created that is an extension of e_a. An internal edit edge is also created from e_c to e_d, hence completing the square. The formalization and visualisation of this is shown in Figure 11.

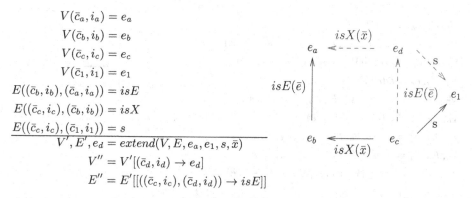

$$V(\bar{c}_a, i_a) = e_a$$
$$V(\bar{c}_b, i_b) = e_b$$
$$V(\bar{c}_c, i_c) = e_c$$
$$V(\bar{c}_1, i_1) = e_1$$
$$E((\bar{c}_b, i_b), (\bar{c}_a, i_a)) = isE$$
$$E((\bar{c}_c, i_c), (\bar{c}_b, i_b)) = isX$$
$$\frac{E((\bar{c}_c, i_c), (\bar{c}_1, i_1)) = s}{V', E', e_d = extend(V, E, e_a, e_1, s, \bar{x})}$$
$$V'' = V'[(\bar{c}_d, i_d) \rightarrow e_d]$$
$$E'' = E'[[((\bar{c}_c, i_c), (\bar{c}_d, i_d)) \rightarrow isE]]$$

Fig. 11. $\langle V'', E'', e_d \rangle = recall(V, E, e_a, e_b, e_c, e_1, s, \bar{x}, \bar{e})$. Given the extension of e_b, where e_b is an edit of e_a, the extension can also be applied to e_a.

Naturally, extensions might only be applicable to the edited entity. Pre-fact recall does not guarantee that recalled entities are semantically valid, so it is suggested that they only be brought into the persisted state of the system if approved by a user.

5   Scalability

Completion operations can have a significant impact on graph size and, as interpretations build, an edit may result in many vertices and edges being created. Figure 12 shows a worked example: A find e_a is edited and extended with a note e_c, then the find is edited again. Finally, the note is edited. With core operations, 6 vertices and 5 edges are needed. With post-fact merging and cross-entity completion this grows to 9 vertices and 14 edges. Adding pre-fact recall, 11 vertices and 20 edges are used. This requires three cross-entity completion operations, due to the entity e_n created in the recall operation: optimised completion uses only two.

The number of references to an entity is significant: for every reference, 3 edges and an entity are created during cross-entity completion. If pre-fact recall is dynamically performed, there are fewer references and the overhead is thus reduced. Similarly, given an extension propagated over a chain of edits via pre-fact recall or post-fact merging, 2n edges and n vertices are created, where n is the number of entities preceding (for pre-fact) or following (for post-fact). If the system only operates on the most recent changes, post-fact has minimal overhead. The most costly post-fact merging operation would occur due to an extension at the oldest point in an edit chain.

Xeros therefore provides a flexible approach to building a scalable system: eager post-fact merging and cross-entity completion minimise storage while ensuring asynchronous operations are handled, and dynamic pre-fact recall provides for the navigation of potential entities in the system.

$$V_1, E_1, e_b = edit(V_0, E_0, e_a, \bar{e}) \qquad \Diamond$$
$$V_2, E_2, e_d = extend(V_1, E_1, e_b, e_c, hasNote, \bar{x}) \quad \Diamond$$
$$V_3, E_3, e_n = recall(V_2, E_2, e_a, e_b, e_d, e_c, s, \bar{x}, \bar{e})$$
$$V_4, E_4, e_e = edit(V_3, E_3, e_b, \bar{e}) \qquad \Diamond$$
$$V_5, E_5, e_o = merge(V_4, E_4, e_b, e_e, e_d, e_c, s, \bar{x}, \bar{e}) \quad \Box$$
$$V_6, E_6, e_f = edit(V_5, E_5, e_c, \bar{e}) \qquad \Diamond$$
$$V_7, E_7, e_g = cross(V_6, E_6, e_c, e_f, e_d, e_b, s, \bar{x}, \bar{e}) \quad \Box$$
$$V_8, E_8, e_h = cross(V_6, E_6, e_c, e_f, e_n, e_a, s, \bar{x}, \bar{e})$$
$$V_9, E_9, e_i = cross(V_6, E_6, e_c, e_f, e_o, e_e, s, \bar{x}, \bar{e}) \quad \Box$$

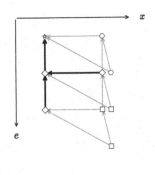

Fig. 12. Operations during a set of edits and extensions. Lines with $\Diamond$ are performed when no completion is used; lines with $\Box$ are added when post-fact and cross-entity completion are used; all lines are performed when every completion operation is used. The diagram shows only the actions on e_a for simplicity.

6   Conclusions

This paper has introduced the Xeros Data Model, its operations, and characteristics. It has been shown that the structure of the model allows for a variety of efficient storage approaches, and that it is robust against asynchronous operations.

Future work on Xeros will provide formalisations for the creation of groups to allow the aggregation of entities, and of the universe: an entity that refers to the leaves of the graph at a single point in time. Editions of the universe allow for these 'snapshots' to be navigated, and users can roll back to any edition of the universe. This approach also caters for the deletion of entities that cannot be removed via reduction: by removing a leaf reference from the universe, the entity can be omitted from visualisations but still exist in the graph.

An HCI study is also being performed, by way of the PoN web application. This is underpinned by the Xeros data model, and the system allows archaeologists to capture their finds and notes in an intuitive manner. Work on PoN will be further informed by the Xeros model, and requirements in the system will feed back into the model's development.

Acknowledgements. This research is funded in part by the EPSRC and AHRC PATINA project through the RCUK Digital Economy programme (EP/H042806/1).

References

[1] Buneman, P., Cheney, J., Lindley, S., Müller, H.: DBWiki: a structured wiki for curated data and collaborative data management. In: SIGMOD Conference 2011, pp. 1335–1338 (2011)

[2] Castro, L.J.G., Giraldo, O.X., Castro, A.G.: Using the Annotation Ontology in semantic digital libraries. In: 9th International Semantic Web Conference, ISWC 2010 (November 2010)

[3] Doerr, M., Ore, C.-E., Stead, S.: The CIDOC conceptual reference model: a new standard for knowledge sharing. In: Tutorials, Posters, Panels and Industrial Contributions at the 26th International Conference on Conceptual Modeling, ER 2007, vol. 83, pp. 51–56. Australian Computer Society, Inc., Darlinghurst (2007)

[4] Dowell, R.D., Jokerst, R.M., Day, A., Eddy, S.R., Stein, L.: The distributed annotation system. BMC Bioinformatics 2, 7 (2001)

[5] Eve, S., Hunt, G.: ARK: A development framework for archaeological recording. In: Layers of Perception. Proceedings of the 35th International Conference on Computer Applications and Quantitative Methods in Archaeology, CAA, pp. 1–5 (April 2007)

[6] Krötzsch, M., Vrandecic, D., Völkel, M., Haller, H., Studer, R.: Semantic wikipedia. Journal of Web Semantics 5, 251–261 (2007)

[7] Moreau, L., Clifford, B., Freire, J., Futrelle, J., Gil, Y., Groth, P., Kwasnikowska, N., Miles, S., Missier, P., Myers, J., Plale, B., Simmhan, Y., Stephan, E., Van den Bussche, J.: The Open Provenance Model core specification (v1.1). Future Generation Computer Systems (July 2010)

[8] Moreau, L., Missier, P. (eds.) Belhajjame, K., Cresswell, S., Golden, R., Groth, P., Klyne, G., McCusker, J., Miles, S., Myers, J., Sahoo, S.: The PROV Data Model and Abstract Syntax Notation. W3c first public working draft, World Wide Web Consortium (October 2011)

[9] Rains, M.: Towards a computerised desktop: the integrated archaeological database system. In: Computer Applications and Quantitative Methods in Archaeology, pp. 207–210 (March 1994)

[10] Theodoridou, M., Tzitzikas, Y., Doerr, M., Marketakis, Y., Melessanakis, V.: Modeling and querying provenance by extending CIDOC CRM. Distributed and Parallel Databases 27, 169–210 (2010), doi:10.1007/s10619-009-7059-2

Using Domain-Specific Data to Enhance Scientific Workflow Steering Queries

João Carlos de A.R. Gonçalves[1], Daniel de Oliveira[1], Kary A.C.S. Ocaña[1], Eduardo Ogasawara[1,2], and Marta Mattoso[1]

[1] COPPE, Federal University of Rio de Janeiro, Brazil
[2] CEFET/RJ, Brazil
{jcg,danielc,kary,ogasawara,marta}@cos.ufrj.br

Abstract. In scientific workflows, provenance data helps scientists in understanding, evaluating and reproducing their results. Provenance data generated at runtime can also support workflow steering mechanisms. Steering facilities for workflows is considered a challenge due to its dynamic demands during execution. To steer, for example, scientists should be able to suspend (or stop) a workflow execution when the approximate solution meets (or deviates) preset criteria. These criteria are commonly evaluated based on provenance data (execution data) and domain-specific data. We claim that the final decision on whether to interfere on the workflow execution may only become feasible when workflows can be steered by scientists using provenance data enriched with domain-specific data. In this paper we propose an approach based on specialized software components, named Data Extractor (DE), to acquire domain-specific data from data files produced during a scientific workflow execution. DE gathers domain-specific data from produced data files and associates it to existing provenance data on the provenance repository. We have evaluated the proposed approach using a real bioinformatics workflow for comparative genomics executed in SciCumulus cloud workflow parallel engine.

1 Introduction

Scientific workflows are used as an abstraction that models and allows for the management of scientific experiments [1]. Many of these workflows are composed by activities that invoke computing and data intensive programs. A workflow may execute for weeks or months, requiring parallel processing in High Performance Computing (HPC) environments. In order to be evaluated and reproduced by third-party scientists or teams, provenance data [2] related to all executions of these workflows has to be captured and organized for further analysis. Capturing provenance in HPC and distributed environments, such as clouds [3], is a very important but also a complicated task.

Provenance, or lineage, of a workflow is related to all metadata associated to the data products generated by a specific workflow execution. Simmhan *et al.* [4] define provenance as the "(…) information that helps determine the derivation history of a data product, starting from its original sources. We use the term data product or

P. Groth and J. Frew (Eds.): IPAW 2012, LNCS 7525, pp. 152–167, 2012.

dataset to refer to data in any form, such as files, tables, and virtual collections (...)". Intuitively, provenance data is mainly used for a *post* analysis of the experiment. This way, many approaches focus on providing techniques for long-term provenance management [5–7]. Specialized models and technologies are being proposed to guarantee the long-term understandability of the preserved data of a workflow. Semantic Web techniques, such as ontologies and annotations [4,7,8], are used for adding semantics to data products and to allow the construction of complex queries.

Long-term provenance data is fundamental for enabling reproducibility and different kinds of *post* analysis [9–11], but these solutions do not allow for provenance analysis during the course of a workflow execution. Even though the workflow execution *log* could be browsed, this is far from provenance data query. Our previous works in supporting workflow scientists from bioinformatics [12] and numerical methods [13] have led us to develop services to query provenance data during the execution [14]. We define this type of provenance as *runtime provenance data*. It means that all derivation history of a data product and the status of all activities (start time, end time, errors) are available for querying as soon as an activity executes and data products are generated.

This runtime data analysis is the basis for workflow steering [15]. Our preliminary experiments in [11] have shown the potential of user steering features in workflows for tracking, evaluating and adapting the execution of a workflow. Workflow steering remains an open issue that could support iterative methods, *i.e.* scientists analyze the status of the execution and interfere by stopping or changing the space of parameters to be explored [11]. This steering mechanism allows for optimizing workflow execution and has gained importance in the last years since HPC environments, such as clouds, are paid according to the time used. In fact, this is highlighted by Gil *et al.* [15] as "a fundamental technology to fully support e-Science".

Provenance generated during the execution course of a workflow is a rich resource to support workflow steering. However, runtime provenance data is not sufficient to support steering mechanisms in workflows. In many cases, the execution has to be suspended or stopped when the approximate solution meets a preset user criterion. The final and complex decision on whether to interfere on the workflow or to reduce the space of parameters to explore, increase or even stop the execution has to be taken by scientists using domain-specific data. This kind of data, associated to the workflow provenance data, provides insight for scientists to perform steering actions. These runtime decisions can be taken based on querying provenance enriched with domain-specific data. Although there are some initiatives to propose workflow steering using runtime provenance [16], none of them allows for performing queries using domain-specific data. In this scenario, the goal is how to provide support for developing steering capabilities in parallel scientific workflows using runtime provenance enriched with domain-specific data.

In this paper, we address the problem of querying provenance data enriched with domain-specific data to provide for steering mechanisms. We contribute with a software solution for scientists to extract domain-specific data from input and produced data files (registered in the provenance repository) and use this data to complement runtime queries on provenance data. This provenance enriched representation is possible due to Data Extractors (DE), which are software components that are deployed in SciCumulus, a cloud workflow engine [17]. Although we used SciCumulus as workflow engine in this paper, the proposed approach can be coupled to other Scientific Workflow Management Systems (SWfMS) especially when it is not possible to modify the underlying workflow engine in order to produce the required, richer provenance metadata for the problem at hand. DE is based on a workflow algebra that uniformly represents workflow data and it allows for extracting domain-specific data and storing it in the provenance repository, *i.e.* a database system, along with information about workflow structure and execution. As a result, DE is independent of application structures, *i.e.* scientists can couple a series of DE to the workflow specification according to their needs.

This paper is organized as follows. In Section 2, we present a motivation workflow for steering while in Section 3, we describe SciCumulus cloud engine and the workflow algebraic approach that provides for the uniform underlying data representation. In Section 4, we detail the proposed approach for enriching provenance with domain-specific data and, in Section 5, we present experimental results. In Section 6, we discuss related work. Next, Section 7 presents final remarks.

2   Motivation: Steering for Comparative Genomics Experiments

This section illustrates a computing-intensive parallel workflow scenario in the comparative genomics bioinformatics domain. We use this example consistently in the rest of the paper. Comparative genomics is one of many bioinformatics fields that aim at computationally comparing hundreds of different genomes [18]. Many types of bioinformatics applications associated to this field, such as multiple sequence alignment (MSA), homologues detection and phylogenetic analysis are increasing in scale and complexity [19]. Managing genomic experiments is far from trivial, since they are computationally intensive and process large amounts of data. One of the main possible usages of comparative genomics workflows is to use profiles hidden Markov models (pHMMs) for improving phylogenetic analyses. One example of this comparative genomics workflow is SciHmm [12]. SciHmm is a parallel workflow based on a cross-validation procedure [12] to decide which MSA method and algorithm offer the best quality in the alignments for a phylogenetic analysis workflow. SciHmm is composed by five main activities: (i) MSA construction, (ii) pHMM build, (iii) pHMM search against a target database, (iv) cross-validation analysis and, (v) generation of Receiver-Operating Characteristic (ROC) curves. A ROC curve is a graphical plot that illustrates the performance of a specific classifier as its threshold is varied. Each ROC curve is generated by plotting the fraction of true positives out of the positives *versus* the fraction of false positives out of the negatives, at various threshold settings.

However, since SciHmm may execute for several hours or even days, scientists may need to analyze if a specific execution is producing the expected results before the workflow finishes. If part of the results is perceived to be under the expectations (*e.g.* sequences that belong to different genes are included in the same input multi-fasta), scientists may interfere on the execution (*e.g.* re-executing choosing specific genes to be processed). These actions certainly spare financial resources and scientists' time. One real steering scenario is when scientists are not aware of the entire content of a produced data file; *i.e.* an aligned multi-fasta file can be formed by a huge volume of biological sequences or, in the worst scenario, sequences belonging to other genes classes. This may lead to incoherent results in ROC curves analysis. Fig. 1 presents a data compilation of a real scenario where the Sensitivity-Specificity (*i.e.* quality analysis parameters of ROC curves) pair value is under the threshold in a ROC curve and scientists may use this information to interfere (calibrate) in the execution. Fig. 1 presents an excerpt of a data file produced by *hmmsearch* comparison using the pHMM (belongs to the gene 6-phosphogluconate dehydrogenase) against protozoan genomes from the RefSeq database. In Fig. 1 underlined lines represent sequences that belong to genes different from 6-phosphogluconate dehydrogenase, which have to be neglected in this case.

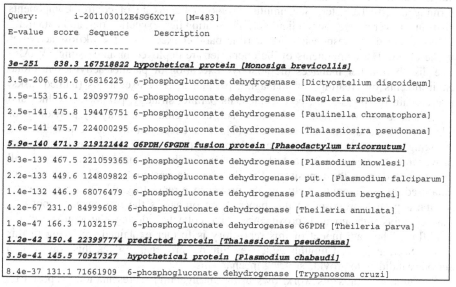

```
Query:       i-201103012E4SG6XC1V  [M=483]
E-value  score  Sequence    Description
-------  -----  --------    -----------
3e-251   838.3  167518822  hypothetical protein [Monosiga brevicollis]
3.5e-206 689.6  66816225   6-phosphogluconate dehydrogenase [Dictyostelium discoideum]
1.5e-153 516.1  290997790  6-phosphogluconate dehydrogenase [Naegleria gruberi]
2.5e-141 475.8  194476751  6-phosphogluconate dehydrogenase [Paulinella chromatophora]
2.6e-141 475.7  224000295  6-phosphogluconate dehydrogenase [Thalassiosira pseudonana]
5.9e-140 471.3  219121442  G6PDH/6PGDH fusion protein [Phaeodactylum tricornutum]
8.3e-139 467.5  221059365  6-phosphogluconate dehydrogenase [Plasmodium knowlesi]
2.2e-133 449.6  124809822  6-phosphogluconate dehydrogenase, put. [Plasmodium falciparum]
1.4e-132 446.9  68076479   6-phosphogluconate dehydrogenase [Plasmodium berghei]
4.2e-67  231.0  84999608   6-phosphogluconate dehydrogenase [Theileria annulata]
1.8e-47  166.3  71032157   6-phosphogluconate dehydrogenase G6PDH [Theileria parva]
1.2e-42  150.4  223997774  predicted protein [Thalassiosira pseudonana]
3.5e-41  145.5  70917327   hypothetical protein [Plasmodium chabaudi]
8.4e-37  131.1  71661909   6-phosphogluconate dehydrogenase [Trypanosoma cruzi]
```

Fig. 1. An excerpt of the output information of SciHmm

In addition, to get the results presented in Fig. 1, scientists have to discover which workflow activities have already finished without errors associated with ROC curves results. For each ROC curve, it is necessary to discover which sequences (*hmmsearch* hits in each multi-fasta file) produced these low quality curves and extract domain-specific data, such as, gene information based on enzyme classification or also species. In the example of Fig. 1, scientists defined that the analysis is based on 6-phosphogluconate dehydrogenase; then, all sequences that do not fulfill this premise have to be excluded (lines underlined). Also, in this particular case, scientists may need to re-execute SciHmm by splitting the input data file in four parts (*i.e.* one for each human pathogens genus (or taxonomic group): *Plasmodium, Trichomonas, Giardia, Toxoplasma,* and Trypanosomatids. However, this steering mechanism is only possible if scientists can query runtime provenance data related to domain-specific data. In this example, species and genus information are not part of the provenance data. Following Simmhan *et al.* definition, provenance is related to data products lineage and domain-specific data is the content of those data products.

3   SciCumulus Engine and Algebraic Workflow Representation

Since the proposed approach has to be implemented in a system that manages the parallel execution of workflows while generating runtime provenance data, we have chosen to use, in the case study, SciCumulus [17]. SciCumulus is an engine that is designed to distribute scientific workflow activities (or even entire scientific workflows) dispatched from an SWfMS, such as, VisTrails [21], Taverna [22], into a cloud environment, e.g. Amazon EC2 [23] to be executed in parallel. SciCumulus creates and manages several parallel tasks associated to each activity and orchestrates the execution of these tasks on a distributed set of virtual machines (VMs), thus forming a virtual cluster. SciCumulus promotes the usage of control components distributed over several tiers: client tier, distribution tier, execution tier, and data tier.

The client tier is responsible for starting parallel execution of workflow activities in the cloud. The components of the client tier are deployed in an existing SWfMS. The distribution tier manages the adaptive execution of parallel activities in cloud environments by creating and managing parallel activity executions (named tasks) that contain the program to be executed, its parallel strategy, parameters values and input data to be consumed. SciCumulus addresses cloud elasticity by providing for adaptive VM addition and removal [17]. The execution tier is responsible for invoking executable codes in many VMs in the virtual cluster and to collect provenance at runtime. As a task execution finishes, it immediately records all provenance data in the repository. Finally, the data tier contains all repositories of data used by SciCumulus, including the provenance repository, which is fundamental for the approach proposed in this paper. It encompasses the provenance repository that contains fundamental provenance data collected during the course of the workflow. The data model of this repository is further explained following in this paper (Section 3). SciCumulus generates runtime provenance data, this way; it is a serious candidate to provide steering mechanisms.

SciCumulus represents workflows using an algebraic representation proposed by Ogasawara *et al.* [24]. This algebra defines its operands as a uniform data representation consistently used throughout the workflow execution, where all data (consumed and produced by each activity) is represented as relations (similar to a database). As in relational algebra, relations are defined as sets of tuples of primitive types (*i.e.* integer, float, string, date) and complex types (*e.g.* a pointer to a data file). The parameter values for the activities are represented as values (attributes) in a tuple, whereas the set of tuples composes the relation to be consumed by an activity. This relation-based representation is a uniform way of introducing new attributes (representing information extracted from produced data files) to represent domain-specific data. By using this algebraic representation, SciCumulus can execute workflows in different domains. In addition, this algebraic representation is fundamental for the proposed approach since it allows for extract information and easily add it to the workflow representation.

4   Enriching Provenance with Domain-Specific Data

Following the definition of Simmhan *et al.*, all provenance data is related to lineage metadata about a specific data file. In fact, each data file is considered as a "black-box" by the traditional provenance definition. Commonly represented provenance data is related to execution time of each activity, input and output files (in the case of retrospective provenance [2]), and details about software involved in the execution (in the case of prospective provenance). Although very useful, this provenance data is not sufficient to provide steering capabilities for scientists. In order to facilitate scientists' work, we present in this section an approach to extract domain-specific data from generated data files and use it to enrich provenance data allowing for queries with more expressivity. First we present Data Extractors (DE) and the adaptations in SciCumulus to incorporate them in the architecture. Then, we present the data model to represent both provenance and domain-specific data for an execution of SciHmm workflow.

SciCumulus Data Extractor

For the domain-specific data acquisition, we designed, developed and incorporated DE into SciCumulus engine. A DE can be implemented as an artificial workflow activity, which invokes an external program (defined) by scientists that analyzes produced data files and extracts domain-specific data from it. These programs encapsulate the domain-specific extraction rules to crawl domain-specific data from generated files, being a fundamental component of the proposed approach. An example of a rule implemented by a program is to verify the format types accepted as input for an activity. In this case, the workflow engine (SciCumulus) generates the OPM *isProducedBy* link (querying its provenance repository) between the activity and data file and the domain contents as depicted in Fig. 2.

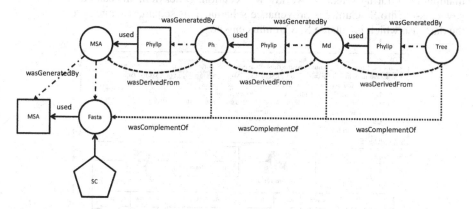

Fig. 2. An OPM graph generated based on SciCumulus' provenance repository

This way, SciCumulus allows for a DE to follow the provenance chain and relate the domain outputs to domain information in the input files. Based on the identification of domain-specific data files, DE can invoke third-party Web services to gather domain-specific data from these files. In the case of bioinformatics workflows, information extracted from data files can be enhanced by querying one of the several available NCBI databases and services. A DE is placed after each activity execution in SciCumulus and the program to be invoked is defined at the workflow specification file (in XML file similar to the one presented on Fig. 3) created by scientists. Once an activity is executed (and a data file is produced) the DE is invoked to extract associated domain-specific data. All data is stored using a unified provenance schema that comprises provenance data (related to activity execution) associated to domain-specific data. This way, each activity execution in SciCumulus presents three phases: (a) a data production phase, (b) data extraction phase and, (c) provenance repository update as depicted in Fig. 3.

Phase (a) invokes a specific program that is part of the workflow. In the case of SciHmm, HMMER and MAFFT are examples of these programs. Each invocation consumes an input tuple Tp_1 and produces an output tuple Tp_2 that indicates the produced files (using a file pointer in the output tuple). The (b) phase invokes DE and consumes Tp_2 to discover the data files to be processed. It produces a new tuple Tp_3, which now contains a pointer to data files and additional attributes to represent extracted domain-specific data. The (c) and last phase is also performed by DE and it is focused on registering domain-specific data (Tp_3) in the provenance repository (in specific schema classes that are explained following in this section).

The DE framework is implemented in Java version 6.31 and can invoke source codes of different languages. This is possible since the interface, in this case, is a relation-based file that contains all tuples that were processed or generated. This way, scientists may invoke programs in Python or Perl, without needing to modify the workflow engine. This approach follows the Strategy design pattern [25] where different extraction algorithms can be coupled to SciCumulus as independent cartridges. These cartridges can be dynamically changed without interference on the engine code. In this sense, the DE is a workflow-oriented approach for data manipulation during scientific workflow execution. Other domains can be modeled as new classes into SciCumulus provenance schema. This schema change is restricted to the database which is outside SciCumulus engine.

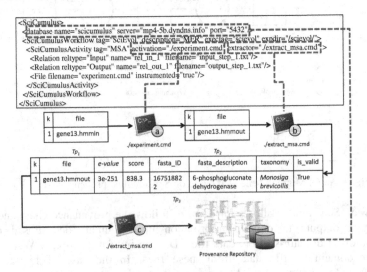

Fig. 3. Three phase activity execution

Coupling Domain-Specific Data to SciCumulus Provenance Model

Since we use a comparative genomics bioinformatics case study (SciHmm workflow), in which scientists are conducting an experiment to identify protein sequence by similarity, we have to couple domain-specific classes to the SciCumulus provenance model in order to store extracted domain-specific data. These classes have to be modeled and coupled to the provenance model by a computer science expert. This is our research focus, but, currently, this part of the approach still has to be done manually. In the case study presented in this paper, several new classes were added to SciCumulus provenance model. *Sequence* is one example of these classes. Sequences in bioinformatics contain biological information about genes, enzymes or other biological data of interest [12]. This way, sequences, genes, enzymes and organisms (including organism's taxonomy, *i.e.* genus, species, phylum, kingdom, class, family) are fundamental information to be used when a scientist is evaluating a result using steering mechanisms, as they represent domain specific terminology. Sequences are used in genomic comparative analyses to identify homologues sequences of a determined gene that are going to be used in other bioinformatics domains such as phylogeny, evolution, o molecular modeling. This way, during the life cycle of SciHmm we have to associate all these domain-specific data to existing provenance data. Fig. 4 presents the extended provenance repository using a UML class diagram. Original SciCumulus provenance classes are represented in white and domain-specific classes are represented in white inside the dashed line.

In Fig. 4 all information of the original SciCumulus provenance model is captured by the components in the execution tier of SciCumulus that captures the information related to the cloud environment. Domain-specific data is captured by DE. This provenance model is composed by four main parts: (i) elements that represent the processes executed in the cloud; (ii) elements that represent the artifacts consumed and produced by a workflow execution, (iii) elements that represent information about the cloud environment and, (iv) elements that represent domain-specific data.

The elements *VirtualMachine, CloudProvider, VirtualMachineType, Account, SecurityPolice, OperationSystem, Image, InstalledSoftware,* and *SoftwareOS* represent all data related to the cloud environment. Some other classes represent the structure of the workflow (*Workflow*) and its activities (*Activity*). Each activity is decomposed in several parallel tasks (*Task*) which consumes parameter values (*Relation, Field* and *Value*) and data files (*DataFile*). Since this provenance schema is based on the OPM recommendation [26], the classes *Activity* and *Task* are mapped as *Processes*. The class *DataFile, Relation* and *Value* are mapped as *Artifacts*. And class *Account* is mapped to an OPM *Agent.* It is important to highlight that all provenance data in SciCumulus is generated at runtime, *i.e.* during workflow execution.

The remaining classes (inside the dashed line in Fig. 4) represent domain-specific data that was extracted using DE and stored associated to provenance data. Sequence represents the smallest grain in a comparative genomic workflow. Each sequence is associated to a specific organism, which is classified using Linnaean taxonomy in

Domain, Kingdom, Phylum, Class, Order, Family, Genus and *Specie*. All this domain-specific data is obtained using NCBI Web services using sequence information extracted from files (Sequence ID). A *Sequence_Group* represents a set of sequences of one gene class present in divergent species. Each *Sequence_Group* is used as input for SciHmm workflow. Once aligned, each *Sequence_Group* produces an *MSA* which is converted to a phylip format thus producing *MSA_Converted*.

Hits represent a specific *MSA_Converted* match with a target database. *MSA*, *MSA_Converted* and *Hits* may be mapped to OPM *Artifact*. By coupling this domain-specific data to SciCumulus provenance data, scientists can perform steering queries using specific terms of the domain. For example, using the proposed data model, scientists are able to discover which organisms or species are considered in a specific ROC curve. If the partial runtime results of the ROC curve are not appropriated, there is no point to continue the execution, especially in paid public clouds. This type of query is important since each ROC curve generation need several hours of processing. If we can reduce total execution time we can spare financial resources in public clouds. Another trial may split a specific sequence group in different new instances of the *Sequence_Group* element and perform the workflow analysis separately. In addition, scientists are still able to *post* validate the execution using domain terminology. All of these features are not possible if domain-specific data is not available. In this case, all queries should be performed based on the name of data files. In the next section, we present steering queries using this data model and an overhead analysis when using DE in a parallel execution.

5   Experimental Results

In this section we present an evaluation of the proposed approach by measuring performance overheads imposed by the execution of DE and present queries for steering mechanisms in scientific workflows using runtime provenance data enriched with domain-specific data. We executed SciHmm workflow in parallel in Amazon EC2 environment using SciCumulus cloud workflow engine.

Environment and Experiment Setup
There are several types of VMs provided by Amazon EC2, such as micro, large, extra-large, high CPU extra-large, and Quadruple Extra Large. In the experiment presented in this paper we have considered just Amazon's micro types (EC2 ID: t1.micro – 613 MB RAM, 30 GB of EBS storage only, 1 core). Each instantiated VM uses Linux Cent OS 5 (64-bit), and it was configured with the necessary software, libraries like MPJ [27], and the bioinformatics applications. All instances are based on the same image (AMI ID ami-7d865614) and it was used to execute SciCumulus. According to Amazon, all VMs were instantiated in the US East - N. Virginia location and follow the pricing rules of that locality.

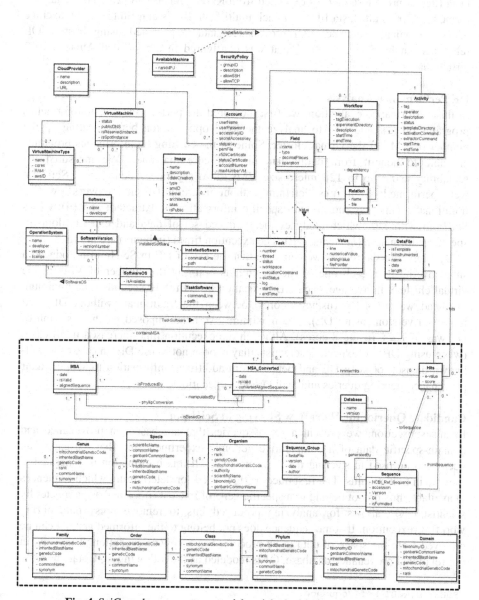

Fig. 4. SciCumulus provenance model enriched with domain-specific data

To execute SciHmm in parallel, our simulations use as input a dataset of multi-fasta files of protein sequences extracted from RefSeq release 48 [28]. This dataset is formed by 200 multi-fasta files and each multi-fasta file is constituted by an average of 10 biological sequences. All provenance data is persisted using PostgreSQL relational database version 8.4.6 that was configured in a dedicated Amazon EC2 virtual machine.

DE Performance Analysis

In this performance evaluation, we first measured the performance of bioinformatics programs on a single VM to analyze the local optimization before scaling up the number of VMs of the virtual cluster. Some of the existing bioinformatics programs are able to benefit from parallelism in multi-core machines. We measured the scalability using up to 128 micro-size VMs. Two separate executions of SciHmm were performed: (i) it runs SciHmm without inserting DE in the workflow (*i.e.* traditional). This way, no domain specific information is extracted; and (ii) it uses SciHmm with DE, which analyzes the produced set of data and extracts domain-specific information (*i.e.* using DE). The execution times (in hours) are in Fig. 5.

By analyzing the results we can state that the use of DE in SciHmm introduced a small overhead in each one of the executions (varying the number of VMs in the virtual cluster). In average, each DE invocation lasted for 10 seconds. The minimum overhead was of 4.1% (using 4 cores) between the traditional (without DE) and improved version (using DE). The maximum overhead imposed by the insertion of DE was of 7.3% (using 8 cores). Although the execution time increased in all cases (when using DE), as expected, scientists may choose not to use DE, in case of a well-known dataset, or keep DE and benefit from additional information to support their provenance steering queries and avoid useless executions.

Candidate Queries for Workflow Steering in SciHmm

In this subsection, we present a set of queries that are based on provenance and domain-specific data of a comparative genomic experiment and that are candidate queries to be used in steering mechanisms since all this information is generated at runtime in SciCumulus. The first query (Q1) is used for determining which sequences in available hits do not belong to a specific gene of interest (informed as parameter by scientists). Q1 allows for analyzing produced hits to remove noisy data during workflow execution. If some sequence does not belong to the informed gene, it can be removed from the space of data to be processed in a new re-execution. This way, in our relational provenance database, Q1 is modeled as the following SQL statement:

```
SELECT S.NCBI_Ref_Sequence
FROM Task T, Hits H, MSA_CONVERTED M2, MSA M1, SEQUENCE_GROUP SG,
SEQUENCE S, ORGANISM O, SPECIE SP, GENUS G
WHERE T.taskid = H.taskid AND H.msacid = M2.msacid AND M2.msaid =
M1.msaid and M1.sgid = SG.sgid AND SG.sqid = S.sqid AND S.orgid =
O.orgid AND O.spid = SP.spid and SP.genid = G.genid AND T.exitStatus = 0
/* No error */ AND G.genus = "PLASMODIUM"
```

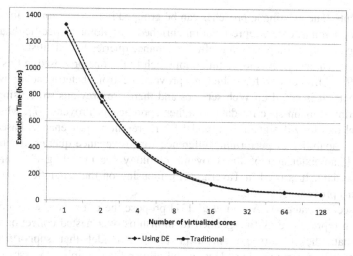

Fig. 5. Performance analysis of DE overhead in SciCumulus

The second query (Q2) is used to determine how many sequences from input data are annotated as putative, hypothetical, similar, and more other similar annotations that denote that sequences are not annotated as "true genes". This value is going to indicate the quality of the ROC curves produced at the end of SciHmm. Query Q2 can be performed after the first alignment activity, *i.e.* when the MSA is produced. However, these sequences annotated as similar, probably can be included in other studies to determine relationships between the "true annotated genes". Scientists are able to filter undesired data to avoid unnecessary processing by Q2. It is important to highlight that in both Q1 and Q2 we have to consider only tasks that have not presented execution errors (based on provenance data). This way, Q2, in our relational provenance database, is modeled as the following SQL statement:

```
SELECT COUNT(*)
FROM Task T, Hits H, MSA_CONVERTED M2, MSA M1, SEQUENCE_GROUP SG,
SEQUENCE S
WHERE T.taskid = H.taskid AND H.msacid = M2.msacid AND M2.msaid =
M1.msaid and M1.sgid = SG.sgid AND SG.sqid = S.sqid AND T.status =
"FINISHED" AND T.exitStatus = 0 /* No error */ AND (S.NCBI_Ref_Sequence
LIKE "%PUTATIVE%" OR S.NCBI_Ref_Sequence LIKE "%HYPOTHETICAL%" OR
S.NCBI_Ref_Sequence LIKE "%SIMILAR%")
```

6 Related Work

There are several provenance management frameworks proposed in the literature. To the best of authors' knowledge, none of them offers support for steering queries based on runtime provenance enriched with domain-specific data. Runtime queries are particularly required in big scientific data, being processed in parallel, in HPC environments. The existing approaches can be grouped in two categories: the first one deals with provenance data representation enriched with domain specific data and the second one provides complex and useful provenance queries for scientists.

In the first category, the most similar approach to the one proposed in this paper is Karma [29], a framework for collecting provenance from heterogeneous workflow environments. It is based on Web services and there are previous work using Karma for extracting domain-specific data. Another approach is Provenir [7], which is an upper-level ontology designed as a model for representing provenance, based on the ontology's capability of performing inference for provenance queries. There is also Janus [30], an extension of the Provenir ontology for modeling domain-specific provenance data. It is used in Taverna [22], focusing on the semantics of a specific domain on a provenance graph.

In the second category, Anand *et al.* [31] propose the effective use of provenance information represented as fine-grained relationships over nested collections of data. Due to that, the authors present a provenance model that supports multiple invocations of the same process. This model allows for multiple processes operating on the same nested data collection. This feature can be useful in domain-specific query and thus can be considered as a first step to acquire domain specific information and associate it to produced provenance data. Gadelha *et al.* [32] introduce a set of query patterns that can be identified in provenance queries of Swift's parallel scripting system [33]. Their provenance management system is focused on large-scale many-task scientific computations. They developed a data model following the OPM specification, with extensions that enrich core structural provenance data, represented as consumption and production relationships between applications and data sets. Domain-specific data is modeled through free text user annotation. They contribute by proposing a query interface to leverage SQL syntax.

Although all of these approaches represent a step forward and many of them can be seen as complementary to our work, none of them provide for provenance data query at runtime. Thus, they can be helpful in planning the next workflow execution, but they cannot be used to provide steering mechanisms based on runtime structured queries. The approach proposed in this paper focus on a different perspective, extracting runtime domain-specific data from data files and representing them related to workflow provenance data.

7   Conclusions

Scientific workflows are used to represent the steps of a scientific experiment. SWfMS manage workflow's programs and data for validating or refuting a scientific hypothesis. Provenance data is fundamental to allow for validation and reproducibility of workflows. Although provenance data is mainly used for a *post* validation and analysis of the experiment, there are other possible usages such as workflow execution steering.

In order to provide workflow steering capabilities, it is necessary that provenance be made available during workflow execution. By steering, scientists may interfere in the execution course interrupting or adjusting parameters based on a runtime analysis. In previous work, we started to provide for provenance data query at runtime [17]. However, scientists cannot decide how to interfere on the execution using provenance data (activity start time, errors, data files produced) disconnected from domain-specific data. In many cases, to suspend or stop an execution, scientists have to analyze if the current solution meets a preset criterion, which is usually based on domain-specific data. This type of data is not available for runtime querying in related work.

This paper proposes an approach for extracting domain-specific data from produced data files and storing them along with provenance data. This allows for scientists to create queries that can be used as a basis for steering mechanisms, thus allowing for verifications based on provenance and domain-specific data at runtime. One of the advantages of our solution is modeling domain-specific data in the same formalism of the workflow algebra [17] underneath the execution engine. This algebra allows for a formal control of the execution, providing for the consistent sequence of the workflow execution, after the scientist's interference. The proposed approach is promising, since it presents small runtime overhead and allows for building complex steering mechanisms based on enriched provenance data with domain-specific data.

Acknowledgments. This work was partially sponsored by CNPq, FAPERJ and CAPES.

References

[1] Taylor, I.J., Deelman, E., Gannon, D.B., Shields, M.: Workflows for e-Science: Scientific Workflows for Grids, 1st edn. Springer (2007)

[2] Freire, J., Koop, D., Santos, E., Silva, C.T.: Provenance for Computational Tasks: A Survey. Computing in Science and Engineering 10(3), 11–21 (2008)

[3] Vaquero, L.M., Rodero-Merino, L., Caceres, J., Lindner, M.: A break in the clouds: towards a cloud definition. SIGCOMM Comput. Commun. Rev. 39(1), 50–55 (2009)

[4] Simmhan, Y.L., Plale, B., Gannon, D.: A survey of data provenance in e-science. ACM SIGMOD Record 34(3), 31–36 (2005)

[5] Factor, M., Henis, E., Naor, D., Rabinovici-Cohen, S., Reshef, P., Ronen, S., Michetti, G., Guercio, M.: Authenticity and provenance in long term digital preservation: modeling and implementation in preservation aware storage. In: First Workshop on Theory and Practice of Provenance, Berkeley, CA, USA, pp. 6:1–6:10 (2009)

[6] Groth, P., Deelman, E., Juve, G., Mehta, G., Berriman, B.: Pipeline-centric provenance model. In: Proceedings of the 4th Workshop on Workflows in Support of Large-Scale Science, Portland, Oregon, pp. 1–8 (2009)

[7] Sahoo, S., Sheth, A.: Provenir ontology: Towards a Framework for eScience Provenance Management. In: Microsoft eScience Workshop, Pittsburgh, PA, pp. 15–17 (2009)

[8] Wolstencroft, K., Alper, P., Hull, D., Wroe, C., Lord, P.W., Stevens, R.D., Goble, C.A.: The myGrid ontology: bioinformatics service discovery. Int. J. Bioinformatics Res. Appl. 3(3), 303–325 (2007)

[9] Crawl, D., Altintas, I.: A Provenance-Based Fault Tolerance Mechanism for Scientific Workflows. In: Freire, J., Koop, D., Moreau, L. (eds.) IPAW 2008. LNCS, vol. 5272, pp. 152–159. Springer, Heidelberg (2008)

[10] de Oliveira, D., Ogasawara, E., Seabra, F., Silva, V., Murta, L., Mattoso, M.: GExpLine: A Tool for Supporting Experiment Composition. In: McGuinness, D.L., Michaelis, J.R., Moreau, L. (eds.) IPAW 2010. LNCS, vol. 6378, pp. 251–259. Springer, Heidelberg (2010)

[11] Missier, P.: Incremental workflow improvement through analysis of its data provenance. In: 3rd USENIX Workshop on the Theory and Practice of Provenance (TaPP 2011), Heraklion, Crete, Greece (2011)

[12] Ocaña, K.A.C.S., Oliveira, D., Dias, J., Ogasawara, E., Mattoso, M.: Optimizing Phylogenetic Analysis Using SciHmm Cloud-based Scientific Workflow. In: 2011 IEEE Seventh International Conference on e-Science (e-Science) IEEE e-Science 2011, Stockholm, Sweden, pp. 190–197 (2011)

[13] Guerra, G., Rochinha, F., Elias, R., Oliveira, D., Ogasawara, E., Dias, J., Mattoso, M., Coutinho, A.L.G.A.: Uncertainty Quantification in Computational Predictive Models for Fluid Dynamics Using Workflow Management Engine. International Journal for Uncertainty Quantification 2(1), 53–71 (2012)

[14] Ogasawara, E., Oliveira, D., Chirigati, F., Barbosa, C.E., Elias, R., Braganholo, V., Coutinho, A., Mattoso, M.: Exploring many task computing in scientific workflows. In: Proceedings of the 2nd Workshop on Many-Task Computing on Grids and Supercomputers, MTAGS 2009, Portland, Oregon, USA, pp. 1–10 (2009)

[15] Gil, Y., Deelman, E., Ellisman, M., Fahringer, T., Fox, G., Gannon, D., Goble, C., Livny, M., Moreau, L., et al.: Examining the Challenges of Scientific Workflows. Computer 40(12), 24–32 (2007)

[16] Dias, J., Ogasawara, E., Oliveira, D., Porto, F., Coutinho, A., Mattoso, M.: Supporting Dynamic Parameter Sweep in Adaptive and User-Steered Workflow. In: 6th Workshop on Workflows in Support of Large-Scale Science WORKS 2011, Seattle, WA, USA, pp. 31–36 (2011)

[17] Oliveira, D., Ogasawara, E., Ocaña, K., Baiao, F., Mattoso, M.: An Adaptive Parallel Execution Strategy for Cloud-based Scientific Workflows. Concurrency and Computation: Practice and Experience (2011) (online)

[18] Miller, W., Makova, K.D., Nekrutenko, A., Hardison, R.C.: Comparative Genomics. Annual Review of Genomics and Human Genetics 5(1), 15–56 (2004)

[19] Clark, A.G.: Genomics of the evolutionary process. Trends in Ecology & Evolution 21(6), 316–321 (2006)

[20] Baldi, P., Brunak, S., Chauvin, Y., Andersen, C.A.F., Nielsen, H.: Assessing the accuracy of prediction algorithms for classification: an overview. Bioinformatics 16(5), 412–424 (2000)

[21] Callahan, S.P., Freire, J., Santos, E., Scheidegger, C.E., Silva, C.T., Vo, H.T.: VisTrails: visualization meets data management. In: SIGMOD International Conference on Management of Data, Chicago, Illinois, USA, pp. 745–747 (2006)

[22] Hull, D., Wolstencroft, K., Stevens, R., Goble, C., Pocock, M.R., Li, P., Oinn, T.: Taverna: a tool for building and running workflows of services. Nucleic Acids Research 34(2), 729–732 (2006)

[23] Amazon EC2, Amazon Elastic Compute Cloud (Amazon EC2) (2010), http://aws.amazon.com/ec2/

[24] Ogasawara, E., Dias, J., Oliveira, D., Porto, F., Valduriez, P., Mattoso, M.: An Algebraic Approach for Data-Centric Scientific Workflows. Proc. of VLDB Endowment 4(12), 1328–1339 (2011)

[25] Gamma, E., Helm, R., Johnson, R., Vlissides, J.M.: Design Patterns: Elements of Reusable Object-Oriented Software. Addison-Wesley Professional (1994)

[26] Moreau, L., Freire, J., Futrelle, J., McGrath, R.E., Myers, J., Paulson, P.: The Open Provenance Model: An Overview. In: Freire, J., Koop, D., Moreau, L. (eds.) IPAW 2008. LNCS, vol. 5272, pp. 323–326. Springer, Heidelberg (2008)

[27] Carpenter, B., Getov, V., Judd, G., Skjellum, A., Fox, G.: MPJ: MPI-like message passing for Java. Concurrency: Practice and Experience 12(11), 1019–1038 (2000)

[28] Pruitt, K.D., Tatusova, T., Klimke, W., Maglott, D.R.: NCBI Reference Sequences: current status, policy and new initiatives. Nucleic Acids Research 37(Database issue), D32–D36 (2009)

[29] Simmhan, Y.L., Plale, B., Gannon, D.: A Framework for Collecting Provenance in Data-Centric Scientific Workflows. In: ICWS, pp. 427–436 (2006)

[30] Missier, P., Sahoo, S.S., Zhao, J., Goble, C., Sheth, A.: *Janus*: From Workflows to Semantic Provenance and Linked Open Data. In: McGuinness, D.L., Michaelis, J.R., Moreau, L. (eds.) IPAW 2010. LNCS, vol. 6378, pp. 129–141. Springer, Heidelberg (2010)

[31] Anand, M.K., Bowers, S., McPhillips, T., Ludäscher, B.: Exploring Scientific Workflow Provenance Using Hybrid Queries over Nested Data and Lineage Graphs. In: Winslett, M. (ed.) SSDBM 2009. LNCS, vol. 5566, pp. 237–254. Springer, Heidelberg (2009)

[32] Gadelha, L., Mattoso, M., Wilde, M., Foster, I.: Provenance Query Patterns for Many-Task Scientific Computing. In: USENIX Workshop on the Theory and Practice of Provenance (TaPP), Heraklion, Crete, Greece (2011)

[33] Zhao, Y., Hategan, M., Clifford, B., Foster, I., von Laszewski, G., Nefedova, V., Raicu, I., Stef-Praun, T., Wilde, M.: Swift: Fast, Reliable, Loosely Coupled Parallel Computation. In: 3rd IEEE World Congress on Services, Salt Lake City, USA, pp. 199–206 (2007)

Network Analysis on Provenance Graphs
from a Crowdsourcing Application

Mark Ebden[1], Trung Dong Huynh[2], Luc Moreau[2],
Sarvapali Ramchurn[2], and Stephen Roberts[1]

[1] Department of Engineering Science, University of Oxford,
Oxford, OX1 3PJ, United Kingdom
{mebden,sjrob}@robots.ox.ac.uk
www.robots.ox.ac.uk/~parg
[2] Electronics and Computer Science, University of Southampton,
Southampton, SO17 1BJ, United Kingdom
{tdh,l.moreau,sdr}@ecs.soton.ac.uk
www.ecs.soton.ac.uk

Abstract. Crowdsourcing has become a popular means for quickly achieving various tasks in large quantities. CollabMap is an online mapping application in which we crowdsource the identification of evacuation routes in residential areas to be used for planning large-scale evacuations. So far, approximately 38,000 micro-tasks have been completed by over 100 contributors. In order to assist with data verification, we introduced provenance tracking into the application, and approximately 5,000 provenance graphs have been generated. They have provided us various insights into the typical characteristics of provenance graphs in the crowdsourcing context. In particular, we have estimated probability distribution functions over three selected characteristics of these provenance graphs: the node degree, the graph diameter, and the densification exponent. We describe methods to define these three characteristics across specific combinations of node types and edge types, and present our findings in this paper. Applications of our methods include rapid comparison of one provenance graph versus another, or of one style of provenance database versus another. Our results also indicate that provenance graphs represent a suitable area of exploitation for existing network analysis tools concerned with modelling, prediction, and the inference of missing nodes and edges.

1 Introduction

Crowdsourcing is an increasingly popular approach for tasks that computers find too difficult to solve; the method distributes tasks among human contributors, often through a website. For instance, citizen-science projects at Zooniverse (www.zooniverse.org) have managed to enlist hundreds of thousands of volunteer "citizen scientists" to classify distant galaxies, transcribe historical naval logs, and more. The volunteers contribute data of a quality that is as varied as their backgrounds and expertise. Usually cross-verification among participants helps to discard inaccurate results, yet challenges remain in anticipating how different human contributors will behave and in designing a robust crowdsourcing application.

P. Groth and J. Frew (Eds.): IPAW 2012, LNCS 7525, pp. 168–182, 2012.

CollabMap (www.collabmap.org) is an online mapping application in which we crowdsource the task of identifying residential evacuation routes, with the eventual aim of helping to plan large-scale evacuations in case of disaster. In an effort to address the aforementioned human challenges, we introduced provenance tracking into CollabMap, capturing in detail how contributors trace buildings and draw evacuation routes, and noting the dependencies among their contributions. The resulting provenance graphs allow us to re-create the situations in which the data were generated and to inspect them for potential inaccuracies. In order to gain an understanding of the common characteristics of these graphs, here we carry out an analytical study on various network measures and report our findings. Other researchers have viewed provenance graphs in alternate ways: Altintas et al. [1] have analysed them as collaboration networks, and Margo et al. [11] have used them as a basis for node classification. The present work offers a deeper level of mathematical abstraction, and our contributions are twofold. First, we estimate probability distribution functions over three selected characteristics of these provenance graphs: the node degree, the graph diameter, and the densification exponent; to our knowledge we are the first to analyse provenance graphs in this way. Second, we devise provenance-specific network measures for provenance graphs, to gauge whether such measures provide a novel insight into provenance graphs, or whether generic network measures are enough. We are also exploring the question of whether provenance graphs, at least those from crowdsourcing contexts, are suitable candidates for existing network methods that support graph modelling, prediction, and the inference of missing nodes and edges.

The remainder of the paper is organized as follows. Section 2 provides a summary of the CollabMap application, including how it works and how provenance was modelled. In Section 3, we describe a range of techniques to extract characteristics from the CollabMap provenance graphs. Section 4 reports our main findings, and the paper is concluded with a discussion in Section 5.

2   CollabMap

In planning the responses to city-wide disaster scenarios, simulating large-scale evacuation is a major challenge, owing in part to the lack of detailed evacuation maps for residential areas. These maps need to contain evacuation routes connecting building exits to the road network, while avoiding physical obstacles such as walls or fences. Existing maps do not provide such routes. To our knowledge, automated techniques to augment current maps with such paths are not available, and direct surveys of city-scale residential areas are usually infeasible owing to the significant effort required. Against this background, CollabMap was developed to crowdsource the drawing of evacuation routes for the public by providing them with two freely available sources of information from Google Maps: aerial imagery and ground-level panoramic views. During a recent two-month trial on the website we established, contributors were awarded cash-prize lottery tickets in proportion to the number of contributions they made. Our ongoing application has so far produced 5,128 provenance graphs for 37,931 micro-tasks completed by over 100 contributors.

2.1   CollabMap Workflow

Based on the Find-Fix-Verify pattern [3], we divide the task of identifying evacuation routes for a single building into smaller activities, called *micro-tasks*, carried out by different contributors. We have designed five types of micro-task:

A. **Building Identification.** The outline of a building is drawn on the map. It serves as the basis for the other micro-tasks.
B. **Building Verification.** The building outline is assessed, with a vote of either valid (+1) or invalid (−1).
C. **Route Identification.** An evacuation route is drawn, to connect an exit of the building to a nearby road.
D. **Route Verification.** The evacuation route is assessed, with a vote of either valid (+1) or invalid (−1).
E. **Completion Verification.** The set of evacuation routes is assessed for exhaustiveness, with a vote of either complete (+1) or incomplete (−1).

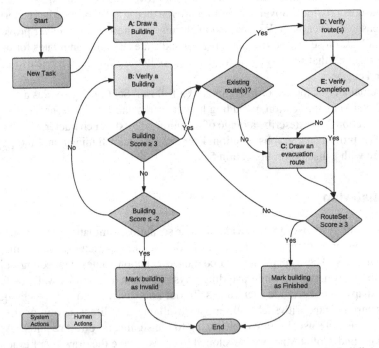

Fig. 1. The CollabMap workflow for identifying evacuation routes of a building

The CollabMap workflow (Figure 1) has two main phases:

Building phase. The outline of a building that has no evacuation route needs to be drawn (**A**). The outline is then checked by other contributors, who vote up or vote down the building outline (**B**) without seeing others' votes. If the total score of the

building, defined as the sum of all the votes, reaches $+3$ then the Building phase
ends and the Evacuation route phase begins. If the score reaches -2, the building
outline is rejected and marked as invalid.

Evacuation route phase. This is the main activity carried out by CollabMap contributors. The first is permitted only to draw a route (**C**). Subsequent contributors are
asked to verify routes (**D**) and are asked whether the set of routes is complete (**E**);
if it is not, they are invited to draw new routes (**C**).

In both phases, in order to avoid biases, a contributor is not allowed to verify his or her
own work.

2.2 Recording Provenance

We adopted the Open Provenance Model (OPM) [13] for capturing the provenance of
data generated in the CollabMap application. The micro-tasks in the previous section
generate data of four different types: building outlines, evacuation routes, route sets
(collections of routes belonging to a building), and votes. The classes for these data
types are **Building Outline**, **Route**, **Route Set**, and **Vote**, respectively (see Figure 2).
In order to keep separate the application-specific data from the provenance-related information, OPM constructs were recorded in their own classes: **Artefact** representing
a data entity (via the *subject* relation), **Agent** a CollabMap contributor, and **Process** an
instance of one of the five types of micro-task above.

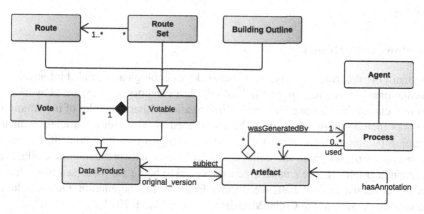

Fig. 2. The UML class model for CollabMap's data and provenance classes. **Data Product** and
Votable are abstract classes.

When a contributor completes a micro-task, this is recorded as a process along with
timing information (namely, how long it takes; see Figure 3 for an example). We also
record the artefacts (equivalently, the corresponding data products) that were generated by the process (via the *wasGeneratedBy* relation), and we record which existing
artefacts were shown to the contributor in the micro-task (via the *used* relation). Own
knowledge of the internal workings of CollabMap also enabled us to assert various

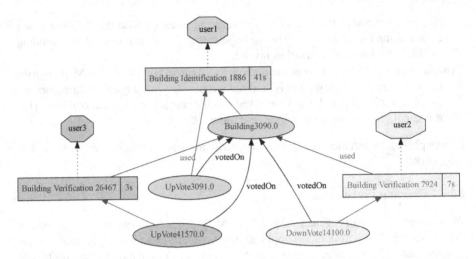

Fig. 3. An example OPM provenance graph recorded by CollabMap showing a building was drawn and voted on by three different users

direct relations between artefacts (via the *hasAnnotation* relation in Figure 2): *wasDerivedFrom*, *wasRevisionOf*, *includes*, and *votedOn*. The last three are special cases of the *wasDerivedFrom* relation, and were treated as such in our analyses in subsequent sections.

2.3   Provenance Graphs

Newman [14] describes four types of network: technological, social, biological, and informational. Provenance graphs fall into the last category, as they are networks describing relationships among elements of information. Other examples of informational networks include those which describe co-authorship of academic articles, semantic relationships among words, and peer-to-peer exchanges of online content. Using the vocabulary associated with the collection of relational network data, our CollabMap provenance graph data are *enumerated* as opposed to being partial or sampled; that is, they are collected in an exhaustive manner from the full population. Our population concerns the totality of the CollabMap data set as of March 2012.

We create a graph $G = (V, E)$, with vertex set V and edge set E. Edges in the present work are unweighted and directed, but our design is extensible to weighted edges, to indicate reliability of connection or other probabilistic phenomena. Five edge types are defined by the OPM: *used*, *wasGeneratedBy*, *wasControlledBy*, *wasDerivedFrom*, and *wasTriggeredBy*. In the current work we recorded all but the last of these, in addition to all three possible node types: artefacts, processes, and agents. Node type is the only vertex attribute currently under study in our provenance graphs, but it is possible to assign additional attributes, either discrete (for example a classification indicating the level of experience of each agent), or continuous (for example, a probabilistic estimate of how often an agent errs during the evaluation of route evacuations).

(a)   b)

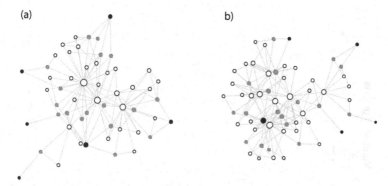

Fig. 4. Provenance graphs for two typical CollabMap tasks, in which artefacts are white, processes are grey, and agents are black. Vertex size increases with degree logarithmically.

To aid graph visualization in Figure 4, vertices in V are represented as circles coloured by node type, and edges in E are represented as straight lines. The graph is drawn in two-dimensional space, but it is possible to imagine the same information appearing in three-dimensional space or on another surface. Vertices are situated according to the Kamada-Kawai free-energy technique in Pajek software [2]. Vertex size is proportional to $\log(d + 3)$, where d is node degree.

The graph in Figure 4(a) contains 54 vertices after 18 processes occurred (18 microtasks), while that in Figure 4(b) contains 59 vertices after the same number of processes occurred. The maximum number of processes occurring in a given provenance graph was 70. Figure 5 gives the distribution of provenance graphs over their maximum process index; it indicates that the majority of tasks were edited at least seven times, and 288 graphs were edited twenty times or more.

3   Methods

To compare the 5,128 networks with those described in the literature, and to see whether the characteristics ascertained from network analysis might be useful, we selected a subset of network properties to investigate. We chose three properties that have been used elsewhere in the analysis of both real and synthetic graphs [10]. They are as follows:

Degree distribution: For many graphs, the degree distribution follows a 'power law' such that the number of vertices N_d with degree d is given by $N_d \propto d^{-\gamma}$, where $\gamma > 0$ is usually called the power-law exponent. We shall examine the degree distribution of an entire provenance graph, and subdivide this into several distributions based on the four edge types and their directionality. In summarizing the information in such plots, we refer to γ as the degree-distribution power-law exponent (DPE), calculated according the method of Clauset *et al.* [5] concentrating on nodes with high degree.

Diameter: The diameter of a graph is the greatest minimum distance between any two nodes. Most real-world graphs exhibit relatively small diameter (the "small-world"

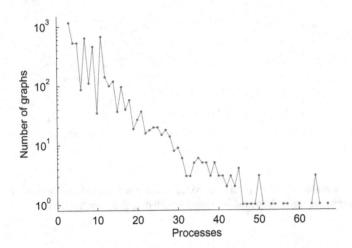

Fig. 5. A plot of the number of CollabMap provenance graphs that contained any given number of processes (micro-tasks)

phenomenon [12]) which tends to stabilize as the number of vertices in a network grows over time (here, as processes occur). Since CollabMap nodes are separated by directed edges, thereby preventing some nodes from forming a path to certain others, strictly speaking the diameter of each graph is infinite; however, by temporarily assuming the edges are undirected, we are able to calculate a diameter and we record its value after each process (micro-task) occurs. In addition, we return to the directed graph to calculate a useful variation on graph diameter: Dijkstra's algorithm [6] provides the minimum path length separating each pair of nodes, and we consider the distribution of the cases in which this path length was a finite number. This distribution determines the maximum finite distance (which we shall refer to as MFD) from one node type to another. We calculate the values of MFD on full provenance graphs as well as on the corresponding data-flow graphs — that is, graphs with only artefacts and *wasDerivedFrom* edges, with no processes involved.

Densification: As a network evolves over time, it generally becomes denser. This can be quantified by comparison of the number of edges to the number of nodes, after each process occurs. The relation between the number of edges $E(t)$ and the number of vertices $N(t)$ in an evolving network after process t ordinarily obeys the densification power law, which states that $E(t) \propto N(t)^a$ for some densification exponent a typically greater than unity [9]. In our provenance graphs, we have chosen to also specialize this relation by node type and by edge type, noting Pearson's product-momentum correlation coefficient in each case. We refer to each coefficient as the edge-to-node correlation (ENC).

Our descriptions of the above three properties have indicated that many graphs which have been studied elsewhere in the literature have a degree distribution following a power law, have small diameter which stabilizes eventually, and become denser over time in a manner that follows a power law as well. To summarize, our methodology for analysing these three properties on each provenance graph results in several plots and includes the following three metrics: DPE, MFD, and ENC.

4 Results and Discussion

We now present the results from the analyses described in the above section for the provenance graph depicted in Figure 4(a) and for the largest provenance graph. In addition, we carried out the same analyses for the whole population of 5,128 provenance graphs recorded by CollabMap and summarize their results here.

4.1 Degree Distribution

Figures 6(a) and (b) plot degree distributions (histograms depicting how many nodes had a certain number of interconnections) which were typical of those for the provenance graphs under study. The tails (high-degree data) conceivably follow a power law, although the low-degree data points (here, for node degrees fewer than three) lie below this trend; this is a pattern observed in many networks elsewhere [15]. The degree-distribution power-law exponents (DPE) for the data in these two figures were 2.1 and 2.0. Over the 5,128 graphs we examined, the mean DPE was 2.4, with a standard deviation of 0.2. In comparison, elsewhere in the literature values tend to fall between 1.4 [15] and 4.3 [5], with the vast majority between 2 and 3 [15]. The full distribution, given in Figure 6(c), is clearly multi-modal; this is because some of the provenance graphs under investigation were small, and the calculation of DPE is only reliable for large graphs. We found that restricting the analysis to graphs with a minimum size of 40 nodes (recognizing that the maximum number of nodes in a graph was 271) led to the emergence of a peak near DPE = 2.2. In summary, our graphs tended to follow a power law, and the values of DPE were in the typical range.

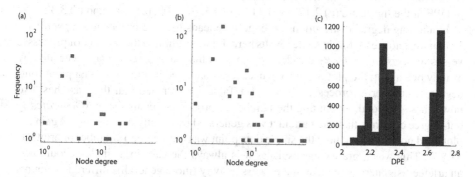

Fig. 6. (a) Distribution of node degrees for the typical provenance graph shown in Figure 4(a). (b) A similar distribution for the largest provenance graph. (c) Degree-distribution power-law exponent (DPE) for all 5,128 provenance graphs.

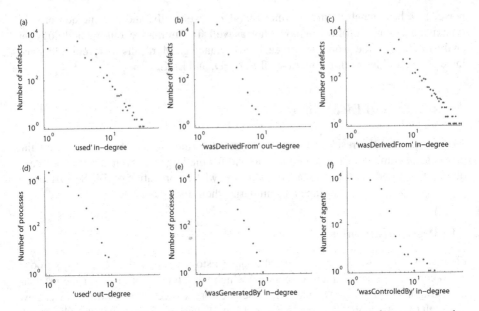

Fig. 7. Degree distributions according to edge type. As the graphs are logarithmic, zeros cannot be plotted; the number of nodes corresponding to zero in-degree or zero out-degree were as follows: (a) 45,194; (b) 5,128; (c) 44,390; (d) 5,157; (e) 34; (f) 0.

Figure 7 shows the degree distribution specialized according to edge type. This figure is probably one of the most useful from a provenance point of view. Since we take into account the directedness of the graph edges in this particular analysis, we can differentiate between 'out-degree' (the number of edges leaving a node; for example, the out-degree of a process is incremented for each artefact it becomes connected to via a *used* edge) and 'in-degree' (the number of edges directed towards a node). In each of the six distributions, the tails can again be well fitted by a power law, with an exponent (DPE) ranging from 1.9 to 4.1. Specifically, from Table 1 it is apparent that the values of DPE in the figure are (a) 2.17, (b) 4.11, (c) 1.86, (d) 3.09, (e) 3.02, and (f) 3.32.

Examining degree distributions by edge type leads to more provenance-specific information, and we highlight some results here. First, examining the number of processes versus the *wasControlledBy* out-degree confirms that each process was controlled by exactly one agent; the plot is not shown since it contained just this one data point (out-degree 1, number of processes 37,931); in Table 1 it is noted that this case has "No power law". Second, examining the number of processes versus the *wasGeneratedBy* out-degree confirms that each artefact was generated by exactly one process. Again the plot need not be shown; here the single data point was out-degree 1, number of artefacts 58,877. This was a gratifying result, as it is always the case in a single account that an artefact is generated by a single process/activity (more generally, different accounts may model what happened from different viewpoints, and the same entity may be recorded as generated from two different processes in two accounts). This confirmation would not be pertinent to normal CollabMap users, but it could be of use to developers

Table 1. Values of the degree-distribution power-law exponent (DPE) for the four types of node inter-connection, when power laws were observed

	used	wasGeneratedBy	wasControlledBy	wasDerivedFrom
in-degree	2.17	3.02	3.32	1.86
out-degree	3.09	(No power law)	(No power law)	4.11

wishing to check the accuracy of the implementation of their software. Third, let us consider the fact that the degree distribution for artefacts is essentially determined by the number of times an artefact is reused. From the distribution in Figure 7(a), we found the average in-degree was 0.80, and the conclusion to draw from this is that each arte-fact was used slightly less than once, on average. Additionally, the range of in-degrees was 0–35; hence some artefacts were used very heavily while some artefacts were not used at all. The latter are mostly user votes (over 43,000), which were recorded for data verification at a later stage and not currently used in any of the micro-tasks. Artefacts that were used at all were used an average of 3.4 times. Similar analysis applies to the other plots in Figure 7.

4.2 Graph Diameter

Figure 8 plots the evolution of graph diameter (the maximum separation between any two nodes) as more and more processes occur. It shows that graph diameter tended to increase quickly for the first few processes before settling to a stable value. Results over all 5,128 provenance graphs are shown in Figure 9. Growth is rapid until approximately the seventh process; thenceforth there is a slow, approximately linear increase in graph diameter. The plots in their entirety are sub-linear. In comparison, in many graphs the diameter grows approximately logarithmically with the number of nodes [4], which is of course another sub-linear pattern, and hence qualitative similarities exist. We have begun to show that the dynamics of provenance graphs bear some resemblance to those of other networks in the literature.

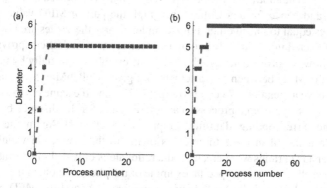

Fig. 8. Plot of diameter versus process number for **(a)** a typical provenance graph, and **(b)** the largest provenance graph

We have also noted a slight difference, one which is due to the type of expansion expected of a provenance graph: the number of artefacts in a chain growing with each process is a complicated function that nonetheless should in many cases contain a small linear term; this in turn leads to the slightly unusual phenomenon of linear growth after a certain number of processes occur. More specifically, revisiting the workflow description in Section 2, consider that the provenance graph depicted in Figure 3 (with a diameter of four) has the capacity to expand downwards through, for example, *wasRevisionOf* edges. If the artefacts downstream are used by processes controlled by agents who have contributed previously to the task, the diameter will not increase, because the agents will have high degree and will act as 'hubs' keeping all nodes within short reach of one another. On the other hand, if new agents control the processes using these downstream artefacts, there is nothing to prevent graph diameter from growing steadily as more and more downstream artefacts appear. Therefore, the linear growth observed in Figure 9 after approximately the seventh process is an indication that, among other things, a fresh supply of agents is readily available, which is the case for crowdsourcing applications in particular.

Recall from Section 3 that the path length between a pair of provenance nodes is measured by the number of directed edges to be traversed in order to travel from one node to another, and the calculation of most path-length data necessitates first ignoring the node pairs with infinite path length between them. Among the remaining node pairs, the maximal finite distance (MFD) between any two processes in a graph was between 1 and 13 edges, inclusive, and the mean was 2.73 edges. The usefulness of this number becomes apparent only when seen in the context of others — namely, the distance required to go from an artefact to a process. In the latter case, the MFD was also 2.73, and hence, the separation statistics were identical in these two cases. This equality is due to the manner in which the CollabMap provenance graphs were created. Under the OPM, two processes are not connected directly but are linked via artefacts. The second process, i.e. the one using the intermediate artefact, will have generated artefacts of its own; hence these artefacts will be separated from the first process by the same distance (i.e. two edges) that exists between the two processes. This is particular to CollabMap, because when an artefact is connected to a process via *wasGeneratedBy*, and that process uses a second artefact, there is always a *wasDerivedFrom* link between the two artefacts. The motif that results (two edges long) is repeated as the provenance graph grows, and hence for any CollabMap graph the pair of MFD values described here are always equal to one another. For example, clearly the values are both 2 for the small graph depicted in Figure 3. In summary, mean separation data can provide a rapid indication of how the provenance graph model was established initially by its designer.

Similarly, the MFD between two artefacts in a given CollabMap provenance graph was found to have a mean of 1.74 edges (range: 1–12), and the same can be said for the distance required to go from a process to an artefact, and for the distance between two artefacts in the corresponding 'data-flow graph' (see Section 3). Again, the separation statistics were identical in these three cases owing to the manner in which the CollabMap provenance graphs were created. The rationale is only a slight variation on the motif described above, and as a specific example of the phenomenon, in the provenance graph depicted in Figure 3 the MFD between two artefacts and the MFD going from

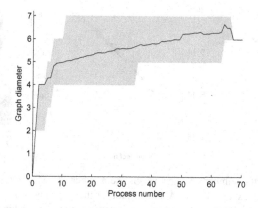

Fig. 9. Evolution of graph diameter with the number of processes (micro-tasks) that have oc-curred, for up to 5,128 CollabMap provenance graphs. The solid line indicates the mean, and the shaded region indicates the point-wise range of values. The number of graphs available for analysis after each process is given in Figure 5.

a process to an artefact are both equal to 1. In an arbitrary provenance graph outside of the CollabMap project, there may exist a different relationship among the MFDs rather than equality; hence, this relationship provides another measure characterizing the design of a provenance graph model. It is necessary to confirm this by repeating the calculation of MFDs on provenance graphs from other applications.

4.3 Densification

Figures 10(a) and 10(b) are included to show densification — that is, the manner in which the number of edges increases with the number of nodes as a graph grows over time. The two logarithmic plots show only minor deviations from the straight line of a power law, and this pattern was typical among the provenance graphs we examined. The densification power-law exponents for these two selected provenance graphs were 1.33 and 1.23, respectively. Over all 5,128 graphs, the mean exponent was 1.31 with a standard deviation of 0.07, and the range was 1.14–1.59. In comparison, the value seen in other networks is never less than unity in a connected graph [10] and typically falls between 1.0 and 1.7 [9]. The full distribution, given in Figure 10(c), is multi-modal as before; however, we found that restricting the analysis to graphs with a minimum size of 40 led to the emergence of a single peak around 1.3. This peak is close to, for example, the value of 1.26 reported by Leskovec *et al.* [8,9] for a person-to-person re-commendation network built from data provided by an online retailer, in which nodes represent users and edges represent recommendations (each time a user purchased a product, they were given the option to send emails recommending the item to friends). More generally, that our results fit in the typical range of 1.0 to 1.7 suggests that proven-ance graphs grow in a manner that has similarities with other graphs. In addition, the observed standard deviation (0.07) was relatively small, which is related to the fact that the provenance graphs grew in a structured manner with each micro-task.

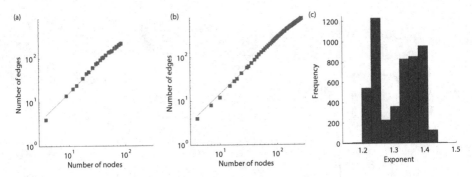

Fig. 10. (a) A plot of the number of edges versus the number of nodes in the provenance graph depicted in Figure 4(a), as it grows. (b) A similar plot for the largest provenance graph. (c) A histogram of the densification exponent a, which is a factor influencing the edge-to-node correlation (ENC), over all 5,128 provenance graphs.

We turn to the values of edge-to-node correlation (ENC), which reflect the densification pattern for particular edge types versus particular node types. Table 2 describes the ENC values among the three node types and the four edge types. In all twelve cases, high values of ENC were observed, which explains the very good line of fit in Figures 10(a) and 10(b). Additionally, there is a deterministic, precisely linear relationship between the number of artefacts and the number of *wasGeneratedBy* edges, or between the number of processes and the number of *wasControlledBy* edges, leading to ENC=1 in either case. This meets with intuition, as each process in CollabMap is linked exactly once to an agent, and (as stated previously) each artefact is generated by exactly one process.

Table 2. Edge-to-node correlation (ENC) coefficients between the number of edges and the number of nodes in a growing graph, averaged over the 5,128 tasks. The three node types are listed on the left and the four edge types are at the top.

	used	*wasGeneratedBy*	*wasControlledBy*	*wasDerivedFrom*
artefact	0.9888	1.0000	0.9929	0.9990
process	0.9948	0.9929	1.0000	0.9894
agent	0.9707	0.9809	0.9807	0.9771

5   Conclusion

In the course of analysing data from a crowdsourcing application, we have highlighted several graph-theoretic metrics to characterize provenance graphs, including DPE, MFD, and ENC. Our first key finding is that CollabMap provenance data possess characteristics similar to those existing in other graphs studied in the literature, including social networks and the World Wide Web [10]. Our second key finding is that our data set is amenable to tools more specific to provenance: our metrics can be used to compare and classify provenance graphs, to help quickly confirm that provenance was recorded properly, and so on.

The first key finding is important because the similarities we have identified indicate that provenance graphs represent a suitable area of exploitation for network analysis tools concerned with modelling, prediction, and inference which exist already in the literature [7]. For example, since the mid-2000s interest has been growing in 'community detection' — that is, identifying groups of nodes that are more densely linked to each other than to the rest of the network. Users in CollabMap (represented as agent nodes) should not form such communities since tasks are assigned at random, and therefore to the extent that community structure is discerned a pathological case is likely. As an example of such a case, CollabMap users have the option to forgo a task and move on to another, thereby allowing them to focus on particular types of task if desired; hence a group of users could agree among themselves to each skip tasks until they recognized a building or buildings of common interest (for example, in a neighbourhood they disliked). The user group could then corroborate each others' bogus building evacuation routes. Community-detection algorithms such as those based on non-negative matrix factorization [16] could help to alert CollabMap designers to inappropiate levels of community structure within the provenance graph, and thus identify and prevent ill-intentioned collaboration among users. As another example, elsewhere we are in the course of developing a link-inference algorithm based on our results here, to assist with the analysis of incomplete provenance graphs.

The second key finding is important because the set of provenance-specific measures from network analysis so far is useful in its own right, in verification and classification, for example. We have shown how degree distributions can be used to confirm provenance graphs were constructed properly, and the plots in Figure 7 illustrate how further properties in a provenance database can be summarized. Other characteristics we have calculated are the maximum path lengths separating given types of nodes, and densification information. In all of the above, the analysis could have been performed on provenance graphs one at a time rather than on an entire database; a useful application of doing so would be to assist the principled comparison of one provenance graph with another. For example, insofar as our metrics are related to completeness and error probability, they can be used in the process of automated verification of the crowdsourced evacuation routes (e.g. confirming that the editing processes were likely to reduce errors acceptably). In machine-learning terminology, the metrics represent the result of 'feature extraction' and as such they have the potential to help learn the differences between high-error graphs and low-error graphs. In general the metrics are of potential use in future software applications which aim to classify tasks based on their provenance graphs.

Acknowledgements. We gratefully acknowledge funding from the UK Research Council for project 'Orchid', grant EP/I011587/1.

References

1. Altintas, I., Anand, M.K., Crawl, D., Bowers, S., Belloum, A., Missier, P., Ludäscher, B., Goble, C.A., Sloot, P.M.A.: Understanding Collaborative Studies through Interoperable Workflow Provenance. In: McGuinness, D.L., Michaelis, J.R., Moreau, L. (eds.) IPAW 2010. LNCS, vol. 6378, pp. 42–58. Springer, Heidelberg (2010)

2. Batagelj, V., Mrvar, A.: Pajek-program for large network analysis. Connections 21(2), 47–57 (1998)
3. Bernstein, M.S., Little, G., Miller, R.C., Hartmann, B., Ackerman, M.S., Karger, D.R., Crowell, D., Panovich, K., Arbor, A.: Soylent: A Word Processor with a Crowd Inside. In: Artificial Intelligence, pp. 313–322 (2010)
4. Chung, F., Lu, L.: The average distances in random graphs with given expected degrees. Proc. Natl. Acad. Sci. USA 99, 15879–15882 (2002)
5. Clauset, A., Shalizi, C., Newman, M.: Power-law distributions in empirical data. SIAM Review 51, 661–703 (2009)
6. Dijkstra, E.W.: A note on two problems in connexion with graphs. Numerische Mathematik 1(1), 269–271 (1959)
7. Kolaczyk, E.: Statistical Analysis of Network Data. Springer (2009)
8. Leskovec, J., Adamic, L., Huberman, B.: The dynamics of viral marketing. In: ACM Conference on Electronic Commerce (2006)
9. Leskovec, J., Kleinberg, J., Faloutsos, C.: Graph evolution: Densification and shrinking diameters. ACM Transactions on Knowledge Discovery from Data 1(1), 2 (2007)
10. Leskovec, J., Chakrabarti, D., Kleinberg, J., Faloutsos, C., Ghahramani, Z.: Kronecker Graphs: An Approach to Modeling Networks. Journal of Machine Learning Research 11, 985–1042 (2010)
11. Margo, D., Smogor, R.: Using provenance to extract semantic file attributes. In: Proceedings of the 2nd Conference on Theory and Practice of Provenance, TAPP 2010, p. 7. USENIX Association, Berkeley (2010)
12. Milgram, S.: The small world problem. Psychology Today 1, 61–67 (1967)
13. Moreau, L., Clifford, B., Freire, J., Futrelle, J., Gil, Y., Groth, P., Kwasnikowska, N., Miles, S., Missier, P., Myers, J., Plale, B., Simmhan, Y., Stephan, E., Van den Bussche, J.: The Open Provenance Model core specification (v1.1). Future Generation Computer Systems (July 2010)
14. Newman, M.E.J.: The structure and function of complex networks. SIAM Review 45(2), 58 (2003)
15. Newman, M.: Networks: an introduction. Oxford University Press (2010)
16. Psorakis, I., Roberts, S., Ebden, M., Sheldon, B.: Overlapping community detection using Bayesian nonnegative matrix factorization. Physical Review E 83(6), 066114 (2011)

Modelling Provenance
Using Structured Occurrence Networks

Paolo Missier, Brian Randell, and Maciej Koutny

Newcastle University, School of Computing Science,
Newcastle upon Tyne, UK
`firstname.lastname@cs.ncl.ac.uk`

Abstract. Occurrence Nets (ON) are directed acyclic graphs that represent causality and concurrency information concerning a single execution of a system. Structured Occurrence Nets (SONs) extend ONs by adding new relationships, which provide a means of recording the activities of multiple interacting, and evolving, systems. Although the initial motivations for their development focused on the analysis of system failures, their structure makes them a natural candidate as a model for expressing the execution traces of interacting systems. These traces can then be exhibited as the provenance of the data produced by the systems under observation. In this paper we present a number of patterns that make use of SONs to provide principled modelling of provenance. We discuss some of the benefits of this modelling approach, and briefly compare it with others that have been proposed recently. SON-based modelling of provenance combines simplicity with expressiveness, leading to provenance graphs that capture multiple levels of abstraction in the description of a process execution, are easy to understand and can be analysed using the partial order techniques underpinning their behavioural semantics.

1 Introduction

Structured Occurrence Nets (SONs) [KR09, Ran11] are a formalism that provides a means of recording the activities of a set of interacting, and evolving, systems. They were initially developed to address problems of validating and synthesizing, and analyzing failures of complex, evolving computer-based systems. SONs are an extension of Occurrence Nets (ON) [BD87], which are "acyclic Petri nets that can be used to record execution histories of concurrent systems, in particular, the concurrency and causality relations between events." [KK11]. In fact ONs are suitable for representing the activities of asynchronous systems whose design is expressed in various different notations, not just Petri Nets; indeed they have, since their invention in the 1970s, been re-invented, and re-named, by many different research communities, e.g. as "strand spaces" by security researchers [KR09], and as "message sequence charts" [HT04] by networking researchers. Moreover, they can be used for modelling the observed or envisaged behaviour of systems whose design is not available, eg. the undocumented process of papers selection and review associated with some publications.

P. Groth and J. Frew (Eds.): IPAW 2012, LNCS 7525, pp. 183–197, 2012.

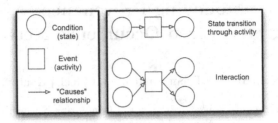

Fig. 1. Basic graphical ON notation

In this paper we show how SONs provide a suitable formal grounding to express the provenance of data that is produced or consumed by multiple interacting systems.

Although SONs can be expressed set-theoretically, in this paper we choose to use a simpler and more immediate graph representation, and completely avoid formal definitions, which can be found in [KR09]. As shown in Fig. 1, the basic ON formalism is very simple. Circles represent conditions (i.e. the holding of a state); an event, represented by a box, can be caused by one or more conditions, and can result in one or more new conditions. Since the arcs are intended to represent causality, ONs must be acyclic directed graphs. In addition, well-formed ONs are defined by two rules, portrayed in the right part of the figure (see Def. 1 in [KR09]): events have at least one incoming arc and one outgoing arc (top in the figure) and states have at most one input and one output arc (bottom).

Fig. 2 shows a simple ON portraying the execution trace of a process, during which information needed to draft a document about some experiment was acquired. This process may have been pre-defined, but it could also have been merely observed. It includes several activities, two of which ("verify experimental results" and "read paper p2") were concurrent. Labels may be associated to states, but they have no formal meaning in the model. In this example, ptd, for "preparing to draft", indicates an initial state for a sequence of actions that lead to a new state, "ready to draft".

An ON is thus simply a means of recording what is observed or believed to have happened, indicating "what caused what". It does not in itself indicate "who" caused a particular event. Rather, the basic formalism implies that the whole of any

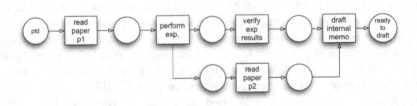

Fig. 2. Simple ON example

given ON represents the (possibly asynchronous) activity of a single un-identified "system" (whose design may or may not have been known). The issue of identifying the various separate systems that together give rise to some given complex activity is one that is addressed by SONs, described in more detail in the next section. Briefly, SONs extend ONs with relationships for describing: (i) *communication* relationships to specify interactions amongst systems; (ii) *behaviour abstraction* relationships, which provide a *dual view between state and system*, whereby a state that appears in one ON unfolds into a whole system, in which internal activities that pertain to that state can be made explicit; and (iii) *temporal abstraction* relationships by which events that appear instantaneous at one level of abstraction, unfold into complex state-event nets at another level. It is worth noting that the formal rules that govern these SON relations take into account the subtle complications that can arise from asynchrony, complications that are not evident in the relatively simple examples shown in the rest of the paper.

In this paper we show how SONs provide a convenient and intuitive formalism for representing data provenance, by introducing modelling patterns that make use of these relationships. A particularly interesting feature exhibited by these patterns is the uniformity of representation of the evolution of data, and *the evolution of the agents that were responsible for performing the activities*. The ability to represent agents as evolving systems has benefits for decision support applications based on provenance. For example, one's provenance-informed judgment on the quality of a document may be affected by the knowledge that the author was aware of certain papers at the time the document was prepared. This knowledge is easily encoded by modelling the author as a system characterized by evolving states, with activities such as "read paper X" that determine state transitions. We give a simple example of this encoding in Sec. 3.3.

1.1 Benefits and Limitations

Some of the benefits expected from this work include seamless modelling of the provenance of data, activities, and agents, all at multiple levels of abstraction. In addition, SONs provide a formal syntax and semantics that will make it possible to carry out formal validation of provenance graphs, including checking whether a temporal logic formula is satisfied, or whether a specific state (or set of states) can ever be reached. This, however, is beyond the scope of this exploratory paper and is left for future work, as is the analysis of the types of queries supported by the model.

Implementation issues, including the encoding of SON graphs in machine-processable form, are being addressed using the WorkCraft platform, developed by the Asynchronous Systems Laboratory at Newcastle[1]. Workcraft provides a flexible, general framework for the visual editing, (co-)simulation and analysis of a variety of Interpreted Graph Models with a common graph structure, including Petri Nets, ONs, gate-level circuits, Static Data Flow Structures and

---

[1] http://www.workcraft.org.

Conditional Partial Order Graphs. Support for SONs that make use of communications relations has recently been added.

1.2 Related Work

The modelling approach proposed in this paper is alternative to others that have been proposed recently, including the Karma model [Sim08], Janus [MSZ⁺10], PASS [HSBMR08], as well as a few that are typically tied to workflow systems, mentioned in Sec. 3.2. While all of these have been developed with particular applications in mind (typically in the area of e-science), the PROV generic model of provenance stands out, as it is, at the time of writing, in the process of crystallizing as a W3C recommendation[2]. PROV follows in the steps of the Open Provenance Model [MCF⁺11].

The PROV approach to modelling provenance is based on the general concept of *entity*, an abstraction for anything that may have a provenance record associated to it, and their relationships to *activities*, which are capable of generating and using entities, and *agents* (including both humans and computer programs) which are responsible for carrying out the activities. A PROV statement is a fact that relates entities to other entities or to activities and agents. For example, one may state that entity e_1 *was derived from* another entity, e_2. A collection of such facts forms a graph of relations that represents an observer's *account* of past interactions amongst the elements mentioned in those facts.

PROV and SON are only superficially similar in the way they represent provenance, differing in at least three main aspects. Firstly, in PROV the notion of causality is deliberately avoided (facts are asserted based on observations or on any form of background knowledge, which is not made explicit), while it is central to the ON and thus the SON models. Secondly, SONs are naturally suited for *modelling the evolution of agents*, because those are simply modelled as systems, a point that is made more concretely in Sec. 3.3. In PROV, modelling agents' evolution is possible in principle, as agents can be viewed as entities themselves, however this involves overloading, or perhaps specializing, the meaning of the `generation` relation (i.e., one could assert that a new version of an agent was "generated by" an activity carried out by the previous version of the same). Finally, and perhaps more importantly, as we will see in the next section SONs extend ONs by introducing a set of relations that provide different forms of abstraction (communication, temporal, behavioural, and spatial). This in turn makes it possible for different abstractions over the same provenance facts to co-exist in the same SONs. In contrast, PROV only defines a single flat space of facts, and completely lacks any mechanism for abstraction[3].

A more detailed comparison between PROV and SON-based provenance regarding these three aspects can be found in Sec. 4. A formal account of the differences between the two approaches is, however, beyond the scope of this paper.

---

[2] PROV will become a W3C recommendation by the end of 2012. The current working draft can be found here: http://www.w3.org/TR/prov-dm/

[3] One can, however, arbitrarily group facts into *bundles*, which can be nested.

1.3   Paper Organization

The rest of the paper is organized as follows. An overview on SONs is provided in the next section, followed in Sec. 3 by the description of SON patterns for modelling provenance. Sec. 5 concludes the paper with a brief discussion on ongoing work.

2   Structured Occurrence Networks

A SON is a set of ONs that are formally related to each other using one or more of a number of different types of relations [KR09]. Here we will make use of just three types of relation, namely behaviour relations, (asynchronous and synchronous) communication relations, and temporal abstraction relations. These provide a direct means of recording which systems give rise to which parts of some overall activity, how these systems interacted during this overall activity, and how these systems have themselves perhaps evolved.

Behaviour relation. The behaviour relation is the means by which some portion of a complex overall activity is associated with a particular system. It embodies the system-state duality alluded to earlier, by allowing the use of the same symbol (a circle representing a condition) at two different levels of (behavioural) abstraction to represent both a system and a state of an activity of that system. Given this, it is then possible to represent an evolving system, and to link appropriate activities to the appropriate versions of this evolving system. This is illustrated in Fig. 3, which uses dashed rectangles to delineate ONs, and portrays the pre- and post-upgrade history of an evolving computer system. The relation is portrayed by a link to the rectangular box enclosing, and hence identifying this set of states and events[4].

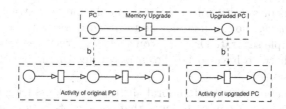

Fig. 3. Duality of systems and states, shown using behavioural abstraction

---

[4] The example refers to a hardware evolution, but it could have equally been a software upgrade. Also, the above example shows offline system evolution, in that there is no direct connection between the final state of the computer's activity pre-evolution and the initial state post-evolution. In contrast, one can use online system evolution, where the final state of an activity pre-evolution is taken as the initial state post-evolution.

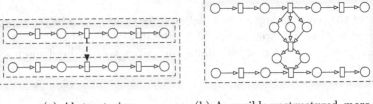

(a) Abstract view   (b) A possible unstructured, more detailed, view of (a)

Fig. 4. Asynchronous communication relation

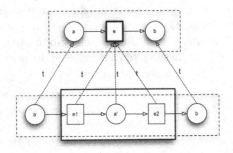

Fig. 5. SON pattern for temporal abstraction

Asynchronous communication relation This relation states a temporal ordering between two events. An example of asynchronous communication between otherwise separate ONs is shown in Fig. 4(a), using a bold dashed arrow[5]. This communication might be very simple, or might in reality be much more complicated, involving sophisticated buffering or networked communication, as in Fig. 4(b).

Asynchronous or synchronous relations[6] enable one to abstract away the details of interactions, should these not be regarded as relevant, and to use a set of relatively simple separate ONs in a conveniently structured representation of what would otherwise have to be shown as an unstructured and hence much more complex single ON.

Temporal abstraction relation Temporal abstraction enables the abbreviation of part of an occurrence net in such a way that some of its actions appear instantaneous to their environment and yet, at a different level of abstraction, they

---

[5] Note that such an arrow connects two events, whereas the directed arcs in a conventional ON connect an event to a condition or a condition to an event.

[6] Synchronous communication [KR09] is used to indicate that two events in separate ONs are perceived as occurring simultaneously. The fact that such a relation is undirected allows one to relax the rule that any ON (and any SON) must be an acyclic directed graph, without however violating conventional notions of causality. This relation is used later in the paper to model activities with a finite duration (Sec. 3.4).

unfold into a possibly lengthy and complex asynchronous activity. One particular pattern involving temporal abstraction is shown in Fig. 5. In this pattern, event e appears instantaneous in the top view of the system, while it expands into multiple events, namely e_1 and e_2, at the more detailed level at the bottom (the latter represents the temporary existence of an intermediate value a', for example). This pattern is useful when using events, which are instantaneous in ON, to model provenance traces that involve activities with a finite duration (see Section 3.4).

3   SONs Modelling Patterns for Provenance

Here we propose, by means of examples, a set of modelling patterns that make use of SONs for representing the provenance of data associated to processes that are at least partially observable, possibly at multiple levels of abstraction.

3.1   Simple Values Manipulation and Variable Assignment

To focus the ideas, we begin with the simplest case of a sequence of operations that act upon data held in a single variable, shown in the ON of Fig. 6(a). As mentioned earlier, the labels associated to the events, i.e., 'r' for read, 'w' for write, are conventional and have no formal meaning. In this example, they are used to clarify whether the events modify the state of the variable. Here the variable name is left implicit. For the more common case where multiple variables are involved, we propose the pattern of Fig. 6(b), consisting on multiple ONs, one for each variable, each labelled with the variable name and linked together by communication relations. For example, the graph in the figure captures the effect of the composed activity "A:=A+1; A:=A+B; B:=A+B" as a SON consisting of a pair of communicating ONs. This SON records how the various data read and write operations occurred, as well as their partial ordering, making it possible to trace the provenance of any particular recorded data value. (A more complex example could show actual use being made of the data obtained by all the various read operations). In each system included in this SON, the activities that occur during the system's lifetime are exposed, including interactions (asynchronous, in this case) with other systems. In this example, the two systems, for variables A and B, interact using read and write operations. Event A:=A+B in particular depends on the current state of B as well as the state of A. This is represented by the asynchronous communication relation connecting the r event in B's activity, to the w event in A's activity. Similarly, the event B:=B+A receives the current value of A from A's SON to compute the new value for B. Note that conveying the state of the system to another system is one of many possible read events that do not modify the state of the system (printing the value is another, shown in Fig. 6(a)[7]).

---

[7] A printing activity would involve communication with a separate printing system, however there is no obligation to represent such interaction, either because it is not of interest for tracing provenance, or because such level of detail is simply not available.

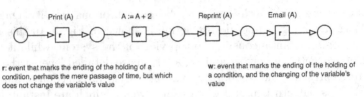

r: event that marks the ending of the holding of a
condition, perhaps the mere passage of time, but which
does not change the variable's value

w: event that marks the ending of the holding of
a condition, and the changing of the variable's
value

(a) Single variable

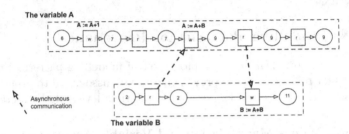

(b) Two variables as interacting systems

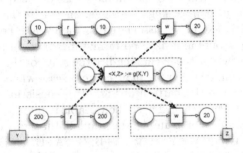

(c) Function application changing the values of
multiple variables

Fig. 6. Capturing the provenance of multiple variables

Expanding on this second example, consider a function application of the
form: $\langle X, Z \rangle := g(X, Y)$, where g doubles the value of its first argument, as well
as of a new variable Z. To capture its execution, we include an additional SON
to represent the function g itself. The resulting pattern is shown in Fig. 6(c).
One advantage of representing g as a system is that its own evolution can be
captured as part of provenance, using behavioural abstraction. We show this
feature in action later (Sec. 3.3).

3.2   Workflow Fragments

The pattern just illustrated in Fig. 6(c) is a stepping stone for modelling the
provenance of data produced by dataflows [LP95], which provide the formal underpinning for a number of workflow systems used across e-science domains and

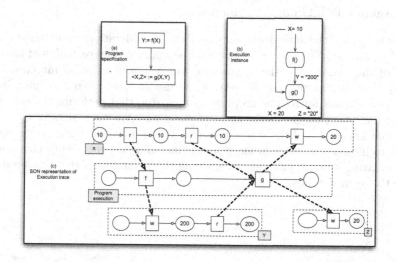

Fig. 7. Dataflow fragment, one execution, and SON portraying the execution trace

applications [DGST09]. A dataflow is a system design (a program) in the form of a graph whose nodes represent executable tasks, and directed arcs denote data dependencies between a source node (producer) and a sink node (consumer). A basic example is given in Fig. 7(a)[8]. Part (b) depicts one execution of this system. The scientific workflow community has been amongst the earliest and most eager to support provenance recording of workflow outputs, motivated by the need to associate an evidence trail to valuable datasets which are destined for publication [ABJF06, MMW11, MPB10, KSM+11]. Provenance is recorded by instrumenting the workflow enactment engine with suitable monitoring
capability.

A possible SON representation of an execution of Fig. 7(b) appears in Fig. 7(c). Note that a choice has been made to model both workflow tasks (the invocation of functions *f* and *g*) as part of the same system, which represents the entire workflow execution. As an alternative, one could associate one SON *to each task*, a modelling choice that makes it possible to capture *the evolution, eg. represented by software updates, of the tasks themselves*. This means that SONs can be used to seamlessly model both workflow execution traces, workflow tasks, and their evolution over time. Only a few other documented provenance data models, including Janus [MSZ+10] and OPMW [GG11] (both of which extend the Open Provenance Model [MCF+11]) and [LLCF10] support the modelling of the dataflow itself, in addition to its execution traces. The VisTrails provenance model [SVKF08] is, to the best of our knowledge, the only model that can describe the evolution of the dataflow, as a tree of its versions.

---

[8] This is a simplified flowchart-like visual depiction. A variety of visual languages are employed in actual systems.

3.3 Agents and Their Provenance

As mentioned in the introduction, one of the considerations that make SONs appealing for encoding execution traces is the uniform representation of the evolution of the data and of the agents that are responsible for its manipulation, namely both as systems (in this setting, we use the term *agent* to refer, informally, to a system, such as a computer or a person, that performs the activities that account for changes in the state of the data). We have already made the point that knowledge of the state of agents, and of how that state evolves in response to interactions with other systems (including other agents), contributes to formulating sensible judgments regarding the reliability of the data products under the agents' control.

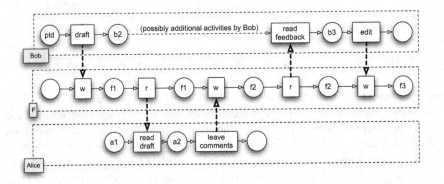

Fig. 8. Alice and Bob collaborate on document editing

Fig. 8 shows an example in which an actor Bob collaborates with Alice in editing a document. The systems modelling follows our familiar pattern: the F ON captures the evolution of the file itself, according to activities that occur in two other ONs ("Bob" and "Alice"). The overall SON unambiguously models the following situation: *"Bob drafts version f1 of file F (he then goes on to perform other activities that are of no interest here). At some later point in time, Alice reads the draft f1 and leaves some comments as part of the same file. This results in a new version f2 of F. Later, Bob reads the comments (this leaves the file unchanged), then performs additional edits which result in the new version f3."* This model makes it explicit that Bob does the edits after reading Alice's feedback, i.e., while he is in state b_3. Contrast this with an alternative model, shown in Fig. 9, in which Bob is unaware of Alice's comments when he performs the editing activity. Arguably, these two models may lead to different conclusions as to the quality of the final document.

An additional advantage of modelling agents within the SON framework (as opposed to other approaches, including PROV) is that behavioural abstraction can be used to expand on the activities that correspond to an agent's state,

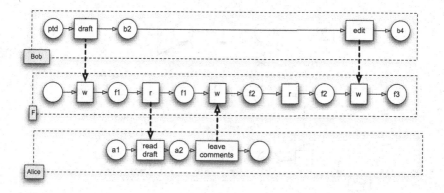

Fig. 9. Bob ignores Alice's comments

thus revealing further details that may be relevant for judgment. This is shown in Fig. 10, where Bob's state `ptd` (preparing-to-draft) expands into a set of activities that describe the preparation phase (shown in Fig. 1 as our initial example). Note that we still do not have a complete picture of how the draft manuscript was produced: for example, we do not know whether the memo was actually used during the drafting of the manuscript. We can, however, easily add this additional information (assuming it is available) by explicitly modelling the internal memo itself as a system, and then adding appropriate communication relations amongst the SONs, using our familiar pattern.

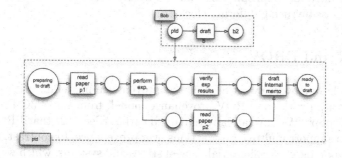

Fig. 10. Bob prepares to draft a manuscript

3.4   Modelling Activities with a Finite Duration

So far we have used ON events, which are by definition instantaneous, to model activities, ignoring that the latter generally span some finite, non-zero time duration. To reconcile this contrast, we introduce a further pattern which makes use of the temporal abstraction relation (see Sec. 2) as shown in Fig. 11.

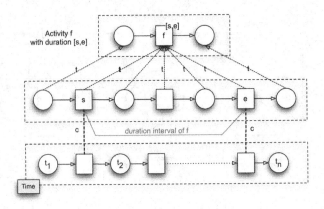

Fig. 11. Representing activities with explicit start and end events, and time

The top ON in the figure includes a new shorthand notation to indicate that activity f is demarcated by start and end events s and e, respectively. This ON is mapped to the one in the middle by way of temporal abstraction relations, following the (graphical) rules set out in Sec. 2. In turn, one can optionally introduce a new ON to represent a time line, and use *synchronous* communication relations to associate a time to events s and e. This type of communication relation appears in [KR09]. It indicates that two events in separate ONs in fact are perceived as occurring simultaneously. Note that this convention leaves the freedom to introduce multiple time lines to account for events seen by different observers, possibly using differing clocks.

4   SON and PROV

We conclude our overview of SON-based provenance modelling with an informal comparison with the PROV provenance model, from the W3C Provenance Working Group[9]. We have already remarked earlier (Sec. 1.2) that PROV is not designed to support multiple abstractions over provenance. In contrast, SONs do this by supporting an explicit dual view of states and systems, which we have described in the paper. We also remarked, in the same section, that it is possible in PROV to model at the same time the evolution of data and of the agents who are responsible for it, a feature we have argued for, but that this involves overloading some of the PROV relations. Indeed, one can assert that agent `ag` was responsible for activity a: `wasAssociatedWith(a,ag)`, that entity `e` was generated by a: `wasGeneratedBy(e,a)`, and because agents can be viewed as entities, which are therefore are entitled to their own provenance, `wasGeneratedBy(ag,a)` is a valid assertion, too. This makes it possible to encode (a simplified version of) the SON fragment of Fig. 9 (reproduced in Fig. 12(a)), as shown in Fig. 12(b).

---

[9] http://www.w3.org/2011/prov/wiki/Main_Page

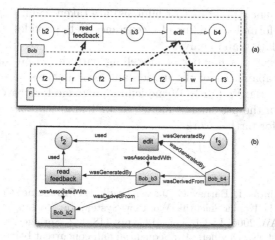

Fig. 12. SON and PROV model fragments for the document editing example

In this encoding, ON states are mapped to PROV entities or agents. In particular, states for agent Bob become agents Bob_b2, Bob_b3, and Bob_b4. Data evolution through an activity is modelled by used(edit,f2) and wasGeneratedBy(f3, edit). Because modelling system evolution is not part of PROV, agent evolution must be encoded using relations such as wasGeneratedBy(Bob_b4, edit), wasDerivedFrom(Bob_b4, Bob_b3). However, f3 and Bob_b4 are now both "outputs" of edit, despite their different nature and role, a confusion that can only be resolved by adding properties to the wasGeneratedBy relations themselves[10].

Other differences concern the use of system communication along with state changes, a SON feature that is missing in PROV and that makes it possible, for example, to expand the communication links into complex system interactions.

5 Conclusions

In this paper we have presented an initial exploration into the use of Structured Occurrence Nets as a model for describing the execution traces of interacting asynchronous systems, and thus as a manifestation of the provenance of data produced and consumed by those systems. Provenance analysis informs the formulation of judgments regarding the quality and reliability of data products. SON-based modelling of provenance makes it possible to view agents, in addition to the data, as evolving interacting systems. This is a distinctive feature of this modelling approach, which leads to potentially more accurate judgments

---

[10] Additonal subtleties make this pattern less than natural: in PROV, from wasDerivedFrom(e2,e1) one can infer the existence of an entity e that used e1 and generated e2. This would be edit, which would therefore both use Bob_b3 and be associated with it.

as the state of agents (programs, or humans) are taken seamlessly into account. In addition, the formal grounding of Occurrence Nets provides a foundation for provenance validation and analysis.

We have presented a number of modelling patterns as an informal demonstration of the capabilities of the model, and Sec. 4 shows an example of how it compares with the W3C PROV modelling language for provenance. A more formal account of the provenance model, as well as a rigorous comparison with PROV, are left for further work.

References

[ABJF06]   Altintas, I., Barney, O., Jaeger-Frank, E.: Provenance Collection Support in the Kepler Scientific Workflow System. In: Moreau, L., Foster, I. (eds.) IPAW 2006. LNCS, vol. 4145, pp. 118–132. Springer, Heidelberg (2006)

[BD87]   Best, E., Devillers, R.: Sequential and concurrent behaviour in Petri net theory. Theoretical Computer Science 55(1), 87–136 (1987)

[DGST09]   Deelman, E., Gannon, D., Shields, M., Taylor, I.: Workflows and e-Science: An overview of workflow system features and capabilities. Future Generation Computer Systems 25(5), 528–540 (2009)

[GG11]   Garijo, D., Gil, Y.: A New Approach for Publishing Workflows: Abstractions, Standards, and Linked Data. In: Proceedings of the Sixth Workshop on Workflows in Support of Large-Scale Science (WORKS 2011), held in conjunction with SC 2011, Seattle, Washington (2011)

[HSBMR08]   Holland, D.A., Seltzer, M.I., Braun, U., Muniswamy-Reddy, K.-K.: PASSing the provenance challenge. Concurrency and Computation: Practice and Experience 20, 531–540 (2008)

[HT04]   Harel, D., Thiagarajan, P.: Message Sequence Charts. In: Lavagno, L., Martin, G., Selic, B. (eds.) UML for Real, pp. 77–105. Springer US (2004)

[KK11]   Kleijn, J., Koutny, M.: Causality in Structured Occurrence Nets. In: Jones, C.B., Lloyd, J.L. (eds.) Dependable and Historic Computing. LNCS, vol. 6875, pp. 283–297. Springer, Heidelberg (2011)

[KR09]   Koutny, M., Randell, B.: Structured Occurrence Nets: A Formalism for Aiding System Failure Prevention and Analysis Techniques. Fundamenta Informaticae 97 (2009)

[KSM+11]   Koop, D., Santos, E., Mates, P., Vo, H.T., Bonnet, P., Bauer, B., Surer, B., Troyer, M., Williams, D.N., Tohline, J.E., Freire, J., Silva, C.T.: A Provenance-Based Infrastructure to Support the Life Cycle of Executable Papers. Procedia CS 4, 648–657 (2011)

[LLCF10]   Lim, C., Lu, S., Chebotko, A., Fotouhi, F.: Prospective and Retrospective Provenance Collection in Scientific Workflow Environments. In: 2010 IEEE International Conference on Services Computing (SCC), pp. 449–456 (July 2010)

[LP95]   Lee, E.A., Parks, T.M.: Dataflow Process Networks. Memorandum 5, UC Berkeley EECS Dept. (1995)

[MCF+11]   Moreau, L., Clifford, B., Freire, J., Futrelle, J., Gil, Y., Groth, P., Kwasnikowska, N., Miles, S., Missier, P., Myers, J., Plale, B., Simmhan, Y., Stephan, E., Van Den Bussche, J.: The Open Provenance Model — Core Specification (v1.1). Future Generation Computer Systems 7(21), 743–756 (2011)

[MMW11]   Marinho, A., Murta, L., Werner, C.: ProvManager: a provenance man-
           agement system for scientific workflows. Concurrency and Computation:
           Practice and Experience, n/a–n/a (2011)
[MPB10]   Missier, P., Paton, N., Belhajjame, K.: Fine-grained and efficient lin-
           eage querying of collection-based workflow provenance. In: Procs. EDBT,
           Lausanne, Switzerland (2010)
[MSZ+10]   Missier, P., Sahoo, S.S., Zhao, J., Goble, C., Sheth, A.: *Janus*: From
           Workflows to Semantic Provenance and Linked Open Data. In: McGuin-
           ness, D.L., Michaelis, J.R., Moreau, L. (eds.) IPAW 2010. LNCS,
           vol. 6378, pp. 129–141. Springer, Heidelberg (2010)
[Ran11]   Randell, B.: Occurrence Nets Then and Now: The Path to Structured
           Occurrence Nets. In: Kristensen, L.M., Petrucci, L. (eds.) PETRI NETS
           2011. LNCS, vol. 6709, pp. 1–16. Springer, Heidelberg (2011)
[Sim08]   Simmhan, Y.L., Plale, B., Gannon, D.: Karma2: Provenance manage-
           ment for data driven workflows. International Journal of Web Services
           Research 5(1) (2008)
[SVKF08]   Scheidegger, C.E., Vo, H.T., Koop, D., Freire, J.: Querying and Re-Using
           Workflows with VisTrails. In: Procs. SIGMOD, pp. 1251–1254 (2008)

DEMO: ourSpaces – A Provenance Enabled Virtual Research Environment

Peter Edwards, Chris Mellish, Edoardo Pignotti, Kapila Ponnamperuma,
Thomas Bouttaz, Alan Eckhardt, Kate Pangbourne, Lorna Philip,
and John Farrington

Computing Science and Geography & Environment, University of Aberdeen,
Aberdeen AB24 5UA, UK
{p.edwards,c.mellish,e.pignotti,k.ponnamperuma,t.bouttaz,a.eckhardt,
k.pangbourne,l.philip,j.farrington}@abdn.ac.uk

Abstract. In this demo we present *ourSpaces*, a Virtual Research Environment designed to support inter-disciplinary research teams. This system has been developed to facilitate collaboration and interaction between researchers by enabling users to create, visualise and manage the provenance of research artefacts and processes.

Keywords: provenance, virtual research environment, eResearch.

1 Introduction

Many of the contemporary challenges facing society such as climate change require researchers from a range of disciplines to work together. Moreover, as scientific research becomes increasingly interdisciplinary in nature, the need for technologies that support collaboration and provide access to heterogeneous data and computational resources becomes ever more critical.

Some of the issues highlighted above have been explored by the PolicyGrid[1] project, a collaboration between human geographers and computer scientists as part of the UK Digital Social Research initiative. As part of this project we have developed *ourSpaces*[2], a web-based virtual research environment which aims to provide a collaboration space for interdisciplinary academic research communities. Groups using *ourSpaces* work in socio-environmental and health-related domains and there are currently around 170 registered users. The system is scalable and, in principle, applicable to any research/policy domain. A screenshot of the *ourSpaces* web interface in presented in Figure 1.

Provenance in *ourSpaces* is crucial in order to support transparency and accountability of the research process by documenting the derivation history of research artefacts. The system utilizes a number of Semantic Web technologies

---

[1] This work is supported by the UK Economic & Social Research Council (ESRC) under the Digital Social Research programme; award RES-149-25-1075.
[2] http://www.ourspaces.net

P. Groth and J. Frew (Eds.): IPAW 2012, LNCS 7525, pp. 198–202, 2012.

such as OWL[3] and RDF[4] in a user interface that shares some of the networking features of on-line social media.

2 Provenance in *ourSpaces*

At the heart of *ourSpaces* is a ontological framework describing different aspects of the provenance of the research process [1]. An extract of this framework is illustrated in Figure 2. In order to support basic provenance we use a Web Ontology Language (OWL) representation of the Open Provenance Model [2]. This ontology defines the primary entities of OPM as well as the causal relationships that link them. OPM is a generic solution and as a result, our framework supports additional domain-specific provenance ontologies that are created by extending the concepts defined in the OPM ontology with domain-specific classes. For example, in a social simulation domain ontology one might have a `Model` as a type of artefact and a `Simulation Experiment` as a type of process. To date we have developed a number of domain-specific provenance ontologies describing aspects of Human Geography and Social Simulation. Using these ontologies it is possible, for example, to describe a physical research activity (e.g. an interview) as an `opm:Process`, and how such an activity causes an `opm:Artifact` to be generated (e.g. interview notes).

For research groups utilising *ourSpaces*, it is important to situate research artefacts and processes alongside people and their associated organisational structures. The current OPM specification supports limited information about a person (agent) controlling a process; there is also little regard for the wider social context. Friend-of-a-Friend[5] (FOAF) is an established RDF vocabulary for describing people and their social networks and we have opted to utilise this within our framework; a `foaf:Profile` is thus a subclass of the `opm:Agent`.

In an environment like *ourSpaces*, online communication is often used to comment about research artefacts or to discuss research issues. Documenting this process in the VRE it is also a crucial requirement for achieving a full and transparent provenance representation. The SIOC[6] (Semantically-Interlinked Online Communities) ontology is designed to describe aspects of online communication by providing a model to express user-generated content such as posting a message in a blog or posting a comment. We have also integrated this vocabulary within our provenance framework, e.g. a `sioc:post` generated by a `foaf:user` can be associated with an `opm:Artifact`, `opm:Process` or `opm:Agent`.

Provenance produced in *ourSpaces* is stored in a repository in the form of RDF statements. Within the system we have developed a service enabling users to visualise short textual descriptions of the provenance of resources. This service translates RDF statements into English sentences, based on the approach described by Bouttaz et al. [3].

---

[3] http://www.w3.org/TR/owl-ref/

[4] http://www.w3.org/RDF/

[5] http://www.foaf-project.org/

[6] http://sioc-project.org/

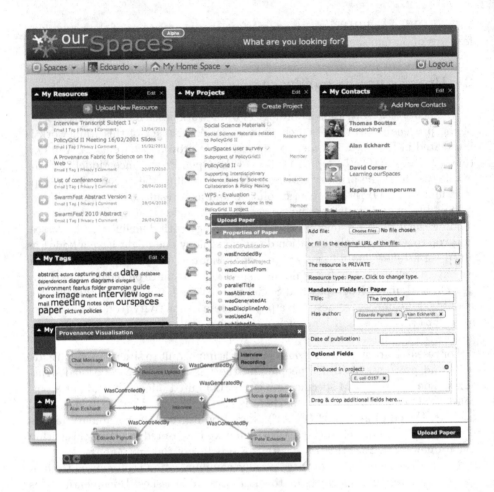

Fig. 1. A screenshot of the *ourSpaces* VRE showing a user's home space, an open upload form and the graphical provenance visualiser

Within the environment, there is also a need to manage users and their behaviours so that they comply with certain policies. For example, a user may impose certain access constraints on digital artefacts that he/she owns, e.g. an artefact may only be accessible to people in my social network. Provenance provides useful contextual information to trigger such policies and influence their outcome. For example, provenance would be useful in order to determine the relationship between a restricted artefact and the person requesting access to it. An artefact may only be accessible to users who are members of a particular project and who contributed towards the creation of the artefact (i.e. were named as a co-author).

We have extended our provenance framework to define such policies as a combination of conditions such as obligations, prohibitions or permissions [4].

We make use of the SPIN ontology [5] to support the use of the SPARQL query language to specify rules and logical constraints necessary to reason about policies. The SPIN ontology allows SPARQL queries to be represented in RDF and associated to classes in an ontology using two pre-defined description properties: `spin:constraint` can be used to define conditions that all members of a class must fulfil; `spin:rule` can be used to specify inference rules using SPARQL CONSTRUCT, DELETE and INSERT statements.

In order to support this policy framework in *ourSpaces* we have developed an event manager service designed to monitor events taking place in the environment, e.g. download/upload artefact, add/remove metadata, etc. When an activity is detected, the event manager initiates a *policy session*. The PolicyReasoner checks if any of the policies stored in the policy repository can be activated by running the SPIN reasoner against the `spin:rule` instances associated with the policies and stores the outcome of the activation in the *policy session*. In order to reason about obligation, permission or prohibition conditions we require a reasoning mechanism able to check conditions over a provenance graph.This can be seen as a semantic matchmaking problem where a functional description of a condition is matched to a subset of a provenance graph. This is done by evaluating each condition defined as a `spin:rule`. For an obligation, conditions have to be met; for a prohibition, the condition cannot be met; and for a permission, the condition might (or might not) be met.

Using this approach in *ourSpaces* we were able to implement a number of policies for use by the project teams using the system. For example, one of the policies specifies the kind of metadata required for artefacts that will be archived to the UK social science data archive - UKDA[7]. More specifically, a policy associated with an interview transcript requires the user to provide information about the provenance of the interview process if this is not already documented in the provenance graph. We have also implemented policies to control the re-use of resources within the VRE. In this context provenance is crucial in order to allow the creation of policies that reason about the derivation of an artefact. For example, in the map visualisation space, only publicly available data (including its sources) can be visualised as stated by the conditions of use of the OS Open Space map service[8] which is integrated into *ourSpaces*.

3 Demonstration Content

During the demonstration, we will present the *ourSpaces* virtual research environment. Key features of the system will be demonstrated such as creation of provenance, provenance policies, visualisation of provenance, provenance of social networks and provenance querying. A video podcast of the demo is available at: http://www.ourspaces.net/ourSpacesDemo.mov

---

[7] http://www.data-archive.ac.uk/
[8] http://openspace.ordnancesurvey.co.uk/

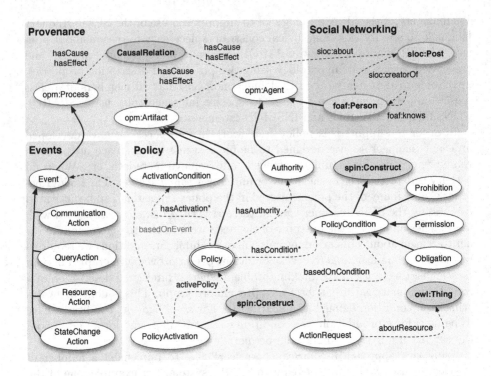

Fig. 2. An extract of the ourSpaces ontological framework

References

1. Pignotti, E., Edwards, P., Reid, R.: A Multi-faceted Provenance Solution for Science on the Web. In: McGuinness, D.L., Michaelis, J.R., Moreau, L. (eds.) IPAW 2010. LNCS, vol. 6378, pp. 295–297. Springer, Heidelberg (2010)
2. Moreau, L., Clifford, B., Freire, J., Futrelle, J., Gil, Y., Groth, P., Kwasnikowska, N., Miles, S., Missier, P., Myers, J., Plale, B., Simmhan, Y., Stephan, E., den Bussche, J.V.: The open provenance model core specification (v1.1). Future Generation Computer Systems (July 2010)
3. Bouttaz, T., Pignotti, E., Mellish, C., Edwards, P.: A policy-based approach to context dependent natural language generation. In: Proceedings of the 13th European Workshop on Natural Language Generation, Nancy, France, pp. 151–157. Association for Computational Linguistics (September 2011)
4. Pignotti, E., Edwards, P.: Using web services and policies within a social platform to support collaborative research. In: Working Notes of AAAI 2012 Stanford Spring Symposium on Intelligent Web Services Meet Social Computing (March 2012)
5. Knublauch, H., Hendler, J.A., Idehen, K.: SPIN - Overview and Motivation. Technical report, W3C Member Submission (2011)

SOLE: Linking Research Papers with Science Objects

Quan Pham[1], Tanu Malik[2], Ian Foster[1,2], Roberto Di Lauro[3], and Raffaele Montella[3]

[1] Department of Computer Science, University of Chicago, Chicago, IL 60637
[2] Computation Institute, University of Chicago, Chicago, IL 60637
[3] Department of Applied Science, University of Napoli Parthenope, Napoli, 80143
quanpt@cs.uchicago.edu, tanum@ci.uchicago.edu

Abstract. We introduce Science Object Linking and Embedding (SOLE), a tool for linking research papers with associated *science objects*, such as source codes, datasets, annotations, workflows, packages, and virtual machine images. The objective of SOLE is to reduce the cost to an author of linking research papers with such science objects for the purpose of reproducible research. To this end, SOLE allows an author to use simple tags to delimit a science object to be associated with a research paper. It creates an adequate representation of the science object and manages a bibliography-like specification of science objects. Authors and readers can reference elements of this bibliography and associate them with phrases in the text of the research paper through a Web interface, in a similar manner to a traditional bibliography tool.

1 Introduction

Prior to the computational driven revolution in science, research papers provided the primary mechanism for sharing data. Papers summarized experiments involving small amount of data, derivations on that data, and associated methods and algorithms. Readers reproduced results through physical experimentation, hand calculation, and/or logical argument. But as scientific methods have become increasingly computational, involving large quantities of data, complex data manipulation and/or numerical simulation, and the use of large and often distributed software stacks, the paper often merely summarizes rather than describes the data and computation. A reader wanting to understand the paper fully requires access to further digital materials. Input and output data may be shared through websites and software may be made available through packages or virtual machine images. Such indirect linkages, however, are typically disconnected from the claims and the results in the paper–not allowing, for example, an equation in a paper to be mapped directly to its implementation.

With the growing emphasis on reproducible research, readers and reviewers increasingly often want to be able to assess the validity of findings and to verify results. Consequently, indirect linkages are not sufficient. Instead, we would like digital materials associated with the works described in a paper–what we term here the paper's *science objects*–to be closely associated with the text so that they can be accessed while reading the paper. Examples of such associations are linking a concept described in the paper to its implementation in source code; linking a description of a dataset to its metadata and digital object identifiers (DOIs); linking a figure in the paper to its derivation and

P. Groth and J. Frew (Eds.): IPAW 2012, LNCS 7525, pp. 203–208, 2012.

workflow, and linking data values referenced from another paper sources to the exact location in that other paper's PDF source.

While associating papers with science objects at this fine granularity may be desirable, the realization of this goal introduces at least three challenges. First, we face the need to transform each science object into a form amenable to linkage with a paper. In our work, this means that important classes and functions in source code files must be associated with URLs and that datasets must be recorded in registries that specify dataset locations and access methods. It also means that data analysis pipelines must be cast as workflows with appropriate wrappers and web services that specify inputs and functional forms, or alternatively associated with software on a adequately provisioned virtual image. A second challenge concerns the manner in which linkages are represented in papers. Using URLs to refer to science objects is often unwieldy, especially when an object is referenced multiple times. A third challenge relates to presentation: Clicking on a science object link should lead to adequate presentation to the user.

We demonstrate Science Object Linking and Embedding (SOLE), a system [15] that eases the process of linking research papers with science objects, such as source codes, datasets, workflows, and virtual images. Authors identify science objects with human-readable tags; SOLE converts each tagged science object into an associated linked data object with an associated URI. For ease of management, the tags, URIs, and accompanying representation are maintained in a registry: what is, in effect, a science object bibliography. To aid authors with the linking process, SOLE also provides a web interface that allows authors to associate groups of words in a research paper with one or more science object tags. Clicking a link in the text results in the display of an appropriate representation of the science object.

In the remainder of this article, we describe how SOLE works to ease author burden and demonstrate how SOLE has been used to enable reproducible research in the RD-CEP project [4] in which research papers must be associated with several computational products.

2   Related Work

It is widely recognized that currently there is a lack of suitable incentives that attribute scientists for conducting reproducible research. However, the merits of conducting reproducible research are also widely accepted–it leads to scientific methods which have higher transparency and are more open. To improve transparency of research papers, some projects have demonstrated the concept of reproducible research paper by focussing on one or more aspects. Utopia [1] reproduces paper by associating concepts in paper with external annotations retrieved from an online meta data store. Annotations are publicly shared and readers can further comment upon them. Vistrails [9] creates reproducible papers by associating figures and results in the paper with executable components. It allows authors to publish workflows and associated provenance and hyperlink to it in a result or figure in the article. Sweave [14] and Dexy [6] are literate programming environments, which if adopted from the beginning of the scientific process can lead to papers with embedded source code and derived results. SOLE is particularly targeted towards authors for whom experimentation and writing research papers continue to remain separate activities, but would like a less burdensome, yet efficient mechanism to associate their research papers *post-hoc* with the inputs and outputs of the scientific process. SOLE has similar goals as provided by websites such as Run-MyCode.org [13], but provides the ability to associate a wider class of scientific inputs and outputs at a finer control.

3 SOLE

SOLE provides command-line tools for authors to create science objects, and a web-based interface for authors and readers to associate phrases in the paper with their corresponding science objects. To create a science object in SOLE, the author puts a tag on the science object with the following syntax:

$begin\ type\ name_1 | \ldots | name_n$
  [science object content]
end

in which *begin* and *end* are delimiters of the tag, *type* defines the kind of science object to create, and $name_1$ to $name_n$ are user-defined names. Thus, the same object can be tagged by more than one name. SOLE processes a tagged file and based on tag *type* definitions creates a science object, which associates a set of metadata elements representing the object, including a reference to the object as a URI. Authors can place tags on source codes and text files to create SOs, such as source code snippets, annotations in PDFs, units of a workflow that can be executed on a given environment, and virtual machine images, described later in the section. After creation of a variety of science objects, authors/readers can load the paper in HTML format and associate phrases in the text with the name of the tag.

In SOLE, four kinds of science objects can currently be created and linked:

Language Objects. The author can import a local source code repository or a public domain code repository, such as Github, to create URIs for language objects defined in the source. Internally, SOLE uses Ctags [5] to create tags for language objects in a file, but appends a URI to the language objects. We have expanded the Ctags utility to allow users to tag more than one language object as a single object to be referenced in a paper. This is useful when an algorithm in a paper must be associated with multiple functions and data structure specifications defined in multiple files.

Annotated PDFs and Datasets. SOLE uses the Poppler library [12] to extract tagged annotations from PDF. The metadata of the tagged annotation includes the URI of the PDF, the exact location in the pdf where annotation was made, and the annotated text. Tagging of a dataset, should ideally retrieve the metadata associated with the dataset, associate a DOI, and provide some methods for data access. However, developing generic tags for all types of datasets is challenging since datasets exist in a variety of formats, and with a wide variety of access tools. Currently, an author can tag the metadata file of NetCDF and ASCII datasets to generate a corresponding URI on the entire dataset. We plan to make dataset tags more versatile by integrating them with DOIs.

Web Services. SOLE creates a web-service specification of functions specified by a user. The functions are delimited in the source file by inserting tags with the workflow

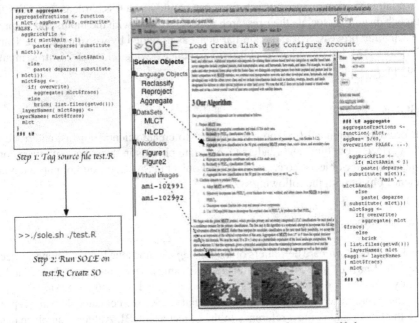

Fig. 1. Figure 1 demonstrates the three easy steps that an author follows to create and associate science objects in SOLE. The author first tags the function *aggregateFractions* in their source code with the user-defined tag name "*aggregate*" (step 1); then runs SOLE as command line tool to create the necessary metadata (step 2); and finally associates the phrase "Aggregate' in the paper with the tag and views the specification of the object (step 3).

tag_{type}. SOLE creates workflow specifications as Galaxy tools, with description about inputs and outputs. Galaxy provides an open, web-based platform for specifying tools and running computational experiments as workflows[10]. Each function is automatically wrapped as an appropriate Galaxy tool definition and hosted on the web-server instance connected with Galaxy. Authors can further specify if web services should accept user specified parameters and types of data.

Virtual images. Authors can also create packages of a source directory, using different package managers, and then with a single click deploy those packages on a virtual machine hosted on a cloud, and obtain a URI that includes machine ID and parameters for the package to be executed. To conduct this operation, SOLE must be configured with the user's account on a cloud infrastructure such as Amazon. SOLE uses a configuration file to specify the package and deploys on the image using recipes in provisioning tools.

The science object URI and its tag is stored in FluidInfo [7], a key-value data store that stores tags for a variety of data objects and provides a simple query language to allow users to search the datastore for specific tags and tag-values.

4 Demonstration Scenario

The Center for Robust Decision making on Climate and Energy Policy (RDCEP) [4] is a collaborative, multi-institutional project that aims to improve the computational models needed to evaluate climate and energy policies and to make robust decisions based on outcomes. Sharing science objects in the form of data, tools, and software is critical; it enables scientists to compare models and to build more accurate models. Currently in RDCEP science objects are shared through a web site. Our demonstration scenario consists of two documents [2,11] produced within the Center which we link with their respective science objects, using SOLE

Scenario 1: To reproduce the first document [2] (a master's thesis; see also the associated paper [3]), the author must associate the text and embedded figures with science objects that include datasets, algorithmic descriptions, computational analysis workflows, and workflow executions. The author tags each science object to create web accessible resources in the form of HTML fragments and web services. The resulting object representations are maintained in the SOLE database.

Scenario 2: To reproduce the second paper [11], the author must associate descriptions in the paper with a set of data values, each of which is embedded in another research paper. We demonstrate that authors can insert an annotations on the PDF, tag it, then use SOLE on PDF files to generate URIs on tagged annotations, and and finally associate with phrases in the research paper.

5 Conclusion

SOLE eases the management and creation of digital objects associated with scientific experiments and associating the objects with research papers. Demonstrated in the domain of policy science, SOLE uses general features and interfaces such as tagging and Galaxy. With minimal effort it can also be applied to other domains such as biology, astronomy, and the geosciences. SOLE is currently under development and will be released to a broader audience at a later date. In the future, we plan to interface SOLE to Globus Online [8] to enable authors to create a richer reproducible environment.

Acknowledgements. We thank Neil Best for the insightful discussions on conducting reproducible research. This work was supported in part by the Center for Robust Decision making on Climate and Energy Policy, under NSF grant number 0951576.

References

1. Attwood, T.K., et al.: Utopia Documents: linking scholarly literature with research data. In: European Conference on Computational Biology, Ghent, Belgium (September 2010)
2. Best, N.: Synthesis of a complete land use/land cover data set for the conterminous United States emphasizing accuracy in area and distribution of agricultural activity, Master's Thesis, Northeastern Illinois University (2011)

3. Best, N., Elliott, J., Foster, I.: Synthesis of a complete land use/land cover data set for the conterminous United States. RDCEP, Working Paper 12-08, http://dx.doi.org/10.2139/ssrn.2051158
4. Center for Robust Decision making on Climate and Energy Policy (RDCEP), http://www.rdcep.org/
5. Ctags, http://ctags.sourceforge.net/ctags.html
6. Dexy, http://www.dexy.it/
7. FluidInfo, http://fluidinfo.com/
8. Foster, I.: Globus Online: Accelerating and democratizing science through cloud-based services. IEEE Internet Computing, 70–73 (May/June 2011)
9. Freire, J., Silva, C.T., Callahan, S.P., Santos, E., Scheidegger, C.E., Vo, H.T.: Managing Rapidly-Evolving Scientific Workflows. In: Moreau, L., Foster, I. (eds.) IPAW 2006. LNCS, vol. 4145, pp. 10–18. Springer, Heidelberg (2006)
10. Goecks, J., Nekrutenko, A., Taylor, J., The Galaxy Team: Galaxy: a comprehensive approach for supporting accessible, reproducible, and transparent computational research in the life sciences. Genome Biol. 11(8), R86 (2010)
11. Johnson, S., Moyer, E.: Feasibility of U.S. Renewable Portfolio Standards Under Cost Caps and Case Study for Illinois. RDCEP, Working Paper 12-07, http://dx.doi.org/10.2139/ssrn.1996621
12. Poppler, http://poppler.freedesktop.org/
13. Run My Code, http://www.runmycode.org
14. Leisch, F.: Sweave, Part I: Mixing R and LaTeX: A short introduction to the Sweave file format and corresponding R functions. R News 2(3), 28–31
15. Science Object Linking and Embedding (SOLE), http://www.ci.uchicago.edu/SOLE

DEMO: Managing the Provenance of Crowdsourced Disruption Reports*

Milan Markovic, Peter Edwards, David Corsar, and Jeff Z. Pan

Computing Science dot.rural Digital Economy Hub, University of Aberdeen,
Aberdeen, AB24 5UA
{m.markovic,p.edwards,dcorsar,j.z.pan}@abdn.ac.uk

Abstract. Human computation systems that outsource tasks to the crowd often have to address issues associated with the quality of contributions. We are exploring the potential role of provenance to facilitate processes such as quality assessment within such systems. In this demo we present an application for managing traffic disruption reports generated by the crowd, and outline the technologies used to integrate provenance, linked data, and streams.

1 Introduction

Part of the original vision for the World Wide Web described by Berners-Lee and Fischetti in *Weaving the Web* [2] was the creation of a human network that would make it possible to create abstract *social machines* on the Web. These machines are described as: "processes in which the people do the creative work and the machine does the administration...". This is very similar to the *human-based computation* concept [5], where certain steps of a computational process are outsourced to humans. Both these visions of the web create a need for an infrastructure to handle the incorporation of human elements within a larger social computing ecosystem. Hendler [3] noted that early social machines already exist on the Web in the form of interactive applications (e.g. Wikipedia[1]). Hendler also highlighted that these applications are limited as their functions are largely isolated from one another (e.g. they are unable to easily share data). We argue that this limitation could be addressed by emerging practices such as linked data [1] - a set of principles for consuming and publishing machine-readable data on the web.

One of the ways of obtaining human input is through harvesting of so-called *collective intelligence* via crowdsourcing methods. Systems using crowdsourcing typically rely on large, diverse crowds, where the number of error generating individuals is small, resulting in minimal effect to overall system performance.

---

* The research described here is supported by the award made by the RCUK Digital Economy programme to the dot.rural Digital Economy Hub; award reference: EP/G066051/1.
[1] http://wikipedia.org

P. Groth and J. Frew (Eds.): IPAW 2012, LNCS 7525, pp. 209–213, 2012.

However, in situations where the crowd size is small (perhaps because of the nature of the task or a limited population of potential participants) the potential for adverse effects caused by unreliable individuals is significant. Within such systems it is therefore critical to reason about the quality of contributions. We propose a solution to facilitate such reasoning operations based on the maintenance of a *provenance* record within the crowdsourcing system. In this context provenance would mean a record of the data generated/maintained by the crowd and the process(es) involved. Another important characteristic of such applications is their dynamic nature, with participants creating, maintaining or validating data continuously over time. We argue that participant interactions should therefore be modelled as a continuous stream of data elements published in compliance with the Linked Data Principles [4]. This necessitates a provenance solution able to interoperate with such streams.

2   Application Scenario

Travel disruption is not easy to predict and even monitoring of disruption poses some challenges (e.g. how to obtain information from the site of an incident). A crowdsourcing application able to gather, manage, and assess disruption reports would provide an obvious solution. For example, consider a system that allows participants to report travel disruption events (e.g. an accident on a particular route) from their mobile device. In addition, they are able to perform other tasks such as the creation of links between disruption reports or validation of data provided by others (evaluation). By linking here we mean the identification of relationships between disruption reports (e.g. queuing traffic caused by an incident five miles ahead). However, this data alone does not provide important contextual detail such as who created it, who performed a maintenance operation, when and how it was performed - all of which are useful when assessing the credibility of participants and the data they contribute. We argue that the provenance record should be able to provide this context, by capturing information about participants and their activities. For example, user John linked two disruption reports as related, but in the past links created by him have always been subsequently reported as incorrect by others.

A disruption event report is likely to trigger a stream of data relating to this event (such as other disruption reports, or validation reports). It is therefore entirely natural to represent these data as a stream of elements, with participants contributing to a stream about a particular event (e.g. an incident on route A90). A system utilising the crowd to manage travel disruption would thus need to be built around a set of such streams. Capturing the provenance of a stream object (e.g. the disruption report that initiated the stream) and the provenance of stream elements (e.g. who created a specific data element, or created a link between elements) would provide additional context to support reasoning about the quality of the data on the stream.

3   System Architecture

We have constructed a system that is able to gather and manage disruption reports from the crowd, and to capture the provenance of these activities; the architecture of this system is shown in Figure 1. A mobile client application (Figure 2) was built using the jQuery Mobile[2] and OpenLayers[3] library. The client collects information from the crowd and communicates crowdsourced results back to users. It is optimised for use on touch screen mobile devices and supports the following functionality: creation of disruption reports, creation of validation reports, creation of reports about relationships (links) between two disruption reports, visualisation of other reports and their links.

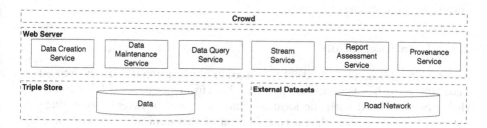

Fig. 1. Provenance-enabled travel disruption system architecture

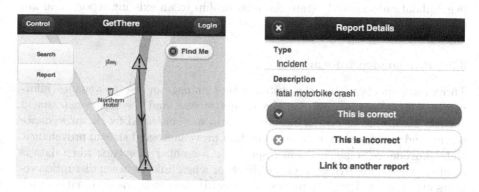

Fig. 2. A mobile client application

The server-side framework was built as a set of RESTful web services. The data within the system is stored in a TDB[4] triple store, and accessed via a Fuseki[5] SPARQL[6] endpoint. The framework is responsible for managing reports

---

[2] http://jquerymobile.com/
[3] http://openlayers.org/
[4] http://jena.apache.org/documentation/tdb/
[5] http://jena.apache.org/documentation/serving_data/
[6] http://www.w3.org/TR/rdf-sparql-query/

created by the mobile client application, managing the provenance of operations within the system, and the storage of this data (both the reports and their provenance). The stream service manages the creation of streams (as an ordered sequence of elements) and is responsible for handling stream operations such as: registering/unregistering queries; inserting reports (with associated provenance); and closing/deleting streams. Stream elements consist of the Unique Resource Identifier that refers to the data stored in a triple store. The provenance service generates annotations and is described further in section 3.2. The report assessment service (described in section 3.3) assesses and annotates reports generated by the crowd. Disruption reports are represented using a travel disruption ontology, describing a set of concepts from the domain of transport and travel disruption; this ontology was developed following a review of a number of UK travel information services.

3.1   Data Integration

To provide additional contextual information about a report, the system automatically records a timestamp, user location (from the phone's GPS receiver), the error associated with the location, and the result of reverse geocoding the location. Each report is thus a combination of this data and the data directly contributed by the participant. When the system receives a report, if a stream already exists for reports in that location (e.g. the street/road), then the report is added to that stream; otherwise, a new stream is created. Some reports (e.g. validation) explicitly state the relationship to an existing report, and are therefore added to the same stream as the report to which they refer.

3.2   Provenance Information

Three components within the system either manage or use provenance information: the *provenance service*, the *stream service*, and the *report assessment service*. Two types of provenance annotations are generated by the provenance service and are stored in a triple store: data provenance and stream provenance. Data provenance is generated in response to a number of events: when data is created; when data arrives from the client; or when links between disruption reports are created. The data provenance record[7] then contains information such as the agent that created the report, the activities involved in creating the report (e.g. acquiring the agent's location, uploading from the client application, and subsequent processing by the web service), and the entities used/generated by these activities. Stream provenance is generated in response to: creation of a new stream; closing a stream; and data being added to a stream. The stream provenance record then contains information such as the activities that triggered the creation/closing of a stream, the activities that added elements to a stream, and the entities used by those activities (e.g. the report that was received).

---

[7] Expressed using terms from the provenance model being developed by the W3C Provenance Working Group (http://www.w3.org/2011/prov)

3.3 Report Assessment

The report assessment service performs evaluation of the submitted reports using the provenance record and other contextual information (other reports, and links between reports). Currently we have implemented two prototype metrics within the service. The first metric is based on the distance between the reported disruption and the participant providing the report: the greater the distance between the location of the incident being reported and the location of the user reporting it, the lower the reliability of that report. The second metric uses a simple reputation model for the report creator, based on how previous reports generated by that user have been validated by others. For example, if a user creates a disruption report, which is later validated as correct by others, that user's reputation for creating disruption reports will increase. However, if others claim the report is incorrect, then the reputation decreases. As every disruption event has a limited lifespan, only validation reports received within that time period should be used when building the reputation of a participant. However, as each disruption event has a different duration, we are investigating how to incorporate crowdsourcing the end of disruption events into the client application.

During the demonstration the following features of the client application and travel disruption framework will be presented: observation (disruption report) contribution via the client application to highlight our ontology-driven solution for creation of the reports and generation of associated provenance data; validation of disruption reports via the client application; creation of links between related disruption reports and provenance associated with this process; reasoning with provenance within the system to identify unreliable disruption reports; and visualisation of the crowdsourced results via the client application.

References

1. Berners-Lee, T.: Linked data, http://www.w3.org/DesignIssues/LinkedData.html (accessed March 10, 2012)
2. Berners-Lee, T., Fischetti, M.: Weaving the Web: The original design and ultimate destiny of the World Wide Web. Harper Collins, NY (1999)
3. Hendler, J., Berners-Lee, T.: From the semantic web to social machines: A research challenge for AI on the world wide web. Artificial Intelligence 174(2), 156–161 (2009)
4. Sequeda, J.F., Corcho, O.: Linked stream data: A position paper. In: 2nd International Workshop on Semantic Sensor Networks (SSN), Washington, DC, US (2009)
5. von Ahn, L.: Human Computation. PhD thesis, Carnegie Mellon University (2005)

Designing a Provenance-Based Climate Data Analysis Application

Emanuele Santos[1], David Koop[1], Thomas Maxwell[2], Charles Doutriaux[3],
Tommy Ellqvist[1], Gerald Potter[2], Juliana Freire[1], Dean Williams[3],
and Cláudio T. Silva[1]

[1] Polytechnic Institute of New York University
[2] NASA Goddard Space Flight Center
[3] Lawrence Livermore National Laboratory
http://uv-cdat.llnl.gov/

Abstract. Climate scientists have made substantial progress in understanding Earth's climate system, particularly at global and continental
scales. Climate research is now focused on understanding climate changes
over wider ranges of time and space scales. These efforts are generating
ultra-scale data sets at very high spatial resolution. An insightful analysis in climate science depends on using software tools to discover, access,
manipulate, and visualize the data sets of interest. These data exploration tasks can be complex and time-consuming, and they frequently
involve many resources from both the modeling and observational climate
communities. Because of the complexity of the explorations, provenance
is critical, allowing scientists to ensure reproducibility, revisit existing
computational pipelines, and more easily share analyses and results. In
addition, as the results of this work can impact policy, having provenance available is important for decision-making. In this paper we describe, UV-CDAT, a workflow-based, provenance-enabled system that
integrates climate data analysis libraries and visualization tools in an
end-to-end application, making it easier for scientists to integrate and
use a wide array of tools.

1 Introduction

This is the first paper describing capabilities of the newly developed UV-CDAT
system, an advanced application that can locally and remotely access ultra-scale
climate data archives, provide high-performance parallel analysis and visualization capabilities to the desktop of a climate scientist, and ultimately, apply these
tools to make informed decisions on meeting the energy needs of the nation and
the world in light of climate change consequences. UV-CDAT has been developed in response to the needs of scientists for access, analysis, and visualization
to computer model output resulting from high-resolution, long-term, climate
change projections performed as part of the U.S. Global Change Research Program. This program is funding a multi-agency effort towards the modeling and
simulation of long-term climate change, and for the past several years, this effort

P. Groth and J. Frew (Eds.): IPAW 2012, LNCS 7525, pp. 214–219, 2012.

has been an extremely important resource for the research community. As an example of the research progress that has been enabled under this effort, the DOE BER-funded Program for Climate Model Diagnosis and Intercomparison (PCMDI) has collected and disseminated Model Intercomparison Project (MIP) simulation output from most of the world's premier climate modeling centers, including the Coupled Model Intercomparison Project, phase 3 (CMIP-3) collections which encompass over 35 terabytes (TB) of data, and more than 1 petabyte (PB) of CMIP-3 data has been distributed to over 4,300 users worldwide, resulting in over 600 peer-reviewed publications evaluating and using simulations from these state-of-the-art climate models.

Leading domain-specific tools [3, 5, 8], such as Climate Data Analysis Tools (CDAT) lack a number of desirable features to enable the analysis of this data. In particular, CDAT is ill-equipped to process very large data sets resulting from future high-resolution climate model simulations, and it lacks provenance and workflow functionality [4, 6] that are key to ensure that results are reproducible and easily accessible across the climate research community. UV-CDAT is built on top of a provenance-enabled workflow system, and all its functionality is integrated through either tightly coupled or loosely coupled software components. This model has allowed us to create a modular design that easily supports the integration of major new packages (and related functionality) in a matter of a few days versus months of efforts rewriting the guts of the system to accommodate for the new software.

To summarize, our main contribution in this paper is to describe the UV-CDAT system, the first provenance-enabled end-user visualization and analysis tool. UV-CDAT presents a novel architecture that seamlessly integrates workflows, provenance, climate data analysis libraries, and visualization tools in an end-to-end application.

2 UV-CDAT Overview

There are quite a number of components to UV-CDAT, and it is out of the scope of this paper to provide a complete description of the system. We focus on the provenance support, and on how this was enabled in a GUI-based end-user application. Below we provide a rough overview of the system. UV-CDAT is available for downloading from http://uv-cdat.llnl.gov/. UV-CDAT is a workflow-based, provenance-enabled system that integrates climate data analysis libraries and visualization tools in an end-to-end application.

The UV-CDAT framework integrates software infrastructure through two primary means (Figure 1). Tightly coupled integration of CDAT Core, VCS and VTK/ParaView infrastructure provides high-performance parallel streaming data analysis and visualization of massive climate data sets. Loosely coupled integration provides the flexibility to use tools such as VisIt, ParaView, R, and MatLab for data analysis and visualization as well as to apply customized data analysis applications within an integrated environment without modifying the main system. VisTrails provides a package mechanism to allow developers to expose their libraries (written in any language) to the system by a thin Python

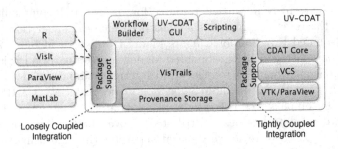

Fig. 1. UV-CDAT system architecture

interface through a set of VisTrails modules [2]. In particular, the DV3D [7] system was integrated into UV-CDAT using this mechanism. DV3D provides the high-level interfaces and tools required to make the analysis and visualization power of VTK readily accessible to users without exposing visualization technical details. Within both paradigms, UV-CDAT provides data provenance capture and mechanisms to support data analysis via the VisTrails infrastructure. Users are able to interact with the system using any of the elements in the top layer: the UV-CDAT GUI, VisTrails' workflow builder or Python scripts. The UV-CDAT GUI, the main window for UV-CDAT, is shown in Figure 2. It is based on a *spreadsheet* (middle), a resizable grid where each cell contains a visualization. By using intuitive drag-and-drop operations, visualizations can be created, modified, copied, rearranged, and compared. Spreadsheets maintain their provenance and can be saved and reloaded. Around the spreadsheet are the tools for building visualizations. The project view (top left) allows you to group spreadsheets into projects, and to name visualizations and spreadsheets. The plot view (bottom left) allows you to use and customize your available plot types. The variable view (top right) allows you to use and edit data variables. The bottom right contains a variable editor widget, making editing a variable similar to using a pocket calculator.

3   UV-CDAT Provenance

One of the key concerns in the design of UV-CDAT was integrating functionality from different sources in a way so that the provenance would be generally understandable. The two core components in accessing and visualizing information in UV-CDAT are variables and plots. A *variable* represents data that may be either the original data from a model or capture or the result of transforming, combining, or filtering some other data. There are many operations that allow the creation of a new variable from existing variables. A *plot* is a computation that generates a visualization given an input variable. In addition, it has many parameters that control the appearance of the visualization.

UV-CDAT uses the same change-based provenance to capture changes to computations as VisTrails, but users can work in an interface that is tailored to cli-

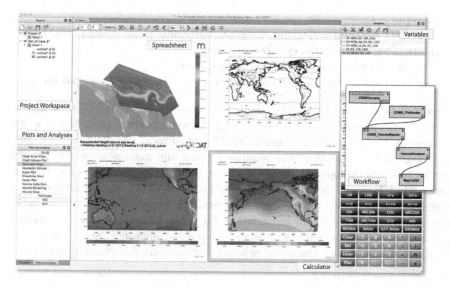

Fig. 2. UV-CDAT Main Window. Spreadsheet (middle), Project View (top left), Plot View (bottom left), Variable View (top right), and Calculator (bottom right)

mate data analysis and exploration. In order to capture provenance, UV-CDAT translates the components of the variables and plots into workflow modules which are automatically stored in a provenance format similar to VisTrails. UV-CDAT also uses the VisTrails infrastructure to capture execution provenance, capturing and storing it via the workflow execution engine. Another key requirement in the design of UV-CDAT was scripting support. We extended the provenance model to automatically generate Python scripts from the stored workflow provenance.

4   Using UV-CDAT as an End-to-End Analysis Tool

As a case study, we present an example of how UV-CDAT is used by a climate scientist performing data exploration and visualization. Some video tutorials can be found on http://uv-cdat.llnl.gov/. The scientist is looking at data from paleoclimate runs on the CCSM3 [1]. The user wants to determine if the variance of the DJF (December-January-February average) 500 hPa heights changes from two different paleoclimate simulations. This should give an indication of the changing location of storm track and could be a test of what happens to extratropical storm tracks in a warming earth. The scientist will also need to be able to do the same analysis for many different periods in the past. The list of steps performed in the analysis are the following:

1. Data discovery: The metadata for the daily model output from the model runs are examined to find the variables.
2. Select a region of interest. For example, the West Coast of the US.
3. Pick a variable and run the variance calculation on the time dimension.

4. Save the data.
5. Plot a 3D Hovmoller diagram (latitude, longitude, time) using DV3D to see the time variation of the geopotential height.
6. Slice the data to examine the region of interest.
7. Plot 2D maps of the subregion, add overlays and manipulate plot parameters.

Figure 2 shows a few of the steps above performed in UV-CDAT. The scientist benefits from the spreadsheet by laying out different kinds of plots in the same spreadsheet. Creating 3D plots using DV3D's set of tools was a simple task. Before UV-CDAT, the scientist was required to save and manage dozens of scripts in order to know the operations and datasets used in the plots. The provenance captured in UV-CDAT is changing all that. The provenance of any plot is readily accessible at any point in time of the analysis. The scripting support was useful to generate scripts to run in batch mode for other time periods in the model run. In addition, the captured provenance allows a student not familiar with the climate model output to learn and repeat the procedure described above.

5   Conclusion

We have described the UV-CDAT system, what we believe is the first provenance-enabled end-user visualization and analysis tool for ultra-scale climate analysis. UV-CDAT presents a novel architecture that seamlessly integrates workflows, provenance, climate data analysis libraries, and visualization tools in an end-to-end application. The system is already available to the climate community. Over the next year and a half, we will continue to refine and extend its functionality with the goal of making it the primary tool for climate scientists. Our future work plans include to further refine UV-CDAT provenance and workflow capabilities to make the integration with other packages as smoothly as possible. We plan to add a more intuitive and powerful provenance browser, and make it easier for scientists to publish their analysis, workflows, and data products on the web.

Acknowledgments. This project has been funded by the U.S. Department of Energy (DOE) Office of Biological and Environmental Research (BER). This is a large project involving many institutions, including LLNL, LBNL, Los Alamos, ORNL, Kitware, NYU-Poly, SCI-Utah, and NASA.

References

1. Community Climate System Model version 3.0 (CCSM3), http://www.cesm.ucar.edu/models/ccsm3.0/ (accessed on March 21, 2012)
2. VisTrails. In: Brown, A., Wilson, G. (eds.) The Architecture of Open Source Applications: Elegance, Evolution, and a Few Fearless Hacks, ch. 23, pp. 377–394. Lulu.com (2011), http://www.aosabook.org/
3. Climate Data Analysis Tools (CDAT), http://www2-pcmdi.llnl.gov/cdat (accessed on March 21, 2012)

4. Davidson, S.B., Freire, J.: Provenance and Scientific Workflows: Challenges and Opportunities. In: Proceedings of SIGMOD, pp. 1345–1350 (2008)
5. Doty, B., Kinter III, J.L.: The Grid Analysis and Display System (GrADS): A practical tool for Earth science visualization. In: Eighth International Conference on Interactive Information and Procession Systems, Atlanta, GA (January 1992)
6. Freire, J., Koop, D., Silva, C.: Provenance for computational tasks: A survey. Computing in Science and Engineering 10(3), 11 (2008)
7. NASA. Dv3d, http://portal.nccs.nasa.gov/DV3D
8. Unidata. The Integrated Data Viewer (IDV), https://www.unidata.ucar.edu/software/idv/ (accessed on March 21, 2012)

Quality Assessment, Provenance, and the Web of Linked Sensor Data*

Chris Baillie, Peter Edwards, and Edoardo Pignotti

Computing Science & dot.rural Digital Economy Research, University of Aberdeen
Aberdeen, UK
{c.baillie,p.edwards,e.pignotti}@abdn.ac.uk

Abstract. This paper presents a quality assessment framework for linked sensor data and discusses a role for provenance in quality assessment.

Keywords: provenance, linked data, quality assessment.

1 Introduction

In this paper we describe a framework for evaluating the quality of linked data and discuss how the provenance of such data could be introduced to the quality assessment process. The open nature of the Web enables anyone (or any 'thing') to publish any content that they choose which means that poor quality data can quickly propagate [1]. Therefore, a mechanism to assess quality is essential if agents (human or machine) are to identify reliable data to support tasks such as decision making and planning.

Data is generally regarded as high quality if it is 'fit for use' in that it meets a number of requirements [2]. These requirements place constraints on certain *quality dimensions* (e.g. *accuracy, timeliness, relevance*) and are described using *quality metrics* (e.g. *timely* data is no more than 10 minutes old). Quality assessments guided by such metrics often require additional metadata describing the context around data, something which can be provided by publishing information as Linked Data. We argue that this context should also include provenance information, a record of the entities and processes involved in data derivation. Provenance has been identified as an essential step in helping users to better understand, trust, reproduce, and validate data [3]. We argue that it should therefore also play an important role in evaluating data quality. Given the scope of the Web, we are investigating quality issues within the Web of Linked Sensor Data [4], a subset of the Web of Linked Data comprising semantic representations of sensors and their observations. In this paper, we provide a motivating example before describing the implementation of our quality assessment framework. We then discuss how provenance can be included in quality assessment and outline our future plans.

---

* The research described here is supported by the award made by the RCUK Digital Economy programme to the dot.rural Digital Economy Hub; award reference: EP/G066051/1.

P. Groth and J. Frew (Eds.): IPAW 2012, LNCS 7525, pp. 220–222, 2012.

2 Quality Assessment Framework

To help us better understand the requirements of quality assessment and the potential for provenance we have examined a number of scenarios. One of these uses data from the mobile phones of public transport users to provide details such as vehicle location, speed, etc. Examples of quality metrics in this scenario include *relevance*, examining the distance between the observation and the accepted route of travel, and *timeliness*, examining how old the observation is when it is used. Following an analysis of this scenario, and others, we have developed a number of requirements for a quality assessment framework: **(1)** data should be evaluated against a number of quality dimensions, **(2)** quality metrics are necessary to guide assessments, and **(3)** quality assessment results should be recorded to enable their re-use.

We represent sensor observations using the W3C Semantic Sensor Network Incubator Group's ontology[1]. This enables us to describe the context around sensor observations such as observed phenomena (e.g. location or speed in the transport scenario) and features of interest (e.g. a journey). Quality assessment is represented using the Data Quality Management[2] (DQM) ontology. *Quality metrics* are defined using SPIN[3] and attached to instances of *dqm:DataRequirement* (requirements 1 and 2); the results of assessment are captured using instances of *dqm:QualityScore* (requirement 3). We associate sensor observations (and their values) to quality scores via the *dqm:plainScore* property. (Fig. 1).

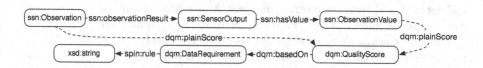

Fig. 1. Quality assessment characterised using the SSN and DQM ontologies

To evaluate our methodology we have developed a number of web services that enable the creation and manipulation of linked data representing sensor observations, quality annotations, and their provenance. The observation service generates RDF representations of sensor observations received from a smartphone app and stores them in a triple store. The quality assessment service takes the URI of an observation as a parameter and performs the evaluation using a SPIN reasoner. Guided by a number of data requirements, the reasoner produces quality scores for the observation and stores them in a dedicated quality annotation triple store, enabling the re-use of quality results. The observation and quality assessment services make use of a provenance service to document how

---

[1] http://www.w3.org/2005/Incubator/ssn/ssnx/ssn
[2] http://semwebquality.org/dqm-vocabulary/v1/dqm
[3] http://www.spinrdf.org

observations and quality annotations were created. This service uses the W3C Provenance Working Group's Prov-O model[4] to represent sensor observations as instances of `Entity` (physical, digital, or conceptual 'things' that one can provide provenance for) and sensing processes as an `Activity` (something that occurs over time and acts upon or with entities). Similarly, we represent data requirements and quality scores as `Entities`, and the quality assessment process as `Activities`. The next section outlines how this provenance information can be used in future quality assessments.

3   Provenance and Quality Assessment

At present, our framework evaluates quality using only the metadata associated with sensor observations. We have identified a number of ways in which provenance can impact upon data quality such as: the reputation of the agent responsible for creating the data, the type of device that created the data, and how the data has been transformed since it was created (e.g. rounded numeric values or type conversion). We therefore intend to implement new quality metrics that can examine observation provenance and make assessments of quality based on this information in addition to the wider contextual information. We also intend to investigate how the provenance of existing quality scores can be used to decide if existing quality assessment outcomes can be re-used instead of executing new ones. We have identified a number of use cases in which this could occur, such as agent A re-using a quality score that was generated after an assessment using agent B's data requirements because they are in the same social network and trust each other, or agent A re-using a quality score generated from a data requirement that matches one of its own requirements.

Finally, we acknowledge that quality assessment is highly subjective and therefore intend to allow users (or their agents) to define their own data requirements that will supersede the system-wide requirements that are in place at the moment.

References

1. Baillie, C., Edwards, P., Pignotti, E.: Assessing quality in the web of linked sensor data. In: 25th Conference on Artificial Intelligence (AAAI 2011), pp. 1750–1751. AAAI Press (August 2011)
2. Furber, C., Hepp, M.: Using semantic web resources for data quality management. In: 17th International Conference on Knowledge Engineering and Knowledge Management, pp. 211–225 (2010)
3. Miles, S., Groth, P., Munroe, S., Moreau, L.: Prime: A methodology for developing provenance-aware applications. ACM Transactions on Software Engineering and Methodology 20(3), 39–46 (2009)
4. Page, K.R., De Roure, D.C., Martinez, K., Sadler, J.D., Kit, O.Y.: Linked sensor data: Restfully serving RDF and GML. In: International Workshop on Semantic Sensor Networks 2009, vol. 522, pp. 49–63 (October 2009)

---

[4] http://www.w3.org/TR/prov-o

Integrating Text and Graphics
to Present Provenance Information*

Thomas Bouttaz, Alan Eckhardt, Chris Mellish, and Peter Edwards

Computing Science, University of Aberdeen, Aberdeen AB24 5UA, UK
{t.bouttaz,a.eckhardt,c.mellish,p.edwards}@abdn.ac.uk

Abstract. We describe two approaches for the visualisation of provenance - one using natural language generation to produce texts, the other using a graphical approach. Our main contribution is a mechanism using a combination of these modalities.

Keywords: provenance, NLG, visualisation, HCI.

1 Introduction

The presentation of provenance should allow users to intuitively understand such information, without requiring any particular knowledge about the underlying model. Therefore, identifying appropriate means to present provenance information to end-users is an issue that needs to be addressed. In this paper, we discuss two ways to present this information, one based on generated textual descriptions and the other based on a graphical visualisation[1]. Our approach was motivated by the needs of multidisciplinary users within a web-based research environment *ourSpaces* [1], but is applicable in other contexts.

ourSpaces[2] enables researchers from different backgrounds to manage their projects by allowing them to communicate and share their research artefacts. The underlying architecture of *ourSpaces* is based on Semantic Web technologies (e.g. OWL, RDF) and at the heart of *ourSpaces* is an OWL representation of the Open Provenance Model [2]. OPM is a generic model and as a result, *ourSpaces* also supports additional domain specific provenance ontologies that are created by extending the concepts defined in the OPM ontology. Several services make use of these ontologies, including *Metadata Access* - provides Java access to a RDF data repository, and *Provenance* - manages provenance data and provides HTTP and Java access.

2 Visualisation Services

Natural Language Visualisation. We have developed a Natural Language Generation (NLG) service that generates short textual descriptions based on

---

* This work is supported by the UK Economic & Social Research Council (ESRC) under the Digital Social Research programme; award RES-149-25-1075.
[1] The software is open source and available at: https://github.com/Policygrid-II
[2] http://www.ourspaces.net

P. Groth and J. Frew (Eds.): IPAW 2012, LNCS 7525, pp. 223–225, 2012.

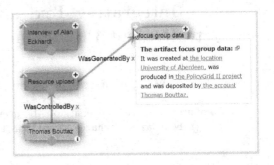

The artifact focus group data: ⬧ It was used by the interview of Alan Eckhardt and was generated by the resource upload process.

The process Interview of Alan Eckhardt: ⬧ It used the focus group data and generated the recording of the interview of Alan Eckhardt. It was controlled by Edoardo Pignotti and Pete Edwards, and involved Alan Eckhardt.

Fig. 1. Example of generated texts containing provenance information

Fig. 2. Integration of textual and graphical visualisations

RDF data. We have implemented two modes for this service: one for generating text about general information regarding an entity (e.g. type, title, date of creation), and one specifically about its provenance (i.e. how it relates to other OPM entities).

The NLG service is composed of two components - *Text Generator* and *Text Formatter*. First, the metadata about an entity is obtained from the *Metadata access* service, which is then used by the *Text Generator* to build a semantic model representing information about the entity. Then the model is transformed into text using the appropriate *Language Specification* files. These XML files are divided into two categories: *Property Language Specifications* contain the linguistic information required to structure the sentence corresponding to a property (e.g. syntactic category, verb tense); *Class Language Specifications* indicate which properties should be used to refer to a particular class.

The *Text Formatter* converts the plain text generated by the *Text Generator* into HTML. Figure 1 shows an example of a text generated by the NLG service. This text contains a description of the provenance of the artefact (*focus group data*) and can be further expanded by clicking on hyperlinks to related entities. This calls the service with the URI of that related entity, appending the resulting description to the original text.

Graphical Visualiser. The *Graphical Visualiser* was developed to visualise provenance information using a graph displaying OPM entities as nodes and OPM causal relationships as directed connections between nodes. It is implemented in HTML and Javascript and divided into two main components - one for communication and one for visualisation. The communication component makes use of the *Provenance* service to query for provenance data, as well to update the provenance graph. The data are then used by the visualisation component to draw the actual graph. The nodes are initially ordered according to timestamp, but the user can control the position of nodes, as well as the level of magnification. Each node has a "plus" icon that loads the provenance of this node when clicked, thus expanding the provenance graph. An example of a graphical visualisation is shown in Figure 2. A user is able to create and edit provenance information using the graphical visualisation. He/she can create new links between nodes, create new processes and delete links.

Combining Visualisations. We have integrated the NLG service within the graphical presentation, by allowing users to generate textual descriptions of the different entities present in the graph. In this way, a user can easily access more information about entities. Figure 2 shows how a user can generate the description of an entity (*focus group data*) by hovering the mouse pointer over its node.

3   Discussion

In order to evaluate this work, we ran a series of focus groups with potential users of *ourSpaces*. Users were presented with the same provenance information presented in different ways and were asked to discuss the main advantages and drawbacks of each. The participants preferred the terminology to adapt to the context of use (e.g. referring to the agent that controlled an interview process as the *interviewer*, rather than with wasControlledBy). This suggests that more adaptation of the underlying representation of provenance information may be required to improve usability. They also felt that some form of temporal information would help them to better understand the provenance presentations. The participants did find that the combination of graphical and textual presentations was useful to better understand provenance.

This work differs from other provenance visualisation services by providing users with two presentation modalities supporting each other, as well as a mechanism to allow users to edit the provenance metadata. In order to further improve this work, we could also implement other "Types" described by [3], such as *Comparison* (comparing the provenance of two artefacts, highlighting their differences) and *Participation* (emphasising the agents involved in the processes) which would be beneficial in the context of a collaborative environment such as *ourSpaces*. Currently, the visualisation conforms with *Timeline* (chronological ordering) and *Result* (focus on the main artefact).

References

1. Edwards, P., Mellish, C., Pignotti, E., Ponnamperuma, K., Bouttaz, T., Eckhardt, A., Pangbourne, K., Philip, L., Farrington, J.: Demo: ourspaces - a provenance enabled virtual research environment. In: 4th International Provenance & Annotation Workshop (2012)
2. Moreau, L., Clifford, B., Freire, J., Futrelle, J., Gil, Y., Groth, P., Kwasnikowska, N., Miles, S., Missier, P., Myers, J., Plale, B., Simmhan, Y., Stephan, E., den Bussche, J.V.: The open provenance model core specification (v1.1). Future Gener. Comput. Syst. 27, 743–756 (2011)
3. Kunde, M., Bergmeyer, H., Schreiber, A.: Requirements for a Provenance Visualization Component. In: Freire, J., Koop, D., Moreau, L. (eds.) IPAW 2008. LNCS, vol. 5272, pp. 241–252. Springer, Heidelberg (2008)

Exploring Provenance
in a Linked Data Ecosystem

David Corsar, Peter Edwards, Nagendra Velaga, John Nelson, and Jeff Z. Pan

dot.rural Digital Economy Research, University of Aberdeen
{dcorsar,p.edwards,n.r.velaga,j.d.nelson,jeff.z.pan}@abdn.ac.uk

Abstract. We describe our work exploring provenance within an open linked data ecosystem being developed in the travel/transport domain. We discuss techniques to infer provenance of sensor data, maintain provenance of third party data, and reference sources not available as linked data within a provenance record.

Keywords: provenance, linked data, intelligent information infrastructures, transport.

1 Introduction

In this paper, we discuss our work exploring provenance within an open linked data ecosystem being developed in the travel/transport domain[1]. Provenance is often cited as a key enabler for trusted information systems [1–3], particularly in dynamic open environments. The ecosystem we are developing integrates several open datasets published by government and online communities, with data generated by the crowd using a mobile phone app. Using these datasets, *GetThere*, a real time passenger information system, provides users with travel information such as timetables, estimated vehicle arrival times, vehicle locations, and details of network disruption. Given the diversity of datasets and providers within the ecosystem, issues such as information quality [4] and trust naturally arise. By providing a record of the agents, entities, and activities involved in producing a resource, provenance has a role to play in addressing these issues. We are exploring how provenance can be used to support the assessment of data within the ecosystem, for the purpose of ensuring passengers are provided with high quality, trustworthy information.

2 Provenance and Open Data

The diversity of data sources within the ecosystem has presented several challenges, a number of which related to provenance. Here we outline those challenges and our solutions to date.

---

[1] http://www.dotrural.ac.uk/irp

P. Groth and J. Frew (Eds.): IPAW 2012, LNCS 7525, pp. 226–228, 2012.

Making Implicit Provenance Explicit. Along with providing users with information, *GetThere* also asks users to act as sensors during their journeys on public transport. Observations generated by passengers are represented within the ecosystem using the Semantic Sensor Network (SSN) ontology[2]. Along with describing sensors and observations, the SSN ontology also captures implicit provenance information (i.e. provenance information not expressed using a provenance model), such as the sensor that generated the observation, the sensing method it used, and the inputs/outputs of that method.

To make this provenance information available explicitly (i.e. expressed using a provenance model), we have defined a series of axioms that map SSN concepts to PROV-O[3], the OWL encoding of the provenance interchange format being developed by the W3C Provenance Working Group[4]. These axioms define two equivalent class relationships between: *ssn:Process* (which represents sensing processes) and *prov:Activity*, and *ssn:Observation* and *prov:Entity*, along with three equivalent properties: *ssn:hasInput* and *prov:used*, *ssn:hasOutput* and *prov:generated*, and *ssn:sensingMethodUsed* and *prov:wasGeneratedBy*. These axioms allow an ontology reasoner to materialise PROV-O information for observations, inferring that an observation is an *Entity*, that the sensing process is an *Activity*, and the relevant *generated/wasGeneratedBy* links.

Associating Provenance with Remote Linked Data. Several of the datasets within the ecosystem are provided by third parties and accessed via remote SPARQL endpoints. Having access to the provenance of this data would provide agents with valuable additional information to use when evaluating such data. Unfortunately, in many cases provenance is not associated directly with the data. For example, the UK Government's public transport linked dataset does not include provenance; however, the web page linking to the endpoint states that the data "dates from March 2010"[5]. As other (non-linked data) versions of this dataset are updated regularly, associating provenance with the linked data would support, for example, automated assessment of timeliness. The main challenge here is determining an appropriate method for associating provenance with third party data only available via a remote SPARQL endpoint.

To address this we use the SPARQL 1.1 Service Design Ontology[6] and PROV-O to describe remote SPARQL endpoints, the data they make accessible, and the data provenance. Each endpoint description consist of individuals representing the *sd:Service* (the endpoint), the *sd:DataSets* accessed by the endpoint, and the *sd:Graphs* within each dataset. By defining *sd:Graph* as equivalent to *prov:Entity*, we can build a provenance record for it, including a description of the *prov:Activity* that generated the graph and the data it contains.

---

[2] http://purl.oclc.org/NET/ssnx/ssn
[3] http://www.w3.org/TR/prov-o/
[4] http://www.w3.org/2011/prov/wiki/Main_Page
[5] http://data.gov.uk/linked-data Accessed May 2012.
[6] http://www.w3.org/ns/sparql-service-description

Including Non-linked Data Resources in a Provenance Record. Several datasets within the ecosystem have been derived from data originally available in formats such as CSV or HTML. For example, the ecosystem includes a bus timetable dataset created by manually scraping the timetable information from the operator's web site into a spreadsheet, which a program then converts into RDF. The main challenge here is recording this and including references to the original resources (for example, the web page), which change over time, so we cannot, for example, reference the web page URL.

We overcome this using the aforementioned technique for representing the provenance of data accessible through a SPARQL endpoint. Here, the provenance record includes details of the timetable scraping process and references to: the program that was used (in a source code repository); a copy of the file(s) used by that program; and a downloaded copy of the scraped web page. Although this record is largely created manually and necessitates storing a copy of all the files used, it does allow agents to verify the linked data by comparing it with the original source data.

3   Conclusion

In order to associate provenance with the data in the ecosystem, it has been necessary to develop various approaches that accommodate the diversity in datasets and providers. Maintaining a provenance record in this environment is challenging, particularly when dealing with data provided and maintained by third parties. The approaches we describe above illustrate how semantic web technologies can be used to provide a starting point for associating provenance with such data. We believe these approaches point the way towards a set of guidelines for provenance management in open, linked data environments.

Acknowledgements. The research described here is supported by the award made by the RCUK Digital Economy programme to the dot.rural Digital Economy Hub; award reference: EP/G066051/1.

References

1. Artz, D., Gil, Y.: A survey of trust in computer science and the semantic web. Web Semantics: Science, Services and Agents on the World Wide Web 5(2), 58–71 (2007)
2. Carroll, J.J., Bizer, C., Hayes, P., Stickler, P.: Named graphs, provenance and trust. In: Proc. of the 14th Int. Conf. on World Wide Web, pp. 613–622. ACM, New York (2005)
3. Dividino, R., Sizov, S., Staab, S., Schueler, B.: Querying for provenance, trust, uncertainty and other meta knowledge in RDF. Web Semantics 7(3), 204–219 (2009)
4. Hartig, O., Zhao, J.: Using web data provenance for quality assessment. In: Freire, J., Missier, P., Sahoo, S.S. (eds.) Semantic Web in Provenance Management. CEUR Workshop Proceedings, vol. 526. CEUR-WS.org (2009)

Enabling Re-executions of Parallel Scientific Workflows Using Runtime Provenance Data[*]

Flávio Costa[1], Daniel de Oliveira[1], Kary A.C.S. Ocaña[1], Eduardo Ogasawara[1,2],
and Marta Mattoso[1]

[1] COPPE, Federal University of Rio de Janeiro, Rio de Janeiro, Brazil
[2] CEFET, Rio de Janeiro, Brazil
{flscosta,danielc,kary,ogasawara,marta}@cos.ufrj.br

Abstract. Capturing provenance data in scientific workflows is a key issue since it allows for reproducibility and evaluation of results. Many of these workflows generate around 100,000 tasks that execute in parallel in High Performance Computing environments, such as large clusters and clouds. SciCumulus is a workflow engine for parallel execution in clouds. Activity failure is almost inevitable in clouds where virtual machine failures are a reality rather than a possibility. We present SciMultaneous, a service architecture that manages re-executions of failed scientific workflow tasks using runtime provenance. Experimental results on clouds showed that SciMultaneous considerably increases the workflow completion and reduces the total execution time of the workflow (considering executions and re-executions) up to 11.5%, when compared to *ad-hoc* approaches.

1 Introduction

Scientific workflows became a *de facto* standard for modeling scientific experiments that are based on computer simulations [1]. Experiments in different domains of science demand high processing power. Scientific workflows can generate 100,000 or more parallel tasks in High Performance Computing (HPC) environments. Recently, clouds [2] emerge as an attractive alternative environment for scientific applications. By using clouds, scientists may avoid acquiring expensive HPC machines by instantiating a multi-processor environment composed by several virtual machines (VM). In addition, scientists benefit by paying only according to the effective use of HPC resources (pay *per* use model [2]). In this paper, we aim at improving reliability of workflow completion by managing workflow re-execution, in the presence of many types of failures. Previous experiments [3] show that failures occur very often in clouds, where the environment is constantly changing. It is a top priority to provide reliability so that scientists do not have to manage the potentially large numbers of failures. To illustrate the effective need of improving the reliability of parallel scientific workflows, we have explored, as case study, a workflow from the bioinformatics domain, SciPhy [3]. Typically, one execution of SciPhy on clouds,

---

[*] This work was partially sponsored by CNPq, FAPERJ and CAPES.

P. Groth and J. Frew (Eds.): IPAW 2012, LNCS 7525, pp. 229–232, 2012.

consuming 50 multi-fasta files, generates 1,250 parallel tasks and demands approximately 4.19 days using 16 virtual cores. Mainly due to performance fluctuations on the cloud environment, a typical execution of SciPhy presents from 2% to 9% of task failures, which may demand up to 10 hours of processing [3].

2   SciMultaneous

SciMultaneous enables re-executions of parallel tasks generated from workflow activities in case of failures in clouds. SciMultaneous benefits from SciCumulus, a cloud workflow engine [4], to obtain runtime provenance data [5] in parallel executions. Differently from the current mainstream, SciMultaneous can detect and manage failures during workflow execution, by using runtime provenance. SciCumulus distributes scientific workflow activities (or even entire scientific workflows) dispatched from a scientific workflow management system (*e.g.* Kepler [6]) into clouds such as Amazon EC2. There are several approaches focused on handling failures on scientific workflows. Ferreira *et al.* [7] introduce a representation of the workflow defining *a priori* the several optional paths to follow when a failure occurs. Crawl and Altintas [8] propose the Scientific Workflow Doctor, a component for Kepler to use prospective provenance data, guaranteeing fault tolerance. However, none of them focus on parallel executions neither provide runtime provenance data.

SciMultaneous architecture follows the Software as a Service (SaaS) model [2]. Three main services are part of SciMultaneous: Task Mapper (TM), VM Configurator (VMC) and Task Executor (TE). The TM searches for any task failure indicative by submitting queries to the workflow engine provenance repository. TM analyzes the generated runtime provenance data and decides which heuristic to use. With the heuristic chosen, TM informs VMC that there is a demand for re-executions. VMC analyzes if there is any idle VM to be used or if VMC has to instantiate new VMs for re-execution. With the environment set, VMC invokes TE that effectively re-executes tasks in each VM created by VMC. TE is also responsible for capturing and storing provenance data (related to the re-executions) in the provenance repository.

SciMultaneous follows two heuristics. In both of them we assume that scientists can access more than one cloud environment. In this case, one of the clouds is chosen as the reliable one with more processing power, consequently presenting higher financial costs. The main idea is to start re-executing failed tasks using the other cloud, less reliable, with lower financial costs. The reliable cloud is left to execute critical tasks or tasks that also failed in their re-executions. The first heuristic (named H1) tries to anticipate failures, by redundantly executing tasks that are considered critical (*i.e.* long-term tasks). In case of failure, a replica is available for substituting the failed task. The second heuristic (named H2) focuses on continuous task monitoring. In case of task failure, SciMultaneous immediately re-schedules it to another VM in the same cloud or even to another cloud. For example, in H2, SciMultaneous follows a hierarchical strategy: firstly it re-schedules the task to the same cloud and in the same VM, assuming that some intermittent problem may have occurred. If the failure persists, another VM is instantiated in the same cloud environment to re-schedule the specific task. Then, if the task is considered critical it is re-scheduled to a powerful VM. Finally, if the failure still persists, SciMultaneous re-schedules the task to a different cloud, using more processing power *per* VM.

3 Experimental Results and Conclusions

SciMultaneous coupled to SciCumulus was evaluated in the Amazon EC2. We executed SciPhy workflow as the case study. Our experiment uses as input, a dataset of 250 multi-fasta files (each file with 10 sequences) of protein sequences extracted from RefSeq database release 48, as detailed in Ocaña *et al.* [3]. This data set generates a total of 6,250 parallel tasks, which approximately 1.96% (thus 123 tasks) presented some kind of failure. We executed SciPhy workflow varying the number of virtual cores used in each execution. We compared the two proposed heuristics of SciMultaneous. For one of the scenarios, both H1 and H2 presented a total execution time lower than *ad-hoc* approaches in all cases. For example, using 32 cores, H1 executed in 9.90 days, H2 in 9.63 days and *ad-hoc* in 10.39 days. In the case of H1, 9.2% of the long-term tasks (*i.e.* ModelGenerator and RAxML programs [3]) were executed redundantly (creating one original task and one redundant). Then, 8% of the original long-term tasks have failed and they were automatically replaced by the redundant task, as soon as, provenance was produced, and queried by SciMultaneous. SciMultaneous reached a performance improvement up to 11.5% when using H1 compared to an *ad-hoc* re-execution approach. In addition, in larger experiments, this performance gain can be higher than the one reached in this experiment. These performance improvements led to a reduction of up to US$ 373.24 in financial costs when comparing H1 execution with *ad-hoc* re-execution approach. However, the highest SciMultaneous gain is reliability improvement by workflow completion. Another advantage of using SciMultaneous is that as it is a service architecture it can be coupled to other approaches for managing workflow execution, as long as, provenance data is provided at runtime. Querying provenance at runtime is fundamental since it allows for online execution adjustments (re-executions) that otherwise would be impossible to be pre-programmed.

References

[1] Mattoso, M., Werner, C., Travassos, G.H., Braganholo, V., Murta, L., Ogasawara, E., Oliveira, D., da Cruz, S.M.S., Martinho, W.: Towards Supporting the Life Cycle of Large-scale Scientific Experiments. International Journal of Business Process Integration and Management 5(1), 79–92 (2010)
[2] Vaquero, L.M., Rodero-Merino, L., Caceres, J., Lindner, M.: A break in the clouds: towards a cloud definition. SIGCOMM Comput. Commun. Rev. 39(1), 50–55 (2009)
[3] Ocaña, K.A.C.S., de Oliveira, D., Ogasawara, E., Dávila, A.M.R., Lima, A.A.B., Mattoso, M.: SciPhy: A Cloud-Based Workflow for Phylogenetic Analysis of Drug Targets in Protozoan Genomes. In: Norberto de Souza, O., Telles, G.P., Palakal, M. (eds.) BSB 2011. LNCS, vol. 6832, pp. 66–70. Springer, Heidelberg (2011)
[4] Oliveira, D., Ogasawara, E., Ocana, K., Baiao, F., Mattoso, M.: An Adaptive Parallel Execution Strategy for Cloud-based Scientific Workflows. Concurrency and Computation: Practice and Experience (2011) (online)
[5] Freire, J., Koop, D., Santos, E., Silva, C.T.: Provenance for Computational Tasks: A Survey. Computing in Science and Engineering 10(3), 11–21 (2008)

[6] Altintas, I., Berkley, C., Jaeger, E., Jones, M., Ludascher, B., Mock, S.: Kepler: an extensible system for design and execution of scientific workflows. In: Scientific and Statistical Database Management, Greece, pp. 423–424 (2004)

[7] Ferreira, J.E., Wu, Q., Malkowski, S., Pu, C.: Towards Flexible Event-Handling in Workflows Through Data States. In: Proc. of the 2010 IEEE 6th World Congress on Services, Miami, FL, pp. 344–351 (2010)

[8] Crawl, D., Altintas, I.: A Provenance-Based Fault Tolerance Mechanism for Scientific Workflows. In: Freire, J., Koop, D., Moreau, L. (eds.) IPAW 2008. LNCS, vol. 5272, pp. 152–159. Springer, Heidelberg (2008)

Access Control for OPM Provenance Graphs

Roxana Danger, Robin Campbell Joy, John Darlington, and Vasa Curcin

Department of Computing, Imperial College London, London SW7 2AZ

The field of provenance in computer science arose from the need to capture the lineage of software data outputs in an automated manner that is semantically consistent across various applications that participated in producing the said outputs. This vision being outside the capabilities of simple text logs, a series of Provenance Challenges investigated the suitability of different approaches, in the process giving rise to the Open Provenance Model (OPM) [3], currently being reworked into PROV, a W3C standard.

Provenance data brings with it a new set of security considerations, since the access permissions to data and to its full lineage may not always coincide. Clinical trial auditor may not be allowed to see a patient's full electronic health record used to gather data for the trial, but may see the trial results, while the patient owns their health record, but may not necessarily access the full trial information. Given that provenance information is commonly represented, and therefore browsed, as causal graphs, access to any individual node in the graph is potentially affected by other nodes connected to it.

Motivation for our work is to provide access policy language and query evaluation method that will offer to the user the maximum permissible amount of information. To that goal, we define ACLP, an extension to XACML, to support such policy definitions, and introduce graph transformations that hide the restricted graph items from the user.

ACLP[1] takes as its starting point the language defined in [1], which is itself an extension of XACML with regular expressions to represent terms of random depth in provenance graphs. Our extension retains their work, and introduces the *transform* construct to support the new query evaluation strategy. SPARQL 1.1 property paths are used for describing complex graph patterns expressions.

A policy in ACLP (Figure 1) is described by a *target* and an optional *condition*, the *scope*, *effect* and *transform* descriptors associated to the target. Full description of these is available in [1], and we only focus on novel elements.

The *effect* element specifies the intended outcome if the applicable rule matches some part of the provenance graph. It can take four values: *Absolute permit* guarantees access to the graph regardless of other policies' outcomes, *Deny* guarantees that certain parts of the graph will never be accessed by users in the subject element, *Necessary permit* describes parts of the graph that need explicit permission to be accessed, and *Permit* describes those graph segments that can be accessed if there are no other policies denying access.

---

[1] The full ACLP XSD is available at:
   http://www.doc.ic.ac.uk/~rdanger/aclschema_new.xsd.

P. Groth and J. Frew (Eds.): IPAW 2012, LNCS 7525, pp. 233–235, 2012.

```
<?xml version="1.0" encoding="UTF-8"?>
<policies>
    <policy>
        <target>
            <subject>ocld:Patient</subject>
            <record>ocld:DiagRecommProcess</record>
            <restriction>ocld:Patient.patId <> ocld:User.id</restriction>
            <restriction>rdf:property*/ocld:Diagnosis/opm:wasGeneratedBy*</restriction>
        </target>
        <scope>transferable</scope>
        <effect>deny</effect>
        <transform>
            <type>subgraph</type>
            <tranformation_scope>ocld:clinicalEvidence</tranformation_scope>
        </transform>
    </policy>
</policies>
```

Fig. 1. Example of access control definition for an EHR system

The *transform* element specifies if and how the graph is transformed to allow access to a subgraph when either *deny* or *necessary permit* policies apply to some nodes within the scope. There are three possible values: *None* denotes that transformations are not allowed and no part of the graph can be returned, *Single* means that the graph may be transformed and modified version returned, and *Subgraph* which also allows graph transformation, and also transfers the access restriction to its children nodes. The scope of this transfer depends on the value of the *transformation_scope* element, which can be either a set of resources, defined through a path query, or 'all' for all reachable nodes.

The example of a fictional EHR system in Figure 1 shows a patient access policy: the patient has no access to any EHRs other than their own, neither to any information associated to a diagnosis that was generated by using an automatic diagnosis recommendation process (*ocld:DiagRecommProcess*) and to the subgraph connecting it with the clinical evidences.

Our query evaluation strategy aims to transform the response graphs so that they conform to the query requestor's authorisation level. In rule conflicts, the strategy takes a *wider-allowed-access-takes-precedence* approach [2], i.e. the algorithm guarantees access to all resources that are not a target of a specific deny rule. The evaluation pseudo-code is shown in Algorithm 1.

To construct the transformed graph, we distinguish between *causality-preserving* and *non-causality-preserving* transformations. The former maintain some causal links between remaining nodes (through previous inferred relations), while the latter change the semantics by removing all connections between some remaining nodes. The algorithm removes all excluded nodes while the overall transformation remains causality-preserving, and when this is not the case, it replaces deleted nodes with the minimal set of *fictitious* artifacts and processes) that act as place-holders for one or more deleted nodes, and maintain the causal dependencies of remaining nodes. This is shown in Algorithm 2.

In this paper, we introduced a novel query evaluation algorithm on provenance data that returns graphs transformed based on user's authorisation levels, and the corresponding extension to XACL to support this in policy definition. The system is currently being implemented.

Algorithm 1. Access policy evaluation

Require: g: OPM graph to access.
    $targets$: Applicable targets filtered by user and validity.
Ensure: $accessibleGraph$: subgraph of g to which the access is granted, or null if the access to the graph is denied.

 {*Step One: evaluate 'absolute permit'*}
 for $target \in targets$ **do**
  if $target.effect = \text{'abs.permit'}$ **and** $eval(target.cond)$ **then**
   return g
 {*Step Two: evaluate 'deny' or 'necessary permit'*}
 $accessibleGraph = g$
 $excludedNodes = \{\}$
 for $target \in targets$ **do**
  if $(target.effect = \text{'deny'}$ **and** $eval(target.cond)$ $)$ **or**
   $(target.effect = \text{'nec.permit'}$ **and not** $eval(target.cond))$ **then**
   if $target.transform = \text{'no'}$ **then**
    return null
   else
    $excludedNodes = excludedNodes \cup getConflictNodes(target, g)$
 $accessibleGraph = transformGraph(g, excludedNodes)$
 {*Step Three: evaluate 'permit'*}
 for $target \in targets$ **do**
  if $target.effect = \text{'permit'}$ **and** $eval(target)$ **then**
   return $accesibleGraph$
 return null

Algorithm 2. Provenance graph transformation

Require: g: OPM graph to access.
    $removedNodes$: set of nodes to be removed
Ensure: g': graph equivalent to g in which all minimal subgraphs associated to the nodes in $removedNodes$ have been transformed.

 {Step One: Selection of 'retain' graph nodes}
 $g' = g$
 for $n \in removedNodes$ **do**
  if $(\exists n_c, n_e, cause(n, n_c), effect(n, n_e) \wedge$
   $\exists n', n' \notin removedNodes, (cause(n, n') \vee effect(n, n'))$ **then**
   $mark(n, \text{'retain'})$
 {Step Two: Transform}
 Delete from g' all $n \in removedNodes, causalityPreserving(n)$ without 'retain'
 Replace all consecutive graph nodes without 'retain' in g' with a fictitious artifact if they are all artifacts, or with a fictitious process otherwise
 Replace all consecutive artifacts with 'retain' in g' with a fictitious artifact
 Replace all consecutive processes with 'retain' in g' with a fictitious process

 return g'.

References

1. Cadenhead, T., Khadilkar, V., Kantarcioglu, M., Thuraisingham, B.: A language for provenance access control. In: Proceedings of the First ACM Conference on Data and Application Security and Privacy, CODASPY 2011, pp. 133–144. ACM, New York (2011)
2. di Vimercati, S.D.C., Foresti, S., Samarati, P., Jajodia, S.: Access control policies and languages. International Journal of Computational Science and Engineering 3(2), 94–102 (2007)
3. Moreau, L., Freire, J., Futrelle, J., McGrath, R.E., Myers, J., Paulson, P.: The Open Provenance Model: An Overview. In: Freire, J., Koop, D., Moreau, L. (eds.) IPAW 2008. LNCS, vol. 5272, pp. 323–326. Springer, Heidelberg (2008)

Improving the Understanding of Provenance and Reproducibility of a Multi-Sensor Merged Climate Data Record

Hook Hua, Brian Wilson, Gerald Manipon, Lei Pan, and Eric Fetzer

Jet Propulsion Laboratory, California Institute of Technology
4800 Oak Grove Drive, Pasadena, California 91109, U.S.A
{hook.hua,bdwilson,gmanipon,lei.pan,eric.j.fetzer}@jpl.nasa.gov

Abstract. Multi-decadal climate data records are critical to studying climate variability and change. These often also require merging data from multiple instruments such as those from NASA's A-Train that contain measurements covering a wide range of atmospheric conditions and phenomena. Multi-decadal climate data record of water vapor measurements from sensors on A-Train, operational weather, and other satellites are being assembled from existing data sources, or produced from well-established methods published in peer-reviewed literature. However, the immense volume and inhomogeneity of data often requires an "exploratory computing" approach to product generation where data is processed in a variety of different ways with varying algorithms, parameters, and code changes until an acceptable product is generated. Furthermore, the data product information associated with source data, processing methods, parameters used, intermediate & final product outputs, and associated materials are often hidden in each of the trials and scattered throughout the processing system(s). We will present methods to help users better capture and explore the production legacy of the data, metadata, ancillary files, code, and computing environment changes used during the production of these merged and multi-sensor data products. By building provenance services on semantic and provenance technologies, we show how to leverage provenance-as-a-service to capture sufficient information to enable users to track processing, perform faceted searches on the provenance record, and visualize the provenance of the products and processing lineage. We will also present services for capturing sufficient provenance information and the associated artifacts to enable some reproducibility of these climate data records.

Keywords: provenance, semantic, open provenance model, reproducibility, multi-sensor, data fusion, climate data, web services, faceted navigation, visualization.

P. Groth and J. Frew (Eds.): IPAW 2012, LNCS 7525, p. 236, 2012.
© Springer-Verlag Berlin Heidelberg 2012

Provenance Tracking in R

Andrew Runnalls and Chris Silles

School of Computing, University of Kent, UK

Abstract. This poster describes current progress and issues in introducing provenance-tracking facilities into the CXXR implementation of the R statistical computing environment.

1 CXXR

The object of the CXXR project (`www.cs.kent.ac.uk/projects/cxxr`) is gradually to reengineer the fundamental parts of the R interpreter from C into C++ in such a way that the full functionality of the standard distribution of R (including the recommended packages) is preserved. In particular, the behaviour of R code is unaffected (unless it probes into interpreter internals), and there is no change to the existing interfaces for calling out from R to other languages such as C or Fortran, nor to the main APIs for calling into R. CXXR achieves a high degree of compatibility with R packages from the CRAN repository, as [1] illustrated.

Work on CXXR started in May 2007, at that time shadowing R-2.5.1. Since then CXXR has been regularly upgraded to keep pace with the major releases of R (usually synching on the .1 minor release), so for example over the last year CXXR has shadowed the increasing deployment of the bytecode compiler within standard R. The current release of CXXR shadows R-2.14.1.

A key difference between CXXR and standard R is in the implementation of R data objects. Standard R provides for only a fixed range of object types (implemented as a C union) to be assigned to R variables, and to participate in the interpreter's garbage collection scheme. In contrast, data objects in CXXR are implemented as a C++ class hierarchy, which can be extended at will. The provenance-tracking variant of CXXR leverages this feature extensively.

2 Provenance Tracking and CXXR

The AUDIT facilities [2] that once formed part of S and S-plus were an invaluable feature, as one of the present authors can testify, and one motivation behind CXXR was to introduce similar but better facilities into the R interpreter. Early work on a provenance-enabled variant of CXXR was presented in [3].

In the terminology of the OPM, the approach used is to regard **bindings** of R symbols (variables) to R data objects as being the OPM **artifacts**, and to regard R **top-level commands** (i.e. expressions entered directly at the interpreter prompt) as being OPM **processes**. At present no use is made of the OPM

P. Groth and J. Frew (Eds.): IPAW 2012, LNCS 7525, pp. 237–239, 2012.

agent concept. The interpreter instruments the reading and writing of bindings within the 'global environment' (R's main workspace), and maintains an audit trail defining the OPM graph leading up to all extant bindings. This provenance information can then be interrogated within the interpreter itself: this marks a difference from the S AUDIT facility, which required a separate tool to query provenance data.

For example, the CXXR command `pg <- pedigree("lm1")` will retrieve the 'pedigree' of the current binding of the symbol `lm1` (presumably to a linear model): `pg$commands` will then return an R list showing, in time order, the history of top-level commands that may have influenced that current value of `lm1`. Other components of `pg` record the dates and times when these commands were issued, and information relating to xenogenesis (Sec. 3).

A recent development in CXXR is to reengineer the way that data are serialized and deserialized between one session and the next, by drawing on the serialization facilities of the well-regarded open-source Boost C++ libraries (`www.boost.org`). This means that not only can developers extend the range of data types usable within the interpreter, they can also—within the new C++ class definitions themselves—specify how objects of that class are saved to and restored from the session archive (which now uses an XML format). This applies not least to the classes implementing the provenance audit trail, so that this is carried forward from one CXXR session to the next.

3 Xenogenesis

Many R functions are pure: their return value depends only on the values of the function arguments. Other functions may have a return value which depends on the values of other variables within the R session, and some functions—for example pseudorandom number generators—may have side effects, modifying the bindings of R variables otherwise than via their return values. Fortunately, none of the preceding presents any inherent problem for CXXR's provenance-tracking mechanism, provided the function's behaviour is entirely mediated by the bindings of R variables.

However, there are some R functions whose behaviour is *not* fully defined by the current state of the interpreter. This may be because the function (e.g. `scan`) reads from an external file or database, or because it accepts user input in some way (e.g. `identify`) or because it calls external non-R code via one of the foreign language interfaces. We call such functions **xenogenetic**, and the bindings they give rise to **xenogenous**: "due to an outside cause".

If a top-level command calls a xenogenetic function (either directly, or indirectly via some other function), this means that the text of the top-level command no longer completely defines the OPM process that maps its input artifacts (bindings) to its output artifacts. To work around this problem, the approach currently being explored is for the provenance record to identify whether a binding is xenogenous, and if so *to record the value* of that binding. So if for example an R function `my.function` was created using an external editor using R's `edit` command, the provenance record will permanently record the value thus given to my.function—permanently, that is, for as long as any artifact depending on that function is retained in the R session.

4   Environments

In R (and CXXR), an **environment** is a container holding a mapping from R symbols to R data objects. As previously mentioned, at present CXXR tracks the provenance of bindings within R's global environment .GlobalEnv. It is straightforward to extend this tracking to other standard environments set up at the start of an R session, though this results in a deluge of provenance data that would rarely be of value.

However, each invocation of a function written in R results in the creation of a local environment. In the overwhelming majority of cases this local environment becomes inaccessible after the function returns, and it is soon garbage-collected. However, there are some exceptions, and it is for example possible to define an R function which in effect has internal state, stored in a local environment and carried forward from one invocation to the next. At present this would result in a 'backchannel' of influence that evades the provenance record, but work is in the pipeline to rectify this.

One remaining concern is that there is currently no method of referring to local environments in a way that is meaningful between R sessions: this can hamper reproducibility, especially in the presence of xenogenesis.

5   Conclusion

This poster has described the current state of work to introduce provenance-tracking facilities into CXXR. The reader will have noted that the tracking is self-contained within the interpreter, and does not rely on any external provenance-tracking tool. A less satisfactory converse is that the implementation does not currently provide for any interoperation with such external tools. The authors would be interested to hear from researchers interested in collaborating to rectify this and other gaps.

References

1. Runnalls, A.: CXXR and add-on packages. In: useR! 2010 (2010), http://user2010.org/slides/Runnalls.pdf
2. Becker, R.A., Chambers, J.M.: Auditing of data analyses. SIAM J. Sci. Stat. Comput. 9, 747–760 (1988)
3. Silles, C.A., Runnalls, A.R.: Provenance-Awareness in R. In: McGuinness, D.L., Michaelis, J.R., Moreau, L. (eds.) IPAW 2010. LNCS, vol. 6378, pp. 64–72. Springer, Heidelberg (2010)

The Provenance Store prOOst
for the Open Provenance Model

Andreas Schreiber, Miriam Ney, and Heinrich Wendel

German Aerospace Center (DLR),
Linder Hoehe, 51147 Cologne, Germany,
{Andreas.Schreiber,Miriam.Ney,Heinrich.Wendel}@dlr.de,
http://www.dlr.de/sc

Abstract. This paper presents the provenance storing system *prOOst* which uses a semi-structured approach to store the provenance data based on the Open Provenance Model (OPM). It uses the graph database "Neo4j" for storage and the graph traversal language "Gremlin" for querying. Furthermore, it provides a REST interface to record data into the store, and a web front end to query the database. The prOOst provenance system was published as Open Source software and is available on SourceForge.

1 Introduction

In [1] the representation of a provenance system is described as follows: A provenance aware application sends information of interest to the provenance store. From this store inquiries and information is gathered, and possibly given back to the application.

To record the information, different approaches have been investigated. In [2] four different realisations are discussed: Relational, XML with XPath, RDF with SPARQL and semi-structured approaches. They conclude semi-structured approaches to be most promising. In semi-structured systems, the used technology has no formal structure, but it provides means of being queried.

In this work, we present the provenance storing system *prOOst* which uses a semi-structured approach to store the provenance data based on the Open Provenance Model (OPM).

2 The Provenance Store prOOst

The Provenance Store prOOst uses the graph database "Neo4j" [3] for storage and the graph traversal language "Gremlin" [4] for querying. Furthermore, it provides a REST interface to record data into the store, and a web front end to query the database. The prOOst provenance system was published as Open Source software and is available on SourceForge[1].

---

[1] http://sourceforge.net/projects/proost/

P. Groth and J. Frew (Eds.): IPAW 2012, LNCS 7525, pp. 240–242, 2012.

It is not the first implementation using a graph database for storage technology. In [5] this approach was already successfully tested. Neo4j was chosen as it is a robust, performant and popular choice for graph storage systems. Additionally it readily connectible with the suitable Gremlin query system to meet our requirements. Further information on the implementation of OPM model provenance assertions using these systems are described in the following two sections.

2.1   Graph Database: Neo4j

"Neo4j is a graph database, a fully transactional database that stores data structured as graphs." (cf. [3])

An advantage of graph databases like Neo4j is that they offer very flexible storage models, allowing for a rapid development. Neo4j is dually licensed (AGPLv3 open source and commercial).

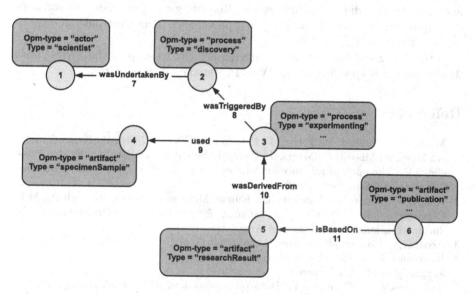

Fig. 1. OPM example in Neo4j

Modelling OPM using Neo4j is described in more detail in [6]. Fig. 1 shows an example of an OPM graph. Each element is represented by a node (vertex) in the database. Nodes are indexed according to the Neo4j standard. The nodes can be annotated with further (OPM specific) information, such as "process" or "artifact". Analogously, also the edges connecting the nodes are indexed and annotated with a label (the OPM relationship).

2.2 Query Language: Gremlin

"Gremlin is a graph traversal language" [4]. Gremlin already provides an interface to interact with the Neo4j graph database. The following example shows its use for querying Neo4j on the example database, searching for the names (identifiers) of all discoveries of a certain scientistX:

```
$_g := neo4j:open('database')
$scientists := g:key($_g, 'type', 'scientist')
$scientistX := g:key($scientists, 'identifier', 'scientistX')
$discoveries := $scientistX/inE/inV[@identifier']
```

3   Conclusions and Future Work

Neo4j was chosen as it is a robust, performant and popular choice for graph storage systems. Additionally it readily connectible with the suitable Gremlin query system to easily perform queries. The provenance store prOOst was evaluated and used by two different applications: Recording the provenance of software development processes [6] and recording provenance in an electronic laboratory notebook system [7].

Future work will concentrate on moving prOOst to support the *PROV Data Model* [8] that is specified by the W3C Provenance Working Group.

References

1. Moreau, L., Clifford, B., Freire, J., Futrelle, J., Gil, Y., Groth, P., Kwasnikowska, N., Miles, S., Missier, P., Myers, J., Plale, B., Simmhan, Y., Stephan, E., den Bussche, J.V.: The open provenance model core specification (v1.1). Future Generation Computer Systems (July 2010)
2. Holl, D.A., Braun, U., Maclean, D., Kumar Muniswamy-Reddy, K., Seltzer, M.I.: Choosing a data model and query language for provenance. In: Proceedings of the 2nd International Provenance and Annotation Workshop (2008)
3. Neo4j.org: Neo4j graph database, http://neo4j.org
4. Rodriguez, M.A.: Gremlin graph traversal language, http://gremlin.tinkerpop.com
5. Tylissanakis, G., Cotronis, Y.: Data provenance and reproducibility in grid based scientific workflows. In: Workshops at the Grid and Pervasive Computing Conference, pp. 42–49 (2009)
6. Wendel, H., Kunde, M., Schreiber, A.: Provenance of Software Development Processes. In: McGuinness, D.L., Michaelis, J.R., Moreau, L. (eds.) IPAW 2010. LNCS, vol. 6378, pp. 59–63. Springer, Heidelberg (2010)
7. Ney, M.: Enabling a data management system to support the good laboratory practice. Master's thesis, Freie Universität Berlin (2011), http://elib.dlr.de/75261/
8. Moreau, L., Missier, P., Belhajjame, K., Cresswell, S., Gil, Y., B'Far, R., Groth, P., Klyne, G., McCusker, J., Miles, S., Myers, J., Sahoo, S.: PROV-DM Part 1: The Provenance Data Model, http://dvcs.w3.org/hg/prov/raw-file/default/model/prov-dm.html

A Comprehensive Model for Provenance

Salmin Sultana and Elisa Bertino

Purdue University
{ssultana,bertino}@purdue.edu

Abstract. In this paper, we propose a provenance model able to represent the provenance of any data object captured at any abstraction layer (workflow/process/OS) and present an abstract schema of the model. The expressive nature of the model makes it potential to be utilized in real world data processing systems.

Keywords: Provenance, Model, Comprehensive, Unified, Generic.

1 Introduction

Existing data provenance systems mostly operate at a single level of abstraction at which they record and store provenance. Provenance systems for scientific data [1][2] record provenance at the semantic level of the application. Other application level provenance systems capture provenance at the granularity of business objects, lines of source code or other units with semantic meaning to the context. Workflow systems record provenance at workflow stages and data/message exchange points. System-call based systems [3][4] operate at the level of system processes and files. While provenance collected at each abstraction layer is useful in its own right, integration across these layers is crucial.

To build a unified provenance infrastructure, defining an expressive provenance model able to represent the provenance of data objects with various semantics and granularity is the first crucial step. Such a model should be able to capture data provenance in a structured way as well as to encapsulate the knowledge of both the application semantics and the system. The model should also support provenance queries that span layers of abstraction, including workflow processes, application objects, and system processes. Despite a large number of research efforts on provenance management, only a few provenance models have been proposed. Most of these models conform only to a particular provenance system's data structure. Although a general provenance model has been proposed by Ni et al. [5], its main focus is on access control for provenance. Also this model is not able to distinguish between application and system level provenance information. In this paper, we propose a comprehensive provenance model that is (i) generic to record the provenance of any data object, (ii) unified to capture and integrate both the application and system level metadata, (iii) focused on interoperability among provenance models and integration of provenance across different systems, (iv) tailored to fine grained access control and originator preferences on provenance, and (v) able to facilitate queries for constructing specialized views of provenance graphs.

P. Groth and J. Frew (Eds.): IPAW 2012, LNCS 7525, pp. 243–245, 2012.
© Springer-Verlag Berlin Heidelberg 2012

2   Provenance Model

Fig. 1 shows the proposed provenance model consisting of entities and the inter-actions among them. To characterize our model, we define the provenance as:

The provenance of a data object is the history of the actors, process, operations, inter-process/operation communications, environment, access control and other user preferences related to the creation and modification of the data. The re-lationships between provenance entities form a data provenance graph (DAG).

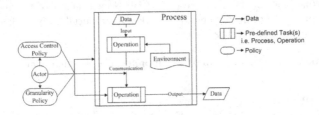

Fig. 1. Proposed Provenance Model

Data creation or manipulation is performed by a sequence of *operations* initi-ated by a *process*. A *process*, consisting of a sequence of operations, may be a service/activity in a workflow, a user application, or an OS-level (e.g. UNIX) process. An *operation* executes specific task(s) and causes manipulation to some system or user data. *Communication* represents the interaction (e.g. data flow) between two processes or two operations in a process. Communication between two operations in a process means the completion of an operation following the start of another operation. When the preceding operation results in data, the communication may involve data passing between the operations. The commu-nication may also contain triggers, specific messages, etc. There might be also no explicit message (i.e. communication record) exchange between two operations. An operation may take data as input and output some data. Each data object is associated with a *lineage* record which specifies the immediate data objects that have been used to generate this data. Processes, operations, and communica-tions are operated by *actors* that can be human users, workflow templates, etc. *Environment* refers to the operational state, parameters, system configurations that also affect the execution of an operation and thus output data.

To address the security and privacy requirements of provenance, we include actor specified *access control policies* that specify whether and how other actors may utilize the provenance records. Since our model can capture the very details of an operation, it might by preferable to allow users to specify the desired level of provenance details. The *granularity policies* allow the users to specify how detailed provenance information they want to be captured and stored.

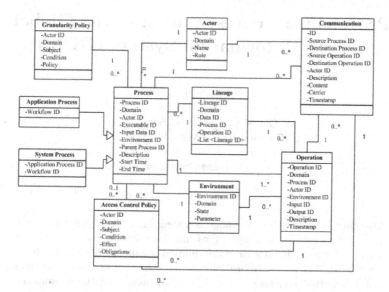

Fig. 2. Class Diagram of Provenance Model

From an implementation perspective, we represent our generic model as relationships among various provenance records as shown in Fig 2. Each provenance record is identified by an ID. Since provenance may be exchanged across different systems, we use *domain* to specify the scope of the records.

3 Conclusion

In this paper, we propose a comprehensive provenance model that can encapsulate the data provenance captured at different stages of a physical/computational process. The model captures the characteristics of standard provenance models which ensures the inter-operability of provenance across different systems.

References

1. Foster, I., Vöckler, J., Wilde, M., Zhao, Y.: Chimera: A virtual data system for representing, querying, and automating data derivation. In: Proc. of the Conference on Scientific and Statistical Database Management (SSDBM), pp. 37–46 (2002)
2. Janée, G., Mathena, J., Frew, J.: A data model and architecture for long-term preservation. In: Proc. of the Conference on Digital Libraries, pp. 134–144 (2008)
3. Frew, J., Metzger, D., Slaughter, P.: Automatic capture and reconstruction of computational provenance. Concurrency and Computation: Practice and Experience 20, 485–496 (2008)
4. Muniswamy-Reddy, K., Holland, D., Braun, U., Seltzer, M.: Provenance-aware storage systems. In: Proc. of the USENIX Annual Technical Conference (2006)
5. Ni, Q., Xu, S., Bertino, E., Sandhu, R., Han, W.: An Access Control Language for a General Provenance Model. In: Jonker, W., Petković, M. (eds.) SDM 2009. LNCS, vol. 5776, pp. 68–88. Springer, Heidelberg (2009)

Provenance Representation in the Global Change Information System (GCIS)

Curt Tilmes

U.S. Global Change Research Program,
1717 Pennsylvania Ave NW, Suite 250
Washington D.C. 20006, USA
Curt.Tilmes@nasa.gov

Abstract. Global climate change is a topic that has become very controversial despite strong support within the scientific community. It is common for agencies releasing information about climate change to be served with Freedom of Information Act (FOIA) requests for everything that led to that conclusion. Capturing and presenting the provenance, linking to the research papers, data sets, models, analyses, observation instruments and satellites, etc. supporting key findings has the potential to mitigate skepticism in this domain.

The U.S. Global Change Research Program (USGCRP) is now coordinating the production of a National Climate Assessment (NCA) that presents our best understanding of global change. We are now developing a Global Change Information System (GCIS) that will present the content of that report and its provenance, including the scientific support for the findings of the assessment. We are using an approach that will present this information both through a human accessible web site as well as a machine readable interface for automated mining of the provenance graph. We plan to use the developing W3C PROV Data Model and Ontology for this system.

1 Background

The U.S. Global Change Research Program (USGCRP)[1] coordinates and integrates federal research on changes in the global environment and their implications for society. The USGCRP began as a presidential initiative in 1989 and was mandated by Congress in the Global Change Research Act of 1990[1] (GCRA), which called for *"a comprehensive and integrated United States research program which will assist the Nation and the world to understand, assess, predict, and respond to human-induced and natural processes of global change."*

Thirteen U.S. federal departments and agencies participate in the USGCRP: Department of Commerce, Department of Defense, Department of Energy, Department of the Interior, Department of State, Department of Transportation, Department of Health and Human Services, Department of Agriculture, National

---

[1] http://globalchange.gov

P. Groth and J. Frew (Eds.): IPAW 2012, LNCS 7525, pp. 246–248, 2012.
© Springer-Verlag Berlin Heidelberg 2012

Aeronautics and Space Administration, National Science Foundation, Smithsonian Institution, Agency for International Development and the Environmental Protection Agency.

The USGCRP is developing a Global Change Information System (GCIS) that will utilize the developing W3C PROV[2] recommendations to eventually represent the provenance for all of the information related to global change across the U.S. federal government. The first implementation will provide provenance for the National Climate Assessment (NCA).

2   National Climate Assessment (NCA)

The GCRA requires a report to the President and the Congress every four years that integrates, evaluates, and interprets the findings of the USGCRP; analyzes the effects of global change on the natural environment, agriculture, energy production and use, land and water resources, transportation, human health and welfare, human social systems, and biological diversity; and analyzes current trends in global change, both human-induced and natural, and projects major trends for the subsequent 25 to 100 years.

The National Climate Assessment and Development Advisory Committee (NCADAC) is a Federal Advisory Committee[2] with 60 members, including 45 non-federal members and 16 federal ex-officio representatives. that provides advice and recommendations for the NCA process. As of this writing, the NCA has defined 30 chapters and selected 62 "Convening Lead Authors" and 180 "Lead Authors." The names and institutional affiliations of 240 contributing authors are a critical part of the provenance of the NCA we will be capturing with the process. All of that information will be of course be part of the printed and web-based text of the document, but will also be represented through machine accessible APIs.

Through an open, public process, the NCA has received over 500 distinct technical inputs, many of which are reports distilling and synthesizing even more information, coming from thousands of individuals around the federal government, non-governmental organizations, academic institutions, etc. The inputs include peer-reviewed scientific publications, model data, observational data (physical, societal, economic), historical data, sectoral and regional assessments, and data at a variety of scales and resolutions. Most original data are archived in long term agency data centers responsible for long term stewardship of the items, but some includes unconventional information collected from public health departments, states and tribes, NGOs, and data collected but not yet reviewed. Where the data are transformed into new graphics, graphs or charts, the process and methods used must be clearly and reproducibly documented.

This poses a tremendous challenge (and opportunity!) for provenance capture, archive, and presentation. We will represent that information using the PROV ontology and make the complete information about the NCA itself as well as all of the inputs to the process available through a publicly accessible web site and

---

[2] http://www.w3.org/TR/prov-dm/

SPARQL end point. The GCIS will provide links from the content and findings of the NCA back to all of their predecessor artifacts.

3   Provenance Representation

The GCIS assigns globally unique, persistent identifiers to all of the entities, activities and agents relevant to our discussions of provenance. These are located in the USGCRP namespace rooted under `http://globalchange.gov/id`. We are linking to existing identifiers where possible and appropriate, using journal or data center assigned DOIs for papers and datasets. NASA's Global Change Master Directory[3] has also assigned reusable identifiers for many of the important datasets and services we are referencing. PROV can be extended with domain defined types and specialized agent roles like the "Convening Lead Authors."

All of the `globalchange.gov` URI identifiers will be resolvable through HTTP content negotiation to either human readable HTML web pages, or machine readable encodings of the metadata describing the item and linking back to the repository for that item (such as a journal site for a paper, or an agency data center for an observational dataset). Where items are derived from other items, they will link back to their predecessor "entities," and "activity" representations with sufficient detail to reproduce the activity.

As an exercise to explore alternative methods of presenting the NCA, the previous report *Global Climate Change Impacts in the United States (2009)*[3] was transformed into a web site[4] with additional pages for each figure and footnote to more information including links back to datasets and data centers.

4   Future Plans

The GCIS is very much a work in progress. We have only begun mapping the myriad of resources into the PROV Data Model. Indeed, at this time, PROV itself is not yet complete, being only a "public working draft." Nevertheless, using PROV to describe the provenance of the NCA will have benefits for each. Beyond the NCA and other synthesis reports, the GCIS will be used to present information about global change from across the agencies of the U.S. Global Change Research Program.

References

1. U.S. Code: Global Change Research Act of 1990 (P.L. 101-606) (1990)
2. U.S. Code: The Federal Advisory Committee Act (5 U.S.C. App.) (1972)
3. U.S. Global Change Research Program: Global Climate Change Impacts in the United States (2009)

---

[3] `http://gcmd.nasa.gov`
[4] `http://nca2009.globalchange.gov`

Integrating Provenance into an Operational Data Product Information System

Stephan Zednik, James Michaelis, and Peter Fox

Rensselaer Polytechnic Institute, Troy NY 12180, USA

Abstract. Knowledge of how a science data product has been generated is a critical component to determining its fitness-for-use for a given
analysis. One objective of science information systems is to allow users
to search for data products based on a wide range of criteria; spatial and
temporal extent, observed parameter, research domain, and organiza-
tional project are common search criteria. Currently, science information
systems are geared towards helping users find data, but not in helping
users determine how the products were generated. An information system that exposes the provenance of available data products, that is what
observations, assumptions, and science processing were involved in the
generation of the data products, would contribute significant benefit to
user fitness-for-use decision-making.

In this work we discuss semantics-driven provenance extensions to
the Virtual Solar Terrestrial Observatory (VSTO) information system.
The VSTO semantic web portal uses an ontology to provide a unified search and product retrieval interface to data in the fields of solar, solar-terrestrial, and space physics. We have developed an extension
to the VSTO ontology that allows it to express item-level data product records. We will show how the Open Provenance Model (OPM)
and the Proof Markup Language (PML) can be used to express the
provenance of data product records. Additionally, we will discuss ways
in which domain semantics can aid in the formulation - and answering
- of provenance queries. Our extension to the VSTO ontology has also
been integrated with a solar-terrestrial profile of the Observation and
Measurement (O&M) model to support domain-specific descriptions of
solar-terrestrial observations; we utilize this integration to connect observation events to the data product record lineage.

Our additions to the VSTO ontology will allow us to extend the VSTO
web portal user interface with search criteria based on provenance and
observation characteristics. More critically, provenance information will
allow the VSTO portal to display important knowledge about selected
data records; what science processes and assumptions were applied to
generate the record, what observations the record derives from, and the
results of quality processing that had been applied to the record and
any records it derives from. We conclude by showing our interface for
showing record provenance information and discuss how it aids users in
determining fitness-for-use of the data.

Keywords: provenance, information systems, observation model, solar-
terrestrial.

P. Groth and J. Frew (Eds.): IPAW 2012, LNCS 7525, p. 249, 2012.

On Presenting Apropos Provenance
for Situation Awareness and Data Forensics

Jing Zhao, Yogesh Simmhan, and Viktor Prasanna

University of Southern California, Los Angeles, CA
{zhaoj,simmhan,prasanna}@usc.edu

Abstract. Provenance for data derived from large-scale workflows across organizations and disciplines can be complex. Users in different roles find their interpretation onerous unless it is presented in a form that is easily consumable for the given task at hand. In this position paper, we motivate the need and discuss key challenges for presenting provenance across different granularities to support data quality forensics for diverse users. We also offer potential modeling and algorithmic solutions.

1 Introduction

As data flows through and is derived from workflows executed across organizations and disciplines, provenance may be collected and reconstructed from different orchestration and execution frameworks [2], and often at different granularities depending on the execution framework in question. For example, for a workflow composed of multiple web services, the workflow management system may collect coarse-grained provenance that describes the data flow and control flow at the granularity of the web service invocations. Further, within an individual web service, detailed provenance may be collected to describe the execution logic of the service. Furthermore, more detailed provenance may be collected on system and OS calls within each execution step.

Understanding and interpreting raw provenance is challenging for users who consume it for diverse uses. The provenance collection mechanism provides a natural "grouping" structure for presenting provenance. However, it presents provenance from the perspective of the "composer" of the workflow rather than the "consumer" of the provenance. An appropriate granularity or view of provenance should be presented to users based on the current task at hand and situation of interest. For example, when using provenance for data quality debugging, fine-grained provenance needs to be provided for data objects and processes that have high impact on quality, whilst other provenance is masked. Users with different roles may also be interested in different views of provenance: business managers may be only interested in high-level business flows, while engineers are interested in detailed steps and the execution logic in the workflow.

An effective provenance presentation approach is thus required. This should determine the suitable view or granularity for provenance based on the context of usage. The presentation approach should support hybrid views that slices across vertical layers and horizontal boundaries and allow navigation across granularities. This requires support from provenance modeling, approaches to solicit

P. Groth and J. Frew (Eds.): IPAW 2012, LNCS 7525, pp. 250–253, 2012.

information on the usage context, frameworks to compose the provenance view, and presentation interfaces to display and navigate the provenance for accomplishing the task. In this paper, we outline key challenges and potential solutions for determining and presenting apropos hybrid provenance views across granularities, analyzed in the context of the Smart Power Grid domain.

2 Presenting Provenance for Data Forensics in Smart Grid

We use a use case from the Smart Power Grids domain as our motivating example. Several workflows, including the Campus Power Consumption Forecast workflow, the Forecast Model Training workflow, and the Building Sensor Integration workflow, are used to reliably forecast future power consumption of the campus, and initiate voluntary and direct-control actions to curtail energy use during peak load periods. A simplified version of the provenance collected for the ecosystem of workflows is shown in Figure 1.

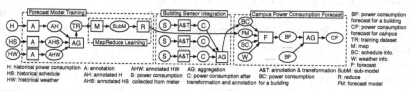

Fig. 1. Simplified provenance graph for power consumption forecast workflows

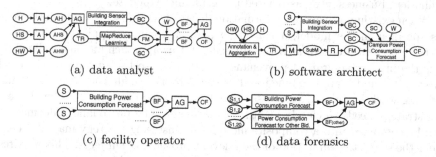

Fig. 2. Provenance graph views for different user roles

Three types of users consume the provenance information: *the software architect*, *the data analyst*, and *the campus facility operator*. Each of them has their own particular interest and usage of provenance collected from the workflow. For example, the data analyst designs machine learning algorithms for generating the forecast model. She is interested in provenance about the execution of the forecast model training and the campus power consumption forecast workflow so that she can verify the quality of the forecast model. Figure 2 shows different provenance "views" for these user roles.

The main usage of provenance in our use case is for data quality forensics. Directly presenting a complete provenance graph with several thousand provenance nodes makes it challenging for users to perform data forensics. The *quality impact*, which indicates how the quality of a process/artifact affects the output quality, is then used to guide users on what processes and data objects they need to exercise more quality control upon. In addition to user roles, we thus also need to consider the provenance usage requirement for its presentation. Figure 2(d) illustrates a provenance view for the facility operator that reflects the granularity requirement based on quality impact. The provenance graph highlights the provenance trace for calculating the consumption forecast of Building 1 since it is the largest building and has the highest quality impact.

3   Determining Apropos Provenance Presentation View

In general, the strategies to determine the suitable provenance presentation view can be classified into a decomposition or a clustering approach. A *decomposition* approach is well suited in the presence of granularities clearly defined in the provenance model. For each individual activity in the workflow, we identify the most appropriate presentation granularity to satisfy the usage requirement and to meet the user's interest. The eventual presentation may be a combination of fine-grained and coarse-grained provenance for different sections of the graph. The approach is based on the provenance usage context information, which includes: 1) the *provenance end use* specifying the activity for which provenance is used, such as data quality forensics or software, and 2) the *user profile* describing the role of the user consuming provenance, which may include the user's affiliation, business level, associated projects, and expertise.

When existing provenance information does not have discrete granularity levels specified in the model, a *clustering* approach can be applied to infer the suitable presentation granularities. In general, this approach incrementally clusters the initial fine-grained provenance information so that groups of low-level provenance nodes are combined and replaced by new higher-level nodes. Some existing work has already discussed problems in this direction [1]. The clustering strategy needs to clearly identify what fine-grained provenance information can be combined into a composite module. A clustering strategy may also consider the semantic connection of the relevant provenance subjects. This requires mechanisms like calculation of connectivity power to be designed.

4   Conclusion

In this paper, we outlined the critical need and key challenges for determining appropriate granularities for presenting provenance. We motivated from the Smart Grid domain and illustrated alternate provenance views when presenting the same provenance to different user roles and end use needs. Our discussions centered around modeling these presentation needs and strategies to determine the appropriate view based on context information.

References

1. Biton, O., Cohen-Boulakia, S., Davidson, S., Hara, C.: Querying and managing provenance through user views in scientific workflows. In: ICDE (2008)
2. Simmhan, Y.L., Plale, B., Gannon, D.: A survey of data provenance in e-science. SIGMOD Rec. 34 (2005)

Author Index

Printed in the United States
by Baker & Taylor Publisher Services

Printed in the United States
by Baker & Taylor Publisher Services